HIDDEN SELVES

By the same author

*

The Privacy of the Self
Alienation in Perversions

HIDDEN SELVES
Between Theory and Practice in Psychoanalysis

by

M. MASUD R. KHAN

INTERNATIONAL UNIVERSITIES PRESS, INC.
New York

ISBN 0-8236-2323-8

Manufactured in Great Britain

To the memory of
ANNA FREUD

CONTENTS

ACKNOWLEDGEMENTS

The years covered by the writings published here were harassed by a nearly lethal physical illness: cancer. I wish to express my indebtedness to the following of my friends who stayed supportive and available whenever I was needy: Professor and Mrs Robert Stoller of Los Angeles; Henri and Martine Cartier-Bresson, J.-B. Pontalis, and Dr Victor Smirnoff, all of Paris; Sardar and Begum Jamil Nishtar of Pakistan; Harry Karnac of London; His Excellency General Yakub-Khan, Ambassador of Pakistan in Washington, Moscow and Paris during these years; Mme Tarfa Salem and her daughters, Lina and Mehreen, who took every care of me when in distress. Also to Dr Barrington Cooper I owe a very private debt for taking continuous medical care of me.

To John Charlton, director of The Hogarth Press, and Patricia White, my literary agent, who kept my writings and my name in public circulation, with an undemanding diligence and goodwill, I would like to express my gratitude with affection.

I would also like to express my gratitude to Marie Glucksman for her help in preparing this volume for press; to Dr John Gibson for compiling the index; and to the editors and publishers of the journals and books in which several of the chapters in this volume first appeared. Details of original publication are given in the Chronological Bibliography on page 189.

February 1983 M. MASUD R. KHAN

PREFACE

> Go, go, go, said the bird: human kind
> Cannot bear very much reality.
>
> T. S. ELIOT, *'Burnt Norton'*

If one has been well nurtured, thrived at times, and been absurdly wasteful at others, then one arrives at a point where the past is the manure by which the present is fructified. This fruition of self is always something much sought after but never fully achieved because we humans are, at root, fearful, even of that which extends us. Hence we live hidden and divided within, sharing a little with the *other*, now and then, but largely holding back, both waking and dreaming.

The clinical work that I recount in this book has no pretensions to offering a 'scientific' explication of the ailment of the *other*. It is an attempt at sharing the discourse between me and the *other*, where each of us made his own contributions, and abstained as well. Hence in the transitional space of Freud's invention, usually called the analytic situation, *encounters* take place that ease only gradually in *un*trust from both sides and enable occasional sharing of the hidden selves of each with the other. In this context curiosity is distracting and our metapsychological vocabulary a hindrance. One learns to tolerate unknowing, so as to facilitate converse and thus engender that unpredictable growth which, if it actualizes, is called 'cure'. And *cure* entails living, and learning, the joyous arduousness of that task.

I have tried to share by metaphor and anecdote how the clinical process gradually involves two persons in a mutuality of relating and, if things fare well, in time enables them to part from each other in a state of grace and awakened unto their hidden selves.

May 1982 M. MASUD R. KHAN

I

Freud and the Crises of Psychotherapeutic Responsibility

'. . . self exiled in upon his ego . . .'

JOYCE, *Finnegans Wake*

In most evaluations of Freud's work it is customary to trace his debt to the tradition and methods of medicine, psychiatry and neurology at the end of the nineteenth century. My argument here is that Freud arrived at a critical point in the evolution of Modernism in European cultures. Trilling (1955) has pertinently remarked:

> The first thing that occurs to me to say about literature, as I consider it in the relation in which Freud stands to it, is that literature is dedicated to the conception of the self. . . In almost every developed society, literature is able to conceive of the self, and the selfhood of others, far more intensely than the general culture ever can.

Since Freud was to concern himself almost exclusively with the fate of self-experience in the individual, he was by the very nature and material of his researches, clinical as well as metapsychological, enmeshed in the tradition of Modernism in European cultures.

Modernism is a historical process that took more than three centuries to crystallize its identity towards the end of the nineteenth century.

T. S. Eliot, in his famous essay, 'The Metaphysical Poets' (1921), has argued: 'In the seventeenth century a dissociation of sensibility set in, from which we have never recovered.'

Foucault (1970), the French historian-philosopher, concludes his book on the epistemology of 'the subject':

> One thing in any case is certain: man is neither the oldest nor the most constant problem that has been posed for human knowledge. Taking a relatively short chronological sample within a restricted geographical area – European culture since the sixteenth century – one can be certain that man is a recent invention within it.

Trilling launches his book *Sincerity and Authenticity* (1972) with the assertion:

> at a certain point in its history the moral life of Europe added to itself a new element, the state or quality of the self which we call sincerity. The word as we now use it refers primarily to a congruence between avowal and actual feeling.

I have quoted from the above authors to establish the fact that a radical change has taken place in the European man's epistemology of self-experience. None can date its exact beginnings: sometime in the sixteenth century the process of Modernism starts. What factors lead to its inception are equally unclear: no two scholars agree on that score. The complexity, as well as the ambiguity, of the myriad forces culturally at work compel each of us to attempt his own abstraction of the crucial elements involved.

Since the beginning of the human cultures, so far as we know, man has always experienced, known and felt his own *being* through *the other*. This *other* was always non-human: a fetish (as in the primitive African cultures); an idol (Buddha is the supreme example); anthropomorphic supra-human presences (the gods of the Greeks abundantly testify to that) or God, that unique invention of the monotheistic religions (Judaism, Christianity and Islam). Sometime in the sixteenth century all this began to change (cf. Gay 1966).

The most revolutionary characteristic of Modernism is the European man's decision to be his own sole witness and exclude God, more and more, from his private relation to himself and his personal relation with others. Nietzsche (1882), in his parable of The Madman, epitomized the end-product of this process:

> Have you ever heard of the madman who on a bright morning lighted a lantern and ran to the market-place calling out unceasingly: 'I seek God! I seek God!' As there were many people standing about who did not believe in God, he caused a great deal of amusement. Why! is he lost? said one. Has he strayed away like a child? said another. Or does he keep himself hidden? Is he afraid of us? Has he taken a sea-voyage? Has he emigrated? – the people cried out laughingly, all in a hubbub. The insane man jumped into their midst and transfixed them with his glances. 'Where is God gone?' he called out. 'I mean to tell you! *We have killed him* – you and I! We are all his murderers!'

Parallel with the European man's rejection of God another process starts to gain momentum: his idolization of the machine. By the end of the nineteenth century machines were not only running the lives of men, but *the machine* itself had become the model in terms of which man was going to explain, understand and regulate his own nature and character. Two consequences of the omnipresence of technics in the affairs of men determine the character of Modernism. The first is the dissociation of words from spoken and shared discourse into printed matter (cf. McLuhan 1962). The second is the invention of the new photographic image. This in time disrupted the humanistic tradition of pictorial arts in Europe and, with the advent of cinematic technics, created an appetite for visual experiences that are as hallucinatory as they are asyntactic (cf. Ortega y Gasset 1948).

So far I have indicated the cultural processes that shape Modernism. Now I shall discuss three persons who have given Modernism its peculiar and specific bias as well as character: Montaigne, Descartes and Rousseau.

Michel de Montaigne (1533–92)

The Essays (1580–88) of Montaigne establish a revolutionary departure in European man's attempt to study and know himself. Their uniqueness rests in the fact that Montaigne stakes his right to be his own exclusive witness, both in his privacy with himself and his relationship with others: 'There is no sure witness except each man to himself.' And what is even more important, Montaigne does not seek after either an absolute knowledge or an ideal experience of man. He concludes one of his last essays, 'Of Vanity', where he accounts his need to have written the essays and to witness his life:

> If others examined themselves attentively, as I do, they would find themselves, as I do, full of inanity and nonsense. Get rid of it I cannot without getting rid of myself. We are all steeped in it, one as much as another; but those who are aware of it are a little better off – though I don't know.

To have shifted the emphasis from wisdom to awareness lent an empirical direction to the epistemology of self-experience. Montaigne, in the same essay, sees through all the contrariness that wisdom entails for us:

> Human wisdom has never yet come up to the duties that she prescribed for herself; and if she ever did come up to them, she

> would prescribe herself others beyond, to which she would aim and aspire, so hostile to consistency is our condition. Man ordains that he himself shall be necessarily at fault.

For Montaigne awareness is of the lived experience, the instrument of self-study is judgement, and the aim is good ordinary living. He does not idealize his vocation as a writer either:

> Whatever I may be, I want to be elsewhere than on paper. My art and my industry have been employed in making myself good for something; my studies, in teaching me to do, not to write. I have put all my efforts into forming my life. That is my trade and my work. I am less a maker of books than of anything else.

And for Montaigne awareness is based on psychology and not morality, since the aim of awareness is to strive after happiness, that is, freedom from pain, but not through repression or denial of the seamy side of human nature. He states this explicitly in his 'Apology for Raymond Sebond':

> I am glad not to be sick; but if I am, I want to know I am; and if they cauterize or incise me, I want to feel it. In truth, he who would eradicate the knowledge of evil would at the same time extirpate the knowledge of pleasure, and *in fine* would annihilate man.

I shall discuss later how Freud was to come to the same conclusion in psychotherapeutics.

I hope these quotations will have given some idea of Montaigne's basic thinking. But there are a few circumstances of his life that need to be mentioned because they are inherent in the evolution of his thought.

Montaigne was reared by a loving father in an affluent feudal home in Bordeaux. The most fateful relationship of his life was with his friend Étienne de la Boétie, who was some three years older than him. They had probably met in 1559 when Montaigne had entered the Bordeaux *parlement*, and their friendship was as short-lived as it was intense and mutual. La Boétie died suddenly, very young, in 1563. It was this friendship that was to be the lasting presence in Montaigne's life. I have discussed the role of this crucial friendship in the genesis of *The Essays* elsewhere (Khan 1970*a*). Frame (1965) is quite justified in his assertion, 'there is much to show that *The Essays* themselves are – among other things – a compensation for the loss of La Boétie.' Some eight years after the death of his friend, in 1571, Montaigne, 'long weary of the servitude of the court and of public employments, while still entire, retired to the bosom of the learned Virgins' in his ancestral home, Chateau de Montaigne. He was barely thirty-eight years of age.

These two facts of his experience deserve special attention, namely, the internalization of a *lost* human relationship that had been mutual and lived, as well as the establishment of a secular space in which to relate to and reflect upon himself. It would be mistaken to think of Montaigne as if he were a sage living in a retreat. His act had little mystical or spiritual motivation. To the end of his life, while he wrote his *Essays*, he kept up a full-blooded interest in life and others. Luther (1483–1546) and Calvin (1509–64) had already placed the European Christian man in direct private relationship with God, without the mediation of the church (cf. Bainton 1967). Montaigne took this a step further and made man his own witness, in privacy with himself and the other humans. In this respect Montaigne in his *Essays* offers us the first private and personal record of self-experience which has no other referents but the lived human life. Montaigne rendered the human condition the exclusive concern of human beings. As Erich Auerbach (1946) has pertinently remarked: 'The obligatory basis of Montaigne's method is the random life one happens to have.' Montaigne, in his essay, 'Of Repentance', had stated his own method incisively:

> Others form man; I describe him, and portray a particular one, very ill-formed, whom I should really make very different from what he is if I had to fashion him over again. But now it is done . . . I do not portray being: I portray passing. Not the passing from one age to another, or, as the people say, from seven years to seventy years, but from day to day, from minute to minute. . . . If my mind could gain a firm footing, I would not make essays, I would make decisions; but it is always in apprenticeship and on trial.
>
> I set forth a humble and inglorious life; that does not matter. You can tie up all moral philosophy with a common and private life just as well as with a life of richer stuff. Each man bears the entire form of man's estate (*l'humaine condition*).
>
> Authors communicate with the people by some special extrinsic mark; I am the first to do so by my entire being, as Michel de Montaigne, not as grammarian or a poet or a jurist. If the

> world complains that I speak too much of myself, I complain that it does not even think of itself.

What Montaigne achieved for man's conscious self-awareness, Freud, some three centuries later, was to reclaim from man's unconscious. Montaigne not only epitomized in his person the European man of the Renaissance but he also prefigured the existentialist man of today, in all his natural flux, veracity and absurdity (cf. Krailsheimer 1971). Hence the acumen of Sainte-Beuve's (1849) remark: 'Il y a un Pascal dans chaque Chrétien, de même qu'il y a un Montaigne dans chaque homme purement naturel.'

The genius of Montaigne's style in *The Essays* is its capacity to sustain an enigmatic undecidedness in the myriad contradictions of self-experience (cf. Olney 1972). Montaigne's *Que sais-je?* is neither doubt nor scepticism; it is the process of self-perception. It is this process that *The Essays* witness and describe. Thus, in Auerbach's phrase, Montaigne 'writes the first work of lay introspection'. Montaigne himself had claimed for his *Essays*:

> I dare not only to speak of myself, but to speak only of myself; I go astray when I write of anything else, and get away from my subject. I do not love myself so indiscriminately, nor am I so attached and wedded to myself, that I cannot distinguish and consider myself apart, as I do a neighbour or a tree. It is as great a fault not to see how far our worth extends, as to say more about it than we see. We owe more love to God than to ourselves and we know him less, and yet we speak our fill of him.

Voltaire, that gnomic high priest of the Enlightenment, in a letter from Paris to Comte de Tressan (21 August 1746), summed up the virtues of Montaigne:

> He bases his thoughts on those of the celebrated figures of antiquity; he weighs them up; he wrestles with them. He converses with them, with his reader and with himself. Always original in the presentation of his objects, always full of imagination, always a painter and what appeals to me is that he was always capable of doubt.

René Descartes (1596–1650)

Some fifty years separate the publication of Montaigne's *Essays* from Descartes' *Discourse on Method* (1637). It is not my intention to discuss the Cartesian philosophy. I wish merely to indicate how, though sharing a certain tradition of scepticism and lay introspection with Montaigne, Descartes splintered that *wholeness* of the individual self-experience that was the high purpose of the Renaissance man (cf. Wade 1971). *Discourse* is written in an autobiographical style, like *The Essays*. In 'Discourse 1', Descartes tells us:

> the only profit I appeared to have drawn from trying to become educated, was progressively to have discovered my ignorance . . . I took to be tantamount to false everything which was merely probable . . . This is why, as soon as I reached an age which allowed me to emerge from the tutelage of my teachers, I abandoned the study of letters altogether, and resolving to study no other science than that which I could find within myself or else in the great book of the world, I spent the rest of my youth in travelling.

One immediately gets an uncanny feeling that Descartes already knows what he is going to find out. This is not the random and multifarious self-awareness of Montaigne. It has a distinctly intent quality to it. In 'Discourse 2', Descartes announces: 'My plan has never gone beyond trying to reform my own thoughts and to build on a foundation which is wholly my own.' Then he tells us the four rules that he has resolved never to fail to observe:

> The first was never to accept anything as true that I did not know to be evidently so: that is to say, carefully to avoid precipitancy and prejudice, and to include in my judgements nothing more than what presented itself so clearly and so distinctly to my mind that I might have no occasion to place it in doubt.
>
> The second, to divide each of the difficulties that I was examining into as many parts as might be possible and necessary in order best to solve it.
>
> The third, to conduct my thoughts in an orderly way, beginning with the simplest objects and the easiest to know, in order to climb gradually, as by degrees, as far as the knowledge of the most complex, and even supposing some order among those objects which do not precede each other naturally.
>
> And the last, everywhere to make such complete enumerations and such general reviews that I would be sure to have omitted nothing.

Here we have the first schema of that obsession with dissecting facts into their component parts for examination, quantification and generalization that was to be the practice of scientific thinking and research for the centuries to follow. And this leads Descartes to postulate: 'as there is only one truth to each thing, whoever finds it knows as much about the thing as there is to be known.' So all things are knowable in an absolute quantitative way. In 'Discourse 3', Descartes informs us that he has formed 'a provisional moral code which consisted of only three or four maxims. . . .' The third maxim deserves special notice:

> My third maxim was to try always to conquer myself rather than fortune, and to change my desires rather than the order of the world, and generally to accustom myself to believing that there is nothing entirely in our power except our thoughts, so that after we have done our best regarding things external to us, everything is for us absolutely impossible.

The irony here rests in the fact that this most humble aim of Descartes was in time to lead to the most militant type of materialism when, with the Industrial Revolution, man as a 'thinking thing' took charge of the total environment for its conquest, 'making ourselves, as it were, masters and possessors of nature'.

It is in 'Discourse 4' that all the basic tenets of Cartesian logic and method are laid down:

> . . . reject as being absolutely false everything in which I could suppose the slightest reason for doubt, in order to see if there did not remain after that anything in my belief which was entirely indubitable . . . But immediately afterward I became aware that, while I decided thus to think that everything was false, it followed necessarily that 'I' who thought thus must be something; and observing that this truth: *I think, therefore I am*, was so certain and so evident that all the most extravagant suppositions of the sceptics were not capable of shaking it, I judged that I could accept it without scruple as the first principle of the philosophy I was seeking. . . . I thereby concluded that I was a substance, of which the whole essence or nature consists in thinking, and which, in order to exist, needs no place and depends on no material thing; so that this 'I', that is to say, the mind, by which I am what I am, is entirely distinct from the body, and moreover, that even if the body were not, it would not cease to be all that it is. . . . Following this, reflecting on the fact

> that I had doubts, and that consequently my being was not completely perfect, for I saw clearly that it was a greater perfection to know than to doubt, I decided to inquire whence I had learned to think of some thing more perfect than myself; and I clearly recognized that this must have been from some nature which was in fact more perfect. . . . With the result that it remained that it must have been put into me by a being whose nature was truly more perfect than mine and which even had in itself all the perfections of which I could have any idea, that is to say, in a single word, which was God. . . . But, because I had already recognized in myself very clearly that intelligent nature is distinct from the corporeal, considering that all composition is evidence of dependency, and that dependency is manifestly a defect, I thence judged it that it could not be a perfection in God to be composed of these two natures, and that, consequently, he was not so composed; but that, if there were any bodies in the world or any intelligences or other natures which were not wholly perfect, their existence must depend on his power, in such a way that they could not subsist without him for a single instant. . . . For, finally, whether we are awake or asleep, we should never let ourselves be persuaded except on the evidence of our reason. And it is to be observed that I say: of our reason, and not: of our imagination or our senses.

I have quoted copiously from such a well-known text because Descartes himself had urged the future generations, in 'Discourse 6', that they were 'never to believe the things people tell them come from me, unless I myself have published them'. It is not my intention to belittle the enormous debt that European thought, and especially science, owes to the Cartesian method. Descartes is the true apostle of the conception of mechanism and asserted that the universe as a whole and in part could be understood only as a mechanized system, and by the mind alone. I only wish to establish the fact that by asserting, 'my essence consists in this alone, that I am a thinking thing . . .' ('Sixth Meditation', 1641), Descartes had firmly established that dissociation between mind and body that Eliot diagnosed in the metaphysical poets as 'a mechanism of sensibility which could devour any kind of experience'.

What was experience, free-floating self-study and essay in Montaigne changed to absoluteness of thought, necessity of doubt and that ideal reality which is God (cf. Hazard 1935).

Wade, in his monumental study of the French Enlightenment (1971), claims:

> Montaigne and Descartes are in full agreement that the making of a personality is fundamentally a problem in epistemology. They agree that the personality requires a certain stimuli in order to express itself. Both are convinced that consciousness of oneself is evidence of the existence of the self; that a guarantee of this self derives from the ability to relate, i.e. to recite, oneself to others. Both undertake this relation in as ingenious and straightforward a way as possible. This injection of the 'je' into the history of the universe is not sufficient though. It must be stimulated by certain procedures: by the determination to observe and compare the different sorts of characters, societies, countries; by travelling as a means of acquiring, at first hand, evidence for this comparison, by extracting from these experiences with the outside world a mode of conduct or at least a general ethical position based on comparison of these countries, their customs, their general character. Finally, these digested experiences should give impetus to knowledge of oneself, one's possibilities, one's own character. In fact, the whole of Descartes' provisional morality is but a repetition of Montaigne's moral position.

There is indeed no doubt that Montaigne and Descartes established two apices of the epistemological triangle, namely, '*Que sais-je?*' and '*Je pense, donc je suis!*' It remained for Rousseau to provide the third apex which would complete the epistemological triangle: '*Moi seul. Je sens mon coeur et je connais les hommes.*'

Jean-Jacques Rousseau (1712–78)

Rousseau is both a more complex person and a more revolutionary thinker than either Montaigne or Descartes. He was not only intent upon his innocent uniqueness but also determined to change the social order of human affairs; he was 'a righter of wrongs' (*Confessions*). Cassirer (1951) has neatly summed up this latter aspect of Rousseau's life and work:

> Rousseau's ethical and political theory places responsibility where it had never been looked for prior to his time. Its historical significance and systematic value lie in the fact that it

> creates a new subject of 'imputability'. This subject is not individual man but society. The individual as such, as he comes from nature's workshop, is still without the pale of good and evil. He follows his natural instinct of self-preservation, and he is governed by his 'self-love' (*amour de soi*); but this self-love has not yet degenerated into 'selfish love' (*amour propre*) whose only satisfaction lies in the subjection of others to its will. Society alone is responsible for this kind of selfish love.

Here I shall be concerned only with Rousseau's contribution to the epistemology of self-experience. Like Montaigne and Descartes, Rousseau experiences and expresses his life-experience in terms of the 'I' (*Je*) – but with what a difference. Whereas Montaigne actualized his experience of himself in life and Descartes found his identity from his thought, Rousseau uses *The Confessions* (1728*a*) as an instrument of becoming himself, his *true* self. His writing *creates* his being. Hence the acumen of Pontalis' (1973) remarks in his Preface to the Folio edition of *Les Confessions*:

> For its author as well as for ourselves this book is primarily an act. An act of confession and not of recall, even if the narrative is chronologically structured. It is a call to the other, seductive and pathetic, which alternately rouses in the reader a sense of intimate complicity and irritated distancing, but it is not a search for lost time. An apology and not a balance sheet. A passionate discourse of a limitless and vagrant subjectivity which declares its rights; and it is not a calm *essai* which a man in his closet has written about himself, finding in his retreat a sure place for his retreating reflections. It is a self-representation which moves from external appearance towards the interior and not a portrait which outlines features. Even more it is a *founding* act and it is our duty to ratify the first words of the proud introductory declaration of: *I have resolved on an enterprise which has no precedent* in order to challenge the second: *and which will have no imitator.*

This *act* was Rousseau's novel use of language and *écriture*. The contents of this *act* are feelings, not thoughts or actions. In Book 7 of *The Confessions*, Rousseau vividly details his method for *creating* his being through his *écriture*:

> I have only one faithful guide on which I can count; the succession of feelings which have marked the development of

> my being, and thereby recall the events that have acted upon it as cause or effect. I easily forget my misfortunes, but I cannot forget my faults, and still less my genuine feelings. The memory of them is too dear ever to be effaced from my heart. I may omit or transpose facts, or make mistakes in dates: but I cannot go wrong about what I have felt, or about what my feelings have led me to do; and these are the chief subjects of my story. The true object of my confessions is to reveal my inner thoughts exactly in all the situations of my life. It is the history of my soul that I have promised to recount, and to write it faithfully I have need of no other memories; it is enough if I enter again into my inner self, as I have done till now.

With these seemingly naive assertions, 'I know my heart and understand my fellow man,' 'I am like no one in the whole world . . . I am different', Rousseau sets out the basic programme for the epistemology of all the Romantics right up to our times. To Descartes' *I think, therefore I am*, Rousseau juxtaposed the corrective, *I feel, therefore I am*. This was to become the concluding apex of the epistemological triangle. And in the space of this triangle all the convolutions and paradoxes were to be lived out by the Romantics and their followers to our days. The basic characteristics of the Romantic sensibility are all there in Rousseau's life and work: a perfervid addiction to subjectivity of self; an idealism about human social life matched only by a militant and egotistical disregard of social conduct; a gnawing but relentless pursuit of alienation of self from others and that *ennui* which is born of an unyielding arrogance of dismay. At the end of his life Rousseau, in the 'First Promenade' of *The Reveries of a Solitary* (1782*b*), states his case with his typical intensity:

> All is ended for me upon the earth; none can now do me good or evil. There remains for me neither anything to hope for nor to fear in this world, and now I am tranquil at the bottom of the gulf, a poor unfortunate mortal but as undisturbed as God . . . alone for the rest of my life, because I cannot find except in myself consolation, hope and peace, I ought not, and do not wish to occupy myself any longer save with myself.

Rousseau (1762), who had claimed for man, 'The supreme enjoyment is in contentment with oneself; it is to merit this contentment that we are placed on the earth and endowed with liberty', found this supreme enjoyment in satisfaction neither with himself nor with anyone else. But what Rousseau did find was the creation of that space and reality in language and *écriture* which actualized his being for himself and for all generations to come. We share experience with Montaigne and think with Descartes, but with Rousseau we partake of an *act* which is his *being* created through the written word. Rousseau did not describe man, like Montaigne, or think him up, like Descartes; he *created* man with language, from imagination and feelings. Starobinski (1971*b*) states Rousseau's case poignantly:

> The eloquence of Jean-Jacques Rousseau is that of an unprovided man, with no claims other than his love of truth, and who feels himself reduced to those resources which he can draw only from his own utterances.

The Romantic Increments: from Blake's Songs of Innocence and Experience *(1789) to Rimbaud's* Une Saison en Enfer *(1873)*

My concern here shall not be with the poetry of the Romantics but with their critical thought and their passions of the mind. From Blake's (1789) pondering:

> Tiger! Tiger! burning bright
> In the forests of the night,
> What immortal hand or eye
> Dare frame thy fearful symmetry?

to Rimbaud's (1873) declamations:

> I have swallowed a famous gulp of poison. Thrice blessed be the counsel that came to me . . . I am burning as I should. There then, demon . . . The hallucinations are innumerable . . . Ecstasy, nightmare, sleep in a nest of flames . . . I am a master of phantasmagoria. Listen! . . . I have all the talents. There is no one here and there is someone: I do not wish to scatter my treasures. Shall it be negro songs, houri dances? Shall I disappear, shall I dive in search of the *ring?* Shall I? I shall make gold, cures.

the inner need of the Western man had changed to a search for self-cure. The poet, in becoming *voyant*, had also become alienated, sick and an exorcist.

How this change had come about within seventy years or so has been debated and argued about at length by literary critics. I shall follow Abrams (1953, 1971), since his discussion of the forces and issues involved strikes me as the most thorough as well as lucid. Abrams argues that with the Romantics a fundamental change had taken place in the relation between the artist and his productions, literary or plastic. The artist was no longer an inspired and ingenious imitator of objects or 'ideas' but had become a creator. And what he created were the expressions of his own feelings. Hence Wordsworth's announcement: 'Poetry is the spontaneous overflow of powerful feelings.' There is nothing novel about it in terms of epistemology, since Rousseau had already established feelings as the true source and content of human experience. What the Romantics did was to break up the unity of feelings into their components of perceptions and sensations. The function of imagination was to lend maximal intensity of experience as well as immediacy of perception and expression to these fragmented sensory experiences (cf. Abrams 1971). Blake, in a marginal note to Lavater's following aphorism:

> Distrust your heart and the durability of your fame, if from the stream of occasion you snatch a handful of foam: deny the stream, and give its name to the frothy bursting bubble.

had ruefully stated:

> *Uneasy: this I lament that I have done.*

Blake, in spite of his lament, established the sovereignty of intensity, immediacy and imagination in poetic experience more than any other English poet: 'Exuberance is beauty'; 'Passion and expression is beauty itself'; 'All things exist in the human imagination'; 'One power alone makes a poet: imagination'. And the enemy of imagination is 'Abstract philosophy' or the reasoning spectre. And finally: 'Imagination has nothing to do with memory' (cf. Damon 1973). It is to Coleridge (1817), however, that we owe the definitive Romantic attitude to imagination:

> The imagination then, I consider either as primary, or secondary. The primary IMAGINATION I hold to be the living Power and prime Agent of all human Perception, and as a repetition in the finite mind of the eternal act of creation in the infinite I AM. The secondary Imagination I consider as an echo of the former, coexisting with the conscious will, yet still as identical with the primary in the KIND of its agency, and differing only in degree,

> and in the mode of its operation. It dissolves, diffuses, dissipates, in order to recreate; or where this process is rendered impossible, yet still at all events it struggles to idealize and to unify. It is essentially VITAL, even as all objects (*as* objects) are essentially fixed and dead.

With Blake, Wordsworth and Coleridge we are still lingering with the transcendental idealistic value systems, and Western man holds on to a noble as well as spiritually elevated notion of his being and purpose in life. He also nostalgically clings to his belief in an innate natural innocence, that is corrupted and lost only through human exchange. It was the French poet Baudelaire (1821–67) who was to fix irreversibly the secularized image of man in aesthetic experience and give innocence itself a fresh and new human value.

It is well known how the appearance of *Les Fleurs du Mal* in 1857 had shocked and scandalized Paris and initiated a new sensibility in poetic experience, namely that of a transparent darkness and an ornate gnawing anguish. What is less often credited to Baudelaire are his contributions to aesthetics and epistemology. In 'The Salon of 1846' he stated:

> Enjoyment is a science, and the exercise of the five senses calls for a particular initiation, which only comes through good will and need. Very well, you need art.

A little later in the same article he states: 'Romanticism is precisely situated neither in choice of subject nor in exact truth, but in a mode of feeling.' What is important to note here is that this 'mode of feeling' ('*manière de sentir*') is no longer innocent and spontaneous but is rooted in *will* and *need*, as well as shaped by them. To this equation Baudelaire was to add two more elements: curiosity and convalescence. Baudelaire (1863) gives a vivid account of it while discussing the work of a painter, Constantin Guys:

> Because convalescence is a kind of return to childhood. The convalescent, like the child, enjoys, to the highest degree, the faculty of lively interest in all things, even those which appear the most trivial. Let us try to go back, through an effort of retrospective imagination, to our youngest and most fresh impressions and we will recognize that they have a strange affiliation with those vividly coloured impressions which we were later to receive following a physical illness, provided that illness had left our spiritual faculties pure and intact. The child

> sees everything *anew*; he is always *intoxicated*. Nothing so closely resembles what we call inspiration as the joy with which the child absorbs shapes and colours. I would dare to go even further; I would claim that inspiration has some connection with a *stroke* and all sublime thought is accompanied by a nervous fit, more or less strong, which rebounds right up into the cerebellum. The nerves of the man of genius are strong, those of the child are weak. For the former, reason occupies a considerable place; for the latter, feeling pervades almost all of his being. But genius is nothing other than willingly *rediscovered childhood*, a childhood now endowed for self-expression with virile organs and an analytic mind which enables him to arrange his randomly collected materials. It is to this profound and joyous curiosity that one should attribute the firm and sensually ecstatic gaze of children when confronted with anything new, be it a face or a landscape, light, gilt, colours, soft fabrics, their enchantment with beauty enhanced by *la toilette*. A friend of mine once told me that when, very young, he watched his father washing and dressing, he would contemplate in a stupor mingled with delight, the muscles of the arm, the gradations of different colours on his skin tinged with pink and yellow, and the bluish mesh of his veins. This external picture was already infusing him with respect and taking over his brain. Already form obsessed and possessed him. Predestination had precociously shown its face. *The damnation* was done.

Abrams (1971) has a succinct and conclusive comment on this passage from Baudelaire:

> The passage in Baudelaire, however, has overtones which signalize a new turn in the aesthetics of the innocent eye. The genius is 'an eternal convalescent' because he suffers from an incurable disease; artistic inspiration is something like a cerebral stroke; and the sustained sense of novelty in perception is a result of hyperaesthesia: 'I dare to press farther; I declare that inspiration has some relation with a cerebral congestion and that every sublime thought is accompanied by a nervous shock . . . which reverberates up to the cerebellum.' The born artist is an *artiste maudit*, for when as a child he showed himself to be 'obsessed and possessed' by external objects and forms, 'predestination' manifested itself in him and 'la *damnation* était faite'.

If Baudelaire had given a new direction and dimension to aesthetics, in his prose-poems ('Le Spleen de Paris', 'Paradis Artificiels', 'Journaux Intimes') he established a new epistemology where self-experience is refracted by a prismatic consciousness and where narrative is replaced by intense and instant lucidities. From here to Rimbaud's celebrated 'Lettre du voyant' to Paul Demeny (15 May 1871) is just a step.

Rimbaud (1973) was not yet seventeen years old when he wrote to his teacher, Georges Izambard, from Charleville (13 May 1871):

> I'm lousing myself up as much as possible. Why? I want to be a poet, and I am working to make myself a *seer*: you will not understand this, and I don't know how to explain it to you. It is a question of reaching the unknown by the derangement of *all the senses*. The sufferings are enormous, but one has to be strong, one has to be born a poet, and I know I am a poet. This is not at all my fault. It is wrong to say: I think. One ought to say: people think me. Pardon the pun.
>
> I is someone else. It is too bad for the wood which finds itself a violin and scorn for the heedless who argue over what they are totally ignorant of!

Two days later Rimbaud had spelt out the whole method of his aesthetic search to his friend Paul Demeny:

> Romanticism has never been carefully judged. Who would have judged it? The critics! The Romantics? who prove so obviously that a song is so seldom a work, that is to say, a thought sung and understood by the singer.
>
> For I is someone else. If brass wakes up a trumpet, it is not its fault. This is obvious to me: I am present at this birth of my thought: I watch it and listen to it: I draw a stroke of the bow: the symphony makes it stir in the depths, or comes on the stage in a leap.
>
> If old imbeciles had not discovered only the false meaning of the Ego, we would not have to sweep away those millions of skeletons which, for time immemorial, have accumulated the results of their one-eyed intellects by claiming to be the authors!
>
> The first study of the man who wants to be a poet is the knowledge of himself, complete. He looks for his soul, inspects it, tests it, learns it. As soon as he knows it, he must cultivate it! It seems simple: in every mind a natural development takes

place; so many *egoists* call themselves authors, there are many others who attribute their intellectual progress to themselves! – But the soul must be made monstrous: in the fashion of the comprachicos, if you will! Imagine a man implanting and cultivating warts on his face.

I say one must be a *seer*, make oneself a *seer*.

The Poet makes himself a *seer* by a long, gigantic and rational *derangement* of *all the senses*. All forms of love, suffering, and madness. He searches himself. He exhausts all poisons in himself and keeps only their quintessences. Unspeakable torture where he needs all his faith, all his superhuman strength, where he becomes among all men the great patient, the great criminal, the one accursed – and the supreme Scholar! – Because he reaches the *unknown*! Since he cultivated his soul, rich already, more than any man! He reaches the unknown, and when, bewildered, he ends by losing the intelligence of his visions, he has seen them. Let him die as he leaps through unheard of and unnamable things: other horrible workers will come; they will begin from the horizons where the other one collapsed!

Western man, who had started the secularization of the Self with such lofty ideals as the authenticity of experience (Montaigne), the sovereignty of thought (Descartes) and the inviolability of feelings (Rousseau), found himself, by the end of the nineteenth century, in the exalted stances of the scientist, the materialist and the *voyant*, on the one hand, and invalided, alienated and his own exorcist on the other.

I am well aware that I have not mentioned the contributions of the novelists to the Romantic sensibility. The poets, through becoming *voyant-exorcists*, had crystallized a new 'objet', the *poem*, sealed in the iconic privacies of its symbolism and hallucinatory imagery, its apotheosis being Comte de Lautréamont's *Les Chants de Maldoror* (1868). The responsibility of *mirroring* the individual in his relation with himself, the others and society had fallen on the novelist. Essentially, the humanistic aspirations of the nineteenth century were to actualize through its novelists and not its poets. One has only to pause and their presence overwhelms one: Scott, Thackeray, Dickens, Charlotte Brontë, George Eliot, Meredith and Hardy in England; Balzac, Hugo, Flaubert, Zola and Maupassant in France; Gogol, Turgenev, Dostoyevsky and Tolstoy in Russia. Yet one has to admit that in spite of their gigantic visions and creations, the novelists failed to establish a new aesthetic. It was the poet, in Rimbaud's apocalyptic idiom, *le grand maudit*, who was to dictate the crises of epistemology in the twentieth century.

Sigmund Freud (1856–1939): the Advent of the Patient as a Person

If Montaigne was his own witness, Descartes his own creator, Rousseau the apostle of his own feelings, and Romantics the exorcists of their sensibility, then Freud's genius and courage lay in becoming his own patient. A decade after starting his private practice, as a neuro-pathologist in Vienna, Freud wrote to his friend Wilhelm Fliess (14 August 1897):

> After a spell of good spirits here I am now having a fit of gloom. The chief patient I am busy with is myself. My little hysteria, which was much intensified by work, has yielded one stage further. The rest still sticks. That is the first reason for my mood. This analysis is harder than any other. It is also the thing that paralyses the power of writing down and communicating what so far I have learned. But I believe it has got to be done and is a necessary stage in my work (1950*a*).

Some three months later we find him telling Fliess (14 November 1897):

> My self-analysis is still interrupted. I have now seen why. I can only analyse myself with objectively acquired knowledge (as if I were a stranger); self-analysis is really impossible, otherwise there would be no illness. As I have come across some puzzles in my own case, it is bound to hold up the self-analysis (1950*a*).

How Freud's 'as if I were a stranger' reminds one of Rimbaud's 'Je est un autre'. Yet what a difference! It was not Freud's intention to abreact himself into language but to know himself through discourse. And he chose to have this discourse with the model case at the end of the nineteenth century: the hysteric. Freud was ideally suited by temperament for this dialogue with the hysteric. The documentation of his youth in Jones' biography leaves one in no doubt about that. In 1882 the twenty-six-year-old Freud had exclaimed to his fiancée: 'If you only knew how mad things look within me at the moment' (1961, p. 33). Freud was a man of intense but *contained* emotions. One could borrow Rousseau's formula and claim for Freud that he knew his own heart and understood the hysteric. And the route to that understanding was a long and arduous one for Freud.

When Freud undertook his pilgrimage to the famous Charcot at Salpêtrière in Paris in 1885–86, the symptoms of the hysteric had already gained a respectable status under Charcot's patronage. In his obituary of Charcot, Freud (1893*f*) gives us a clear picture of the hysteric's new status and fate:

> This, the most enigmatic of all nervous diseases, for the evaluation of which medicine had not yet found a serviceable angle of approach, had just then fallen into thorough discredit; and this discredit extended not only to the patients but to the physicians who concerned themselves with the neurosis. It was held that in hysteria anything was possible, and no credence was given to a hysteric about anything. The first thing that Charcot's work did was to restore its dignity to the topic. Little by little, people gave up the scornful smile with which the patient could at that time feel certain of being met. She was no longer necessarily a malingerer, for Charcot had thrown the whole weight of his authority on the side of the genuineness and objectivity of hysterical phenomena. Charcot had repeated on a small scale the act of liberation in memory of which Pinel's portrait hung in the lecture hall of the Salpêtrière. Once the blind fear of being made a fool of by the unfortunate patient had been given up – a fear which till then had stood in the way of a serious study of the neurosis – the question could arise as to what method of approach would lead most quickly to a solution of the problem. A quite unbiased observer might have arrived at this conclusion: if I find someone in a state which bears all the signs of a painful affect – weeping, screaming and raging – the conclusion seems probable that a mental process is going on in him of which these physical phenomena are the appropriate expression (p. 19).

But Freud overstates the case for Charcot. The hysteric in Charcot's famous neurological unit was still an *exhibit*, taken into medical care but not understood, exposed to public examinations but not talked with or listened to.

The hysteric had travelled a long and chequered route in European cultures: burnt as a witch in medieval times; confused with the mad and the insane and confined to leprosariums from the fourteenth to the eighteenth century, only to find further total constraint from medical procedures in the Age of Reason. Freed by Pinel from chains after the French Revolution, the hysteric was still being identified by the stigma of anaesthesia to become a legitimate neurological case for Charcot, just as the devil's patch had identified the hysteric as a witch to her Inquisitor. (Cf. Foucault 1965, Veith 1970.)

It was to be Freud's unique contribution to the responsibility of psychotherapeutics that he found a method, psychoanalysis, by which the symptoms of the hysteric could be deciphered through interpersonal discourse (the transference).

Freud himself has given us two succinct accounts of his struggles in finding his true vocation in life (Freud 1914*d*, 1925*d*). Medicine had not been a profession of choice for Freud, but there were very few prospects open to an ambitious and talented Jewish youth in the Hapsburg Vienna. He had a sense of destiny. From Paris, in 1886, he had written to his fiancée: 'I feel it in my bones that I have the talent to bring me into the "upper ten thousand".' It turned out to be an understatement. He was to be one of the two who would radically change man's relation to himself and others in the twentieth century. Karl Marx was the other. Looking back, decades later, Freud was to write about himself:

> After forty-one years of medical activity, my self-knowledge tells me that I have never really been a doctor in the proper sense. I became a doctor through being compelled to deviate from my original purpose; the triumph of my life lies in my having, after a long and roundabout journey, found my way back to my earliest path. . . . In my youth I felt an overwhelming need to understand something of the riddles of the world in which we live and perhaps even to contribute something to their solution. The most hopeful means of achieving this end seemed to be to enroll myself in the medical faculty; but even then I experimented – unsuccessfully – with zoology and chemistry, till at last, under the influence of Brücke, the greatest authority who affected me more than any other in my whole life, I settled down to physiology, though in those days it was too narrowly restricted to histology. By that time I had already passed all my medical examinations; but I took no interest in anything to do with medicine till the teacher whom I so deeply respected warned me that in view of my restricted material circumstances I could not possibly take up a theoretical career. Thus I passed from the

> histology of the nervous system to neuropathology and then, prompted by fresh influences, I began to be concerned with the neuroses. I scarcely think, however, that my lack of genuine medical temperament has done much damage to my patients. For it is not greatly to the advantage of patients if their physician's therapeutic interest has too marked an emotional emphasis. They are best helped if he carries out his task coolly and, so far as possible, with precision (Jones 1953, pp. 28–9).

Freud never felt the need to exorcise the ailment of others or become its accomplice. He was convinced that insight and self-knowledge were the only instruments that would help. I have already discussed this in two papers (Khan 1970*b*, 1972*d*); here I shall briefly detail the route which led him to the discovery of his psychoanalytic method.

The mystery of the hysteric's predicament had struck Freud very early. When he had qualified in 1881, the meagre medical techniques for 'dealing with' (I use the verb advisedly, because they were little more than that) the hysteric were hypnotism and electricity, both galvanic and faradic. Already in 1883, while treating his first private patient whom he had taken charge of during Breuer's absence, he wrote to his fiancée, Martha Bernays: 'In such cases one treats more with one's personality than with the instruments' (Jones 1953, p. 201). But Josef Breuer (1842–1925), a well-known physician in Vienna and the first patron-friend of Freud's in his early struggling years, had already confided to Freud his fateful encounter with a talented hysteric, who has since then become celebrated as a classical case of hysteria, Frl. Anna O. (Freud 1895*d*). Fräulein Anna O., a girl of twenty-one, of unusual intelligence and 'completely unsuggestible', had developed a veritable museum of symptoms related to her father's fatal illness. Even more interesting were her two states of mind: 'The patient was split into two personalities of which one was mentally normal and the other insane' (Freud 1895*d*, p. 45). When Breuer had first encountered his patient, in 1880, she was in one of her 'somnolent states', that is, auto-hypnotized. The patient had made a very positive attachment to Breuer and he had responded with a matching sympathy. It was Frl. Anna O. who compelled Breuer to listen to her 'talking cure' or 'chimney sweeping' (both her terms) through which narrative her symptoms would disappear. To spend time daily witnessing one hysteric was indeed a noble act of devotion on Breuer's part and most unusual at that time. Breuer's account of his case ends as follows:

> she was moreover free from the innumerable disturbances which she had previously exhibited. After this she left Vienna and travelled for a while; but it was a considerable time before she regained her mental balance entirely. Since then she has enjoyed complete health (Freud 1895*d*, pp. 40–41).

Some seventy years later Jones (1953) was to recount what had actually led to the end of the treatment of Frl. Anna O., as Freud had told him in confidence:

> Freud has related to me a fuller account than he described in his writings of the peculiar circumstances surrounding the end of this novel treatment. It would seem that Breuer had developed what we should nowadays call a strong countertransference to his interesting patient. At all events he was so engrossed that his wife became bored at listening to no other topic and before long she became jealous. She did not display this openly, but became unhappy and morose. It was a long time before Breuer, with his thoughts elsewhere, divined the meaning of her state of mind. It provoked a violent reaction in him, perhaps compounded of love and guilt, and he decided to bring the treatment to an end. He announced this to Anna O., who was by now much better, and bade her good-bye. But that evening he was fetched back to find her in a greatly excited state, apparently as ill as ever. The patient, who according to him had appeared to be an asexual being and had never made any allusion to such a forbidden topic throughout the treatment, was now in the throes of an hysterical childbirth (pseudocyesis), the logical termination of a phantom pregnancy that had been invisibly developing in response to Breuer's ministrations. Though profoundly shocked, he managed to calm her down by hypnotizing her, and then fled the house in a cold sweat. The next day he and his wife left for Venice to spend a second honeymoon, which resulted in the conception of a daughter; the girl born in these circumstances was nearly sixty years later to commit suicide in New York (pp. 224–5).

When Freud had travelled to Paris in 1885 he had this case in mind and tried to discuss it with Charcot, but Charcot showed little interest in it. Freud was in search of a question, and all he found were answers that begged the question. There is no doubt that Charcot's personality, genius and manner of working fixed Freud's attention on the hysteric as the model case, but in fact he learnt little from Charcot.

When he set up in private pactice in 1886, he tried every method then in vogue and abandoned them as futile. Freud was certain that a psychical process accounted for the hysterical symptoms, but its nature and function were all confused by the neurophysiological techniques and the rigmarole of hypnotic ruses. He had absorbed two disparate traditions: during his adolescence, the humanist tradition of imaginative curiosity about the individual's self-experience; later, from the medicine at the time, the scientific mechanistic tradition of arduous laboratory observation of facts. Freud was never adept at hypnosis; bullying was neither his nature nor his character. He even travelled to Nancy in 1889 to learn more about hypnotism from Bernheim's spectacular feats with his patients. Freud persuaded a recalcitrant female patient of his to accompany him to see if Bernheim could hyponotize her more effectively. It did not work, but it convinced Freud even further that the essence of the hypnotic treatment lay in the emotional relationship the patient built up with his doctor. In his autobiography (1925*d*), Freud recounts a misadventure with a patient of his during his early years of practice in the 1890s that finally convinced him of the futility of hypnosis:

> Increasing experience had also given rise to two grave doubts in my mind as to the use of hypnotism even as a means to catharsis. The first was that even the most brilliant results were liable to be suddenly wiped away if my personal relation with the patient became disturbed. It was true that they would be re-established if a reconciliation could be effected; but such an occurrence proved that the personal emotional relation between doctor and patient was after all stronger than the whole cathartic process, and it was precisely that factor which escaped every effort at control. And one day I had an experience which showed me in the crudest light what I had long suspected. It related to one of my most acquiescent patients, with whom hypnotism had enabled me to bring about the most marvellous results, and whom I was engaged in relieving of her sufferings by tracing back her attacks of pain to their origins. As she woke up on one occasion, she threw her arms around my neck. The unexpected entrance of a servant relieved us from a painful discussion, but from that time onwards there was a tacit understanding between us that the hypnotic treatment should be discontinued. I was modest enough not to attribute the event to my own irresistible personal attraction, and I felt that I had now

> grasped the nature of the mysterious element that was at work behind hypnotism. In order to exclude it, or at all events to isolate it, it was necessary to abandon hypnotism (p. 27).

When Freud discovered the *free association* method is not certain, but it was sometime between 1889–1895. Since Freud was always guided by the needs of his patients, one can pick out two other significant episodes that led to its discovery. The first is reported in his case history of Frau Emmy von N., where he was still using hypnosis:

> I *requested* her to remember by tomorrow. She then said in a definitely grumbling tone that I was not to keep on asking her where this and that came from, but to *let her tell me* what she had to say. I fell in with this. . . . (Freud 1895*d*, p. 63).

I have italicized 'requested' in the above quote because Freud was the first clinician in psychotherapy who sought the truth from the patient instead of dictating it to her. Neither Charcot, nor Bernheim nor Breuer talked with the patient. They isolated the symptom as a foreign body and attacked it with the aim to rid the patient of it. Charcot's famous case history of Ler, in his *Lectures on the Diseases of the Nervous System*, gives a vivid account of the patient treated as an exhibit. Freud learnt from the *persons* whose *symptoms* had rendered them into *patients* how to speak to them and help them to speak to him. Hence I have also italicized 'let her tell me'. Freud was also the first psychiatric clinician who, instead of explaining away symptoms, looked for their meaning for the patient. Freud established the function of the symptom as an intrapsychic communication, using the body for its language, especially in the hysteric. It was a long route yet before he would arrive at the full structure of his analytic method. But he was progressively shedding the techniques he had inherited from his teachers. In the case of Frl. Elizabeth von R., he decided to dispense with hypnosis altogether:

> When one first starts upon a cathartic treatment of this kind, the first question one asks oneself is whether the patient herself is aware of the origin and the precipitating cause of her illness. If so, no special technique is required to enable her to reproduce the story of her illness. The interest shown in her by the physician, the understanding of her which he allows her to feel and the hopes of recovery he holds out to her – all these will decide the patient to yield up her secret. From the beginning it

> seemed to me probable that Fräulein Elizabeth was conscious of the basis of her illness, that what she had in her consciousness was only a secret and not a foreign body. . . . In the first instance, therefore, I was able to do without hypnosis, with the reservation, however, that I could make use of it later if in the course of her confession material arose to the elucidation of which her memory was unequal. Thus it came about that in this, the first full-length analysis of a hysteria undertaken by me, I arrived at a procedure which I later developed into a regular method and employed deliberately. This procedure was one of clearing away the pathogenic psychical material layer by layer, and we liked to compare it with the technique of excavating a buried city. I would begin by getting the patient to tell me what was known to her and I would carefully note the points at which some train of thought remained obscure or some link in the causal chain seemed to be missing. And afterwards I would penetrate into deeper layers of her memories at these points by carrying out an investigation under hypnosis or by the use of some similar technique. The whole work was, of course, based on the expectation that it would be possible to establish a completely adequate set of determinants for the events concerned. . . . The story which Fräulein Elizabeth told of her illness was a wearisome one, made up of many different painful experiences. While she told it she was not under hypnosis; but I made her lie down and keep her eyes shut, though I made no objection to her occasionally opening them, changing her position, sitting up, and so on (Freud 1895*d*, pp. 138–9).

By 1897 Freud had found and established all the crucial elements of his psychoanalytic method. Let us examine how Freud had distributed therapeutic responsibilities between the patient and the analyst.

The essential responsibility of the analyst was that he undertook to try and understand, with the patient's help, the meaning of the illness for the patient (cf. Pouillon 1972). The symptom was no longer to be treated as a 'foreign body' to be exorcised out of the patient. He took it to be a specific way of communicating for the patient, no matter how garbled, distorted and unbeknown even to the patient himself. In order to decipher this communication, Freud offered the patient three basic rights: a total privacy of space; an agreed frequency of measured time for sessions; and a relationship that was contractual for both parties concerned and entailed working with each other. The patient could take his or her own time saying, without censorship from within or without, whatever came to his mind. This is what is usually referred to as free association. In this encounter the patient's incapacity to communicate was allowed for and understood as the result of repression, that is, as the consequence of intrapsychic processes. Similarly, the patient's refusal to cooperate was not taken for a malevolent negativity towards the person of the analyst but a resistance which was the inevitable interpersonal manifestation of the same forces that had led to repression. The analyst offered a vigilant and unobtrusive attention. But if Freud offered so much to the patient by way of care and understanding, his *method* also asked a lot of the patient. Primarily the patients had to accept responsibility for their symptoms. In spite of the suffering entailed, symptoms were a person's own specific creations and could not be understood without that person's willingness to undertake the responsibility of being their author. And discourse was to be the exclusive instrument of relating between the analyst and the patient: 'Nothing takes place between them except that they talk to each other' (Freud 1926*e*, p. 187). It was this peculiar and specialized way of relating to each other that was Freud's unique invention of shared therapeutic responsibility between the analyst and the patient. In his autobiography (1925*d*) he says:

> It is perfectly true that psycho-analysis, like other psychotherapeutic methods, employs the instrument of suggestion (or transference). But the difference is this: that in analysis it is not allowed to play the decisive part in determining the therapeutic results. It is used instead to induce the patient to perform a piece of psychical work – the overcoming of his transference-resistances – which involves a permanent alteration in his mental economy. The transference is made conscious to the patient by the analyst, and it is resolved by convincing him that in his transference-attitude he is *re-experiencing* emotional relations which had their origin in his earliest object-attachments during the repressed period of his childhood. In this way the transference is changed from the strongest weapon of the resistance into the best instrument of the analytic treatment. Nevertheless its handling remains the most difficult as well as the most important part of the technique of analysis (pp. 42–3, Freud's italics).

Freud's method demands a lot both of the analyst and of the patient. It demands an effective dissociation towards the self in each. The patient has to be able to experience, observe and report on himself. Similarly the analyst offers his mind and an 'evenly-suspended attention' (Freud 1912*e*, p. 111) to the patient. It is this last demand that has made most of those who come to psychoanalysis abandon it or try to modify it, because this 'evenly-suspended attention' in the analysis is conditional on the analyst being *free* from grossly repressive mechanisms in himself. In fact, Freud was asking in a therapeutic relationship what Coleridge had asked of the poet and the critic, 'a willing suspension of disbelief', by each of the parties concerned.

Let us hear a little more from Freud himself about his therapeutic method:

> The cathartic method had already renounced suggestion; Freud went a step further and gave up hypnosis as well. At the present time he treats his patients as follows. Without exerting any other kind of influence, he invites them to lie down in a comfortable attitude on a sofa, while he himself sits on a chair behind them outside their field of vision. He does not even ask them to close their eyes, and avoids touching them in any way, as well as any other procedure which might be reminiscent of hypnosis. The session thus proceeds like a conversation between two people equally awake, but one of whom is spared every muscular exertion and every distracting sensory impression which might divert his attention from his own mental activity (1904*a*, p. 250).

This was Freud's first definitive statement of his method.

But for Freud, with the discovery of his therapeutic method in 1897, the struggle had just started. The person he had to struggle with most was *himself*. He had found out the *how* of his method but not the why (the *meaning*) of the material. To discover this Freud realized that the analyst had to find it in himself before he could find it in the patient. Hence he launched his own self-analysis in 1897. This was Freud's most heroic undertaking and one that none can repeat because, after Freud, no one will ever be *innocent* again as to what he is undertaking.

In order to understand the meaning of what constituted the psychic realities of the hysteric, Freud decided to look into himself. The instrument of cure, the analyst, must know himself first and foremost.

This was Freud's arduous humility towards the task he had undertaken.

Introspection was not enough! One must have a witness to talk with. Introspection had already yielded its harvest: to Montaigne his *Essays*, to Descartes his '*method*', to Rousseau his *Confessions*. The nineteenth century abounded in intimate confessions of the self-experience (cf. Girard 1963).

Freud decided neither to solicit attention by confession nor to be his own alienated accomplice (like Rousseau). He chose to *share* and speak. The person he elected for this strange journey was Wilhelm Fliess – a man two years younger than himself. The tale of this odyssey we find in his letters to Fliess (Freud 1950*a*). I have already quoted the significant statement by Freud to Fliess. But he was to learn something deeper and larger from his self-analysis: *the impossibility of it.* Hence Freud's (1912*e*) insistence that every analyst must first undertake to be analysed himself:

> But if the doctor is to be in a position to use his unconscious in this way as an instrument in the analysis, he must himself fulfil one psychological condition to a high degree. He may not tolerate any resistances in himself which hold back from his consciousness what has been perceived by his unconscious; otherwise he would introduce into the analysis a new species of selection and distortion which would be far more detrimental than that resulting from concentration of conscious attention. It is not enough for this that he himself should be an approximately normal person. It may be insisted, rather, that he should have undergone a psychoanalytic purification and have become aware of those complexes of his own which would be apt to interfere with his grasp of what the patient tells him (p. 116).

It was through his self-analysis that Freud discovered the ubiquitous role of infantile sexuality, the Oedipus complex and castration anxiety in the 'modern' human being becoming a person. How Freud's self-analysis helped him refine further the psychoanalytic method, I have discussed elsewhere (Khan 1962). The climax of Freud's self-analysis and therapeutic work in the late nineties is *The Interpretation of Dreams* (1900*a*). The insights into the dreamwork led Freud to revolutionize man's understanding of his inner psychic and emotional reality. The discovery of the dynamic unconscious and its specific laws of functioning enlarged human consciousness to include what up till now had either threatened it or been kept out by it. It is not an accident that the first specimen dream Freud analyses is his own dream relating to a patient, which today would be called a countertransference dream. By taking this bold step, Freud established irrevocably the twofold and reciprocal nature of the therapeutic undertaking between the patient and his analyst. This was a hazardous and novel step forward in sharing the responsibilities in therapeutic relating. With this, the issue is no longer merely that of sickness but of authenticity. Freud was to revise and expand his conceptual structures of theory many times, but he had launched the twentieth century with a new humanistic vision, where man's inner reality was as much the concern of the other as his social experience. I shall let Trilling (1972) sum up Freud's case:

> The increased degree of systematic intentionality which psychoanalysis had discovered in what it designates as the unconscious did not make any the easier the task of bringing it into the comprehension of what it calls the conscious. On the contrary: the extreme complication of the topography and dynamics of the ego and the 'special work' it called for gave pause to the earlier therapeutic optimism of psychoanalysis, at least in point of the length of time required for successful treatment, leading Freud to write his paper with the disquieting title, 'Analysis Terminable and Interminable'. The increased refractoriness of the unconscious is to be laid at the door of a newly discerned principle of inauthenticity, the extent of whose duplicity is suggested by its success in appropriating the reason and authority of society for its own self-serving purposes. The virtually resistless power of this principle of inauthenticity is the informing idea of Freud's mature social theory.

An interesting paradox confronts us *vis-à-vis* the growing complexity of Freud's theories. Trilling is right in deciphering a new form of *resistance* entering the therapeutic alliance with the patient, that from the superego. But as Freud's thought permeates the sensibility of European cultures, a different situation actualizes with writers and painters. In Joyce's pun, from *Finnegans Wake*, their preoccupation becomes: 'Let us pry.' And what they pried into was the unconscious. Gradually the awake and rational ego began to *envy* the dreaming ego its access to the unconscious. Hence in this century most creative writing and painting takes on the hallucinatory imagery of dreams. The aim of the artists and writers becomes a frenzied pursuit of the unconscious. Joyce's *Finnegans Wake* is the extreme, absurd and unique attempt to make language speak with the grammar of dreams: condensations, displacements, puns, inversions, disregard of temporal and spatial relations, etcetera. Freud's therapeutic responsibility helped the patient recall his repressed past into a significant self-narrative. With the Cubists, Dadaists and Surrealists, the narrative becomes utterly suspect. The artists strive to make of the image (in word or plastic idiom) an absolute space and reality from which they do not awaken themselves. Joyce was to claim: 'Since 1922 my book has been a greater reality to me than reality.' Molly Bloom's nocturnal soliloquy, as it ends *Ulysses*, is a critical point in that crisis of consciousness which was to become the fate of Modernism in our times. Most creative effort was to become autotherapeutic and explore the dream-space. Joyce, in *Finnegans Wake*, gives the diagnosis and the new therapeutic responsibility in an epiphanic conundrum:

> Shem Macadamson, you know me and I know you and all your shemeries. Where have you been in the uterim, enjoying yourself all the morning since your last wetbed confession? I advise you to conceal yourself, my little friend, as I have said a moment ago and put your hands in my hands and have a nightslong homely little confiteor about things. Let me see. It is looking pretty black against you, we suggest, Sheem avick. You will need all the elements in the river to clean you over it all and a fortifine popespriestpower bull of attender to booth.

2
Beyond the Dreaming Experience

> God's my life! stol'n hence, and left me asleep! I have had a most rare vision. I have had a dream – past the wit of man to say what dream it was. Man is but an ass, if he go about to expound his dream. Methought I was – there is no man can tell what. Methought I was, and methought I had – but man is but a patched fool, if he will offer to say what methought I had. The eye of man hath not heard, the ear of man hath not seen, man's hand is not able to taste, his tongue to conceive, nor his heart to report, what my dream was. I will get Peter Quince to write a ballad of this dream: it shall be called Bottom's Dream, because it hath no bottom . . .
>
> SHAKESPEARE, *A Midsummer Night's Dream*

Since this is my third attempt to clarify and state my work on dreams, I shall give only a brief outline of my earlier hypotheses. The fundamental bias of my thinking is that psychoanalysis tries to abstract and make sense of the very private subjective experiences in a person. This person can be a patient, the analyst himself or a *mélange* of both.

In my Edinburgh Congress paper (Khan 1962) I had postulated the concept of a 'good dream' and argued that certain intrapsychic functions and ego-capacities were necessary for a person to be able to put together a 'good dream' from his sleep experience. Prominent among these were the ego's capacity to sustain the sleep-wish, controlling excessive influx of the primary process and appropriate dosage of 'day residues' to structuralize the latent 'dream wish' into a contained dream text. I had further stated that it entailed a capacity in the ego for narcissistic gratification from the dream experience in lieu of the more primitive narcissism of the pure blank sleep-state or the concrete satisfactions from reality. The capacity to utilize symbolization and dream work was also necessary for the articulation of the dream text. I had further tried to show how Freud had based the salient features of the analytic situation on the intrapsychic conditions that prevail in sleep, which are conducive to a 'good dream'. I had not given clinical material there because what was then available to me from my practice could not be exposed for professional reasons. Today, some fourteen years later, I can describe the two dreams from two patients that had guided me to write that paper.

The first dream is from a female patient, Mrs X, whose treatment I have described in an earlier paper (Khan 1960). She had come through a very regressed and dependent phase in analysis. She had been an alcoholic and was used to petty stealing, which had got her into trouble with the police a few times, and I had to rescue her. Towards the end of her treatment, when she was about to leave to take up a responsible job, she had dreamt:

> I find myself in the hospital dispensary. I collect a few bottles of sleeping tablets and walk out. Then I get confused and cannot find my way. Eventually I find myself in the occupational therapy room. I see there are paints and brushes and paper lying around. Since there was no one present I arrange the bottles and start making a still-life painting of them. As I am about to finish I become aware someone is watching me. I become terrified and nearly tear up the drawing, then realize that it is not the drawing but the bottles that I should be concerned about. I had stolen them. I turn round and the man strikes me as odd: he is short, grey-haired and looks like a Gestapo officer. Yet he had a kindly permissive face. I leave everything and walk back to my bedroom.

I shall briefly recount that the patient had come to analysis after she had taken an overdose of sleeping-pills and had gone out to drown herself in a nearby lake. She had become confused and had been aimlessly wandering when she was found by the warden and taken back to the house of her friends. The Gestapo officer had more disastrous and guilty associations. The patient had come to London from Central Europe and money was to be delivered to her here with which she was to help bring the rest of her family to London. The money had been delivered all right but her drinks had been laced with a strong sedative. When she had woken up in the restaurant, all the money was gone. Though she was by profession a qualified doctor, she had signed up as a nurse and worked in that capacity all through the war. The whole of her family had perished in Nazi gas chambers.

That this patient should dream this particular dream just as she was about to embark on an honourable and responsible professional career was very important indeed. It showed that she had acquired enough ego resources to cope with her guilt, on the one hand, and to sublimate her deprivation experiences into an aesthetic effort. She had not swallowed the pills, but started to paint them. The transference reference to me as the one watching her benignly also showed an intrapsychic shift from regressive dependence on an idealized me to use of me as a discriminating but noncensorious internal figure. The treatment of this patient had revealed to me most vividly how a person can hide her 'true self' behind the most bizarre psychopathology, but given the right holding-environment her untried ego capacities can begin to function with amazing intactness and efficiency. This to me constituted a 'good dream', because it integrated into a coherent experiential narrative what had so far been split-off and denied aspects of the self.

The second dream is from a patient about whom I have also written earlier (Khan 1963*b*). This patient had come in a very disturbed state, which had improved considerably in analysis. The dream I shall report is from the third year when he became well enough to take up a more responsible and lucrative job. It was a 'bizarre dream', to use the patient's own words. The dream was:

> I am watching two dogs playing. An older large dog and a very lively puppy dog. Suddenly the puppy dog mounts the large dog and the large dog collapses on his four feet.

The patient had woken up from the dream in tears: a rare occurrence for him. The meaning of the dream was very clear to the patient himself and he complimented himself on being able to cry about his father's debility (the old bigger dog in the dream). The whole of this patient's childhood had been cramped by his father's sudden collapse into an acute melancholic state, which lasted till his death some twenty years later. A gay and lively home had turned into a morbid nursing home. The father had lost all capacity to play with his sons or to take any joy in living. I was also taken in by the patient's sense of elation at expressing sadness and distress. He had not been able to show any sign of grief when his father died. It looked at the time as if this patient had achieved enough inner psychic growth to deal with the cumulative trauma from his father's decay into inertia and apathy. He did start the new job but, alas, his own character stayed rigidly negativistic towards the possibilities of new life.

It was material of this kind that led me to write my second paper, 'The Use and Abuse of Dreams' (Khan 1972*e*). In the intervening decade I had become progressively more sensitive to how the whole dream as an experiential entity can have quite a different value and function for a person than the component parts of the dream text. I began to suspect that the remembered dream, which I am calling here the dream text, can be a negation of *dreaming*. Following a hint from Winnicott (1971*a*), I began to scrutinize more vigilantly a person's *use* of the dream text in his total psychic experience of the self. Living with the 'dream text' can be an escape from external reality as well as internal psychic functioning, which inevitably draws upon primary process functioning and is enriched by it. But what had been pertinent for me from my clinical experience was the discovery of the *dream space*. I offered the hypothesis that the *dream space* has to be considered as an area where new experiences are initiated, to be affirmed or negated. I gave two clinical examples. I had compared the dream space to the transitional space of the paper which Winnicott (1971*b*) utilized in his squiggle-game consultations. Looking back, I can see that Mrs X used the dream space to extend and establish her freedom from guilt whereas the male patient failed to use the dream space for a new experience. The old dog collapses, as in the childhood reality. Hence the dream, in spite of its affective release, had the function of a negative therapeutic reaction.

I hope I have indicated enough of my earlier arguments. The new hypothesis that I wish to present for discussion is that we should distinguish between the *dreaming experience* and the meanings of the remembered *dream text*. My clinical work leads me to believe that *dreaming* is quite a different psychic event and experience from the remembered *dream text*. In our literature, dreaming and the remembered dream text are not sufficiently differentiated from each other. Yet I feel that Freud himself was aware of this distinction. His statement (Freud 1925*i*), 'those dreams best fulfil their function about which one knows nothing after waking', seems to imply more than merely the dream's function of preservation of sleep. About the defensive function of dreams, Freud (1923*c*) was explicitly clear:

> In some analyses, or in some periods of an analysis, a divorce may become apparent between dream-life and working-life, like the divorce between *the activity of phantasying* and waking life which is found in the 'continued story' (a novel in day-dreams . . .).

Jean Starobinski (1970), in his illuminating essay, 'Hamlet et Oedipe', has postulated:

> The unconscious is not only language; it is dramaturgy. That is to say, words in theatrical production, spoken action between the extremes of clamour and silence.

He further argues from it that:

> There is nothing behind Oedipus, because Oedipus is depth itself. Hamlet, on the other hand, invites us to ask a thousand ways the irksome question of what is behind Hamlet: his motivations, his past, his childhood, all that he dissimulates, all that he is unaware of, etc.

Following Starobinski's model, I am suggesting that the dream text has the same relation to the dreaming experience as Prince Hamlet to King Oedipus. Oedipus does not dream. He is the actualized event of a cultural dreaming experience. Hence the awe we feel at the end of Sophocles' *King Oedipus*. Oedipus is destiny:

> Born thus I ask to be no other man,
> Than that I am, and *will know who I am*.

Hamlet is fatedness:

> The time is out of joint: O cursed spite,
> That ever I was born to set it right!
>
> (I.V. 190)

Furthermore, Hamlet is haunted by his dreams:

> O God! I could be bounded in a nut-shell, and count myself a king of infinite space; were it not that I have bad dreams.
>
> (II. ii. 253)

Inherent to the dream text is the 'fatedness' of the person concerned. And it is this which lends the dream text its urgent demand to be shared with the other, interpreted and understood in order for things to be set right.

Ernst Hartmann (1973) has good reason to postulate: 'dreaming sleep has a function quite independent of what one recalls about one's dreams.'

It is precisely this function of *dreaming sleep* that I wish to examine. And I would like to make a variation on Pontalis' (1955) aphorism, 'The speaking subject is the entire subject' ('Le sujet parlant est tout le sujet'), and say, 'The dreaming subject is the entire subject.' The dreaming experience is an entirety that actualizes the self in an unknowable way. The dream text gets hold of some aspects of this dreaming experience and works into it the conflictual data from the *vécu* (remembered or repressed) of the person, to make a narrative that can be communicated, shared and interpreted. Dreaming itself is beyond interpretation.

Few will contest the assertion today that our clinical use of the reported dream text has changed significantly from what we find in the classical literature (cf. Sharpe 1937). We do not pursue the dream as a hermeneutic fetish. It is treated like all other reported or expressed behaviour, a piece of psychic reality and functioning to be evaluated and interpreted, *relatively*, in the here and now of the total transference situation. To say this is not to undervalue the unique character of dreams as 'the royal road to the unconscious' (Freud 1900*a*). The dream still provides us with the most condensed, vivid and complex specimens of the conflictual intrapsychic, intersystemic, as well as the interpersonal experiences in any given individual. Furthermore, one has to admit that though our clinical usage of dreams has changed, our understanding of dreams is not significantly more than where Freud left it. To my knowledge the only new conceptual hypotheses offered by analysts since Freud are those by Bertram Lewin (1946) of the dream screen and by Pontalis (1974) of the dream as an object. My concept of the dream space locates the dream more precisely but adds little to the understanding of the mechanisms of dream formation. It was an attempt to define significantly the space-potential of the dream towards self-experience. And it is this issue of the role of the self in dreams that I wish to elaborate further by distinguishing between the dreaming experience of sleep and the remembered dream text.

The difficulty here is of presenting pertinent clinical material. We have a vast literature on conflictual data, in dreams and otherwise. But those quiet and somewhat paradoxical vicissitudes of the self between 'the clamour and the silence' within are very hard to put into words, largely because our patients do not, either! These are inferentially assembled through a mutuality of playing dialogue between the analyst and the patient in an atmosphere of trust in unknowing.

My clinical attention was first drawn to the possibility of this distinction from treating young drug-addicts. I was impressed by the repetitive quality of their dreams and the banality of the imagery entailed. This paralleled their account of their 'trips', which were in the spoken narrative always repetitious and cumbersomely prosaic, in contrast to their subjective feeling that they had lived through a very intense, vivid and unique experience in the 'trip' itself. I began to suspect that the verbal recall failed as well as screened, even negated at times, the experience in the actual 'trip'. A chance phrase of a gifted and successful young pop-musician in analysis 'clicked' the issue into focus for me. He had smoked a lot of pot the night before and was dismayed at the paucity of his recall of what had happened to him. He had paused and then remarked:

> Let me try saying it this way: when I hear the right tune in that state I *am* that tune which I am also hearing. This may sound silly to you but it is true to my experience. There are four of us: the tune, me listening to the tune, and the tune and me as one. And yet again we are also all one. That is the joy of it.

Trying to link up with his trend of thought, I quoted him George Braque's statement about his cubist collages, where shapes are superimposed upon each other: 'Il ne s'agit pas de reconstituer une anecdote, mais de constituer un fait pictural.' ('It is not a case of reconstructing an anecdote, but of stating a pictorial fact.') This made sense to him and he elaborated it further by saying that in some ways the complete song undoes the auditory absoluteness of the tune. This had then led me to interpret to him that we were speaking of the distinction between the dreaming experience and the dream text; that in the dreaming experience the anecdote is absent, whereas the dream re-establishes the anecdote. I had then reminded him that when he had come to analysis it had not been to seek relief from any definite symptoms but to inquire into his feeling, which he had stated as: 'I am with life but not in it. I know others experience living differently and more fully than me. I am an onlooker.' He also had a keen awareness that there was something he experienced in sleep and in the 'trips' that he could never get hold of in his ordinary consciousness. This meant his staying almost suspended in a somewhat somnambulistic state while awake, hoping to lapse back into a sleep-state where he might re-find the experience. This stance of existing had proved to be very taxing for his wife and he had sought treatment largely to escape her pressure on him to become fully awake and to participate in family life.

It was in this climate of clinical work that I began to view the reported dreams as the sign of a failure to be in and with the *dreaming experience* outside sleep, and even in sleep. In this patient I began to see rather clearly how he used banal dreams and shallow sleep as a way to control his sinking deeper towards the dreaming experience. The search for this dreaming experience had, however, led him into smoking pot and taking LSD. The 'trips' *did* something for him, but again, on regaining his ordinary consciousness, he could not 'hold' or get in touch with that experience. The danger had arisen of him taking more frequent 'trips' and wishing to stay longer in them. This meant going deliberately absent from his waking or sleeping self and staying forever in a satellite psychic state of the 'trip'.

I am not satisfied with my description of how I learnt from this patient, but one thing is clear to me, namely, what I learnt: that there is a dreaming experience to which the dream text holds no clue; that the two are not complementary or antithetical to each other. In the total self-experience of a person they can sometimes be superimposed and at others stay separate and unrelated. But one has to be able to allow for the fact that the dreaming experience exists and influences the behaviour of the person, even though it cannot be cognized or brought into anecdotal narrative (pictorially or verbally); that one has to work with the *absence* of a *lived* experience in the person without seeking for its articulation through the secondary process thinking.

What I am searching to say is that the dreaming experience is not symbolic in the way we know the various dream structures to be. If that is so, then what sort of psychic process plays the crucial role in the actualization of the dreaming experience? The only feasible answer seems to be: the primary process. Here we encounter another area of contemporary analytic thinking and clinical work which is different from the classical approach. We do not consider the role of the primary process thinking or imaging as antithetical to secondary process thinking, as Freud did (cf. Laplanche & Pontalis 1973). Nor do we think that the primary process is inevitably and exclusively aligned to the pleasure principle (cf. Rycroft 1962, 1975). Today it is possible to envisage psychic states that further and actualize self-experience through predominantly primary process functioning. I am inclined to think that Winnicott's (1971*b*) squiggle game consultations depended for their success on the child's and therapist's alliance towards that relaxed mutuality of confidence and effort where something very near to the dreaming experience could crystallize. Case III, Eliza, aged seven and a half, is a good example of it. Looking back on the consulation reported, Winnicott says: 'The main part of this work was the child's own discoveries, or ordered sequence of discoveries, culminating in her being able to use the dream which she had had but from which she had not been able to derive full benefit until she was able to produce it and to draw it for my benefit in the therapeutic consultation.'

It is in Marion Milner's (1969) subtle account of her clinical encounter with her patient, Susan, that a person's struggle to gather something vital from the dreaming experience that has been lost, is most poignantly described.

Who can communicate the whole of his self-experience through verbalization, to himself or the other? An essential part remains inaccessible. Freud, I believe, covered this by his concept of the primal repression. What is entailed, however, is a certain type of psychic experience that never becomes available for ordinary mental articulation. I advisedly use the word 'ordinary' because it seems that poets, painters and writers have access to it through their imaginative functions. Hence William Blake's claim: 'The imagination is not a state: it is the Human Existence itself.'

To my earlier hypotheses of 'the good dream' and 'the dream space', I am adding a third: *the dreaming experience*. My argument is that a person in his dreaming experience can actualize aspects of the self that perhaps never become overtly available to his introspection or his dreams. And yet it enriches his life, and its lack can impoverish his experience of others, himself and his sleep.

3
Grudge and the Hysteric

In human cultures the hysteric has worn the mask that reflects the overt morality and the hidden sexual aspirations of the contemporary ethos. Hence if the hysteric has been at times identified as a witch and burnt, he or she has also been sanctified and celebrated as a saint. It was only toward the end of the nineteenth century that Charcot established the status of the hysteric's predicament as a specific clinical syndrome worthy of attention. But even with Charcot the understanding of the hysteric's predicament went little further than treating it as a prestigious psychiatric exhibit. It was left to the genius of Freud to define the nature and character of the hysteric's ailment. And Freud arrived at his insights through respecting the hysteric's 'resistance' to being known and his refusal as well as unwillingness to cooperate in his own cure. Freud (1895*d*) had argued that the hysterical patient's *not-knowing* was in fact a *not wanting to know* and he had concluded that this was 'a not wanting which might be to a greater or less extent conscious'. It is well known that Freud had at first ascribed this *not-knowing* to episodes of actual sexual seduction in childhood and later corrected it to fantasies of seduction that had been repressed and which the patient now expressed through a somatic language but refused to become aware of psychically.

Throughout history the bizarre sexuality of the hysterics had been castigated as the characteristic feature of their personality. What distinguished Freud's approach to the hysteric was that, in determining the aetiology of the hysterical symptoms, he had emphasized the predominant, and almost exclusive, role of infantile sexuality. This changed the whole approach to the hysteric's predicament. The hysteric was no longer to be maltreated as a psychopathic liar or a depraved sensualist but to be seen as a person trying to cope with experiences in early development that were vastly beyond the means of the emergent personality and for which there was little understanding available in the child's care-taking human environment.

In some seven decades since Freud's earliest writings on hysteria, psychoanalytic researches have added little to our further understanding of the hysteric. Instead, the clinical status of the hysteric has become confused with more severe personality disorders. In this essay, my argument is that the hysteric in early childhood deals with the failures of good-enough mothering and care by precocious sexual development. The primitive anxieties and affects generated by the failure of a phase-adequate holding-environment, and the resultant threat to the coherence of the emergent ego, are coped with by intensification, as well as exploitation, of the sexual apparatuses of the body-ego. Hence, from the beginning, a dissociation is established between sexual experience and a creative use of ego-capacities. It is this dissociation and specific technique of coping with excitement and anxiety that gives the hysteric's personality in adult life its peculiar and bizarre sexual character, both in behaviour and symptomatology. If in adult life the hysteric deals with anxiety by sexualization, in object-relations the hysteric employs sexual apparatuses of the body-ego in lieu of affective relating and ego-functions. Both the promiscuity and the inhibitions in the hysteric's sexual experiences result from this. The hysteric tries to achieve through use of sexual apparatuses what, otherwise, a person achieves through ego-functioning. This accounts for the craving for sexual experience in the hysteric, which is matched only by the hysteric's inability to sustain or be nurtured by any loving relationship. Hence, in their self-experience, the hysterics live in a perpetual psychic state of *grudge*. They feel that something is either being withheld from them or their wishes are not being recognized for what they are. What in the childhood experience was an incapacity of the emergent ego that failed to receive adequate coverage from the care-taking human environment, in the adult life is projected and experienced as a refusal by others to recognize their wishes (largely sexual) and to gratify them. Every hysteric, male or female, devoutly believes that gratification of his sexual wishes and desires would cure his illness. They attribute their inability to achieve this gratification through any partner to a lack in their partner's total acceptance and love of them.

If the hypothesis that the hysteric in his early psychosexual development has substituted sexual exploitation of body-ego for development of ego-functions is true, then one can understand why the hysteric is not only fundamentally ambivalent and hostile towards his own innate ego-capacities, but is also maliciously hostile and envious of any ego-functioning in the loved-object in adult life. The *promise* of the hysteric's ego-potential is a large component of his charm as a person, both as a patient and in society. But this ego-potential in the hysteric is continuously sabotaged, unconsciously, for the sexual solution. Hence the hysteric is at root pitted against his own ego assets.

Hysteria is essentially an illness that finds its character and shape at puberty, through adolescence. This corroborates my hypothesis because at puberty, once again, the struggle between sexuality and ego-functioning achieves a new, critical confrontation. And the hysteric's choice, preconditioned by childhood experiences, is inevitably for the sexual solution. Hence the intrusive omnipresence of infantile pregenital, as well as genital, sexual fantasies and their displacement to ego-functions in the identity formation of the hysteric. For this reason the hysteric seeks, omnipotently, to solve new life tasks with sexual reverie and complicity with the adult humans, and beseeches them to take over the necessary and required ego-functions. The overdependence of the hysteric on the adult loved-object is a technique for handing over personal ego-functions in order to live from the sexual solution. And even when a hysteric finds the sexual solution with someone, it never works for long. It inevitably, through its innate hidden logic, ends in grudge and complaints. Why?

The answer to this question is threefold. From my clinical experience I get the impression that the hysteric does not discover genital sexuality at puberty as a new and novel potential of the maturing body-ego. In the childhood psychosexual development of hysterics there has been a flight to premature 'genital' sexuality as a way of coping with ego immaturity. This 'genital' sexuality is by necessity overloaded with pregenital impulses and fantasies. Hence the emergent genital sexuality at puberty does not surprise and enrich the personality of the hysteric as a new experience, but revivifies all the earlier pregenital fantasy-systems, which now conflict acutely with the moral code and values that the person has imbibed en route. In this conflictual inner climate the hysteric experiences himself a 'victim' of instinctual forces and moral prejudices that are felt to be not of his creating and making. To act out seems the only feasible solution. But because of the dissociation between sexual fantasy and ego-functions, the hysterics stay passive and expectant, waiting for someone who will help them act out their bizarre amalgam of pregenital and genital sexuality. In treating perverts, I was struck by the fact that often their accomplices ('victims') were hysterical women. The hysteric needs the other's sexual facilitation, as it were, to act out the latent and repressed sexual fantasies. Hence hysterics always feel innocent in all that actualizes as sexual experience in their lives. They feel more done to than doing, more sinned against than sinning. Furthermore, consciously and overtly the hysteric rarely seeks an object for explicit sexual experience. The sexual desire and intent are expressed more as a tease and a provocation than as a self-acknowledged need. The clamour for sexual gratifications often emerges when the object-relationship has already become soured and the loved-object has begun to despair about finding an emotional mutuality with the hysteric. At the end of their relationships the hysterics discover, in a most sad and ironic way, the true need that was denied by them at the beginning. What the hysteric seeks through the sexual solution is essentially the facilitation of inadequate ego-functioning. It is this fundamental dissociation between body-ego and ego-functions that creates another dire predicament for the hysteric. The success of the sexual solution unconsciously means castration of ego-capacities. Sexual surrender to the object entails the threat of annihilation to the ego. Hence the hysteric's basic refusal of the sought and desired object.

Here we come to the second factor that militates against the success of the sexual solution with an external object. In all object-relating between the hysteric and others there is a basic *méconnaissance*. The object reads the hysteric's gestures as expressing sexual wishes and desires, and meets them as such, whereas they are essentially a symbolic body language for expressing primitive needs for care and protection. Hence the sexual experience for hysterics constitutes often a betrayal of trust and a crude exploitation of their sexual body-potential. A female patient, at the end of her perfervid love-affair with a very worthy man, exclaimed her grudge: 'What I needed was to be loved and all I have got out of it is being whored.' This mistrust of the gratifying adult object is preconditioned in hysterics by the character of their early childhood experiences. Their body-needs had been met but their ego-needs had not received the recognition and facilitation that was necessary. Furthermore, the hysterics project their own betrayal of the ego-process through precocious sexual development onto the adult objects in the new life situation. The essence of the hysteric's grudge, in this context, is that the new love object has also failed to distinguish between id-wishes and ego-needs in them.

This brings me to the third reason why the sexual solution fails for the hysteric. One of Freud's unique contributions to the epistemology of human experience is that he established the fact that hysterical symptoms are a *communication*, and this mode of communicating has its own peculiar grammar in human psychic functioning. Freud had spelt out how the hysterical symptoms communicate repressed and unconscious wish-systems, largely appertaining to infantile sexuality. Winnicott added to this hypothesis another dimension when he distinguished between unconscious (id) wish-systems and unconscious (ego) need-systems. His argument is that wish-systems can be dealt with by intrapsychic processes, for example, displacement, projection and repression, whereas need-systems demand actual external facilitation and support from the care-taking environment for the emergent ego-capacities in the child to become gradually capable of autonomously coping with them in time. In trying to understand the nature of affective and psychic functioning in delinquent children, Winnicott (1956) introduced the concept of the antisocial tendency.

Briefly stated, Winnicott's hypothesis is that an antisocial tendency can be found in all personality disturbances. The presence of an antisocial tendency indicates that 'there has been a true deprivation' in the person's early childhood, relating to good experiences in the ongoing life of the child, which were then disrupted or lost over a length of time during which the child was not capable of sustaining a memory of what had been good and positive. In later life the person acts out these traumatic experiences through an antisocial tendency. What characterizes the antisocial tendency is 'an element in it which compels the environment to be important'. Furthermore, the antisocial tendency implies 'hope' and represents 'a tendency towards self-cure'.

I find Winnicott's concept of the antisocial tendency extremely valuable for an understanding of the hysteric's predicament. It seems to me that the hysteric expresses the antisocial tendency through exclusively sexual experiences. In the developmental process the hysteric has dealt with what Winnicott calls mother's failure 'in catering for ego needs' by precocious sexual development. This makes the adult sexuality in the hysteric not so much the vehicle of instinctual gratification and nourishment as an idiom to communicate deprivation, and a technique for expressing hope that the object will heal the dissociation through reading the ego-needs that are unconsciously expressed through overt sexual compliance and instinctual seeking. Hysterics are notoriously gifted in finding suitable objects, only to defeat and dismay them. The 'promise' of the hysterical personality carries more of a hope in it than a wish or capacity.

Lastly, I would revert to Freud's original hypothesis of the role of *actual* trauma (seduction) in the aetiology of hysteria. There *is* an *actual* trauma in the aetiology of hysteria but it is not of a sexual nature. It relates more to the failure of the mother to cater to the ego-needs of the child. The child's 'self-cure' of this trauma by premature sexual exploitation of body-ego experiences sets the hysteric's basic model for all future situations of stress and conflict. It also conditions his use of objects as well as his own ego-capacities, and accounts for the fact that the hysteric is such a promising and recalcitrant patient. Analytic therapy works through provision of a highly specialized object-relationship. It is precisely in the area of object-relating that the hysteric has suffered his earliest traumata and learnt to be mistrustful. Hence the hysteric oversexualizes the transference, that is, tries to compel the sexual solution on the analytic process. What looks like the hysteric's acute intolerance of sexual frustration is in fact his basic mistrust that the external object will meet his ego-needs. Just as in life, so in the transference, the hysteric establishes that peculiar psychic reality – *the grudge* – through which he or she can relate without mutuality and communicate without the risk of being known and helped.

If the hysteric has been the initiator of the analytic therapeutic process, the hysteric also pushes it to its limits. In the past decade many analysts have questioned the analysability of the hysteric. Zetzel (1968) pertinently sums up the contemporary status of the hysteric in analytic psychotherapeutics when she states that the hysterics 'may have developed an intense, highly sexualized transference neurosis, but with little evidence of a stable analytic situation. None of them appeared to have made any genuine progress towards analytic resolution of their presenting problems.' I consider that the reason for this is our misunderstanding of the hysteric's mode of communication. The hysteric communicates with himself and others through symptom formation. The ability of the hysteric to create, manifest and exploit symptoms screens his basic incapacity to use psychic mental functioning, as well as affectivity, in relating to the self and the object. Anna Freud (1952) has postulated that in the pervert the central dread is that of emotional surrender to the object. In the hysteric the basic dread is that of psychic surrender to the object. The passivity and suggestibility of the hysteric misguide us clinically in truly evaluating his negativity toward pyschic functioning. The grudge in the hysteric further defends him against being helped to face this incapacity. The hysteric compels the environment to act upon him, or for him, but does not become accessible to mutuality of psychic dialogue and sharing.

If my argument that in the developmental process in childhood the hysteric has substituted precocious sexual development for ego-integration is true, then it is possible to postulate that the dread of psychic surrender for the hysteric entails discovering that there is little true creative psychic functioning or affectivity in him. This blankness constitutes the hysteric's essential predicament and militates most against a positive use of the analytic process towards self-knowing and personalization. Hysteria is not so much an illness as a technique of staying blank and absent from oneself, with symptoms as a substitute to screen this absence.

The question arises: what has necessitated this need for blankness and caused this dread of psychic surrender through the early mother-child relationship in the hysteric? Or to put it differently: why does the hysteric's inner life become a cemetery of refusals? I shall report on current work in the analysis of a young married woman to throw some light on the nature of the mother-child disturbance that underlies the hysteric's refusal of object-relating in favour of oversexualization of part-object gratifications.

After a year of very productive analysis, which had helped this patient to understand a great deal of her difficulties, having to do both with sexual frigidity and intellectual inhibitions, suddenly the whole clinical process came to a standstill. For six weeks she was unable even to speak in the analytic situation. Alongside this, her symptoms of frigidity returned in her marital life and she could not even open a book to read. Inertia pervaded all her behaviour inside and outside analysis. The first thing that became clear was that she had moved from an overexcited idealization of me to a passive denigration of me. I had become as useless as everyone else had been before in her life experience. She also became unable to eat anything. All this led me to interpret to her that the regression was now to a very archaic oral mode of desiring me, where my function as a person providing understanding and insight was experienced as a threat to her well-being. Little of this had any effect on her and she continued to punish me by turning up regularly and staying begrudgingly mute in the sessions. Eventually in one session she dozed off and was startled by a hypnogogic image that she had. It was not a dream. The image was that she was sucking my phallus. But as she became aware of it, she also perceived that I as a whole person was not there at all. There was only the phallus. From this it was possible for me to interpret to her that regressive part-object sexual incorporation of me through fellatio was her way of sustaining herself while rejecting me as a threatening person. From this point she was able to recall vividly how, from her very early childhood, she was aware of her mother's indulgent care of her person, particularly in terms of feeding her, but also acutely aware of a certain emotional mood in her mother from which she felt she must protect herself.

One could postulate from all this material, the complexity of which I cannot report here, that in the hysteric's childhood there is a precocious awareness of the mother's subjective mood as a person intruding upon the mother's care-taking function. The child in these circumstances regressively sexualizes a part-object relationship (gratification by the breast or its substitutes) in order to refuse that intrusion by the mother's emotionality and intimacy of mood with which a child's nascent ego-capacities cannot cope. It is this threat from mutuality that sets up in the hysteric a lifelong battle between seeking an exciting object and refusing it through the very act of gratification. Hence my statement that the inner world of the hysteric is a cemetery of refusals. Furthermore, as Freud himself stressed, the hysteric remembers par excellence through repetition. The hysteric remembers from early childhood largely somatic memories deriving from maternal care, which do not lend themselves to psychic elaboration and verbalization. Hence comes the hysteric's demand in the clinical situation for sensual gratification; because this demand cannot be met, his proclivity is to act out. It is this bias of the hysteric's sensibility to remember by repetition that pushes the analytic process to its limits. The ego-coverage that maternal care provided to the infant and young child's id-needs had in it, in the hysteric's case, an excess of intrusive personal needfulness of the mother, so that its satisfactions became idealized as a safe experience where there is a beginning and an end. By contrast, the ego-needs in the child become hidden or are expressed only through id-wishes. This sets up a perpetual confusion in the hysteric's subjective experience between true id-wishes and ego-needs. In adult life, and particularly in the analytic situation, what starts off as a demand for object-relating towards understanding of the self very soon changes to a confused clamouring for id satisfactions. In this context the interpretative function of the analyst is experienced by the hysteric as a phallic attack or seduction. Hence the hysteric has to refuse the whole relationship and return to the safety of that blankness which is a negation of both the self and the object.

4
None Can Speak His/Her Folly

This narrative of my clinical encounter with a young girl and the vicissitudes of madness, psychotic states, being in health, etcetera, is not a 'case-history' in the accepted analytic sense of that word, in so far as it eschews the use of metapsychological concepts. I have chosen to present the 'case history' first, followed by my theoretical discussion, because I do not wish to pre-empt the reader's freedom to experience and evaluate the clinical narrative.

Judy, age fifteen

This young patient had been compelled upon me by her physician, with whom I had worked for years, for urgent consultation, because she had attempted suicide a few days earlier. She was a plain but wholesome looking, buxom, puppy-fat girl. She was wearing the tightest jeans she could possibly have squeezed herself into. Her blouse was unbuttoned to an indecent point. She sat down and was very silent and sullen at the start. She had evidently tried committing suicide by cutting both her wrists, which were heavily bandaged, and which she flaunted by constantly shifting her arms. I concluded that at this visit she was certainly not going to 'speak' to me, but merely establish her presence by exhibiting herself. I decided to go along with her antics.

After some twenty minutes of mutually provocative silence, she asked in an aggressive way: 'You know what has led to all this?' I replied: 'No!' 'Don't you read the papers?' I replied: 'No.' 'Then what do you read?' 'Books,' I said. 'Well I can tell you it was headline in all the evening papers four days ago: the scandal, and it will be on the nine o'clock TV news again tonight.' I simply said: 'I don't see TV either,' and that even if I did, I would not see it tonight. Instead, I would wait until she was less ashamed and could trust to tell me the whole scandal herself. She sank into a raging silence for another ten minutes or so. I waited. Then, with a strange authority in her voice, she demanded: 'If you really want to help me, then get me out of school. I cannot go back. I am too ashamed, and I shall really kill myself next time.' I asked her how I could get her out of the school.

She said: 'Are you a fool. Ring the headmistress and tell her you are advising me not to return to school. And ring my father and tell him you have done it.' I told her that I would do it the other way around. I asked her to ring her father and ask him to speak to me. She did. When her father came on the phone, I introduced myself and said that I had now *seen* his daughter. 'She feels too ashamed to return to school,' I told him, 'and I am sure she means it when she says that if she returns, she will succeed in killing herself this time. So if I could have your agreement, I will ring the headmistress and inform her of "our" decision.' He requested me to do so.

Judy rang her school and the headmistress came to the phone. She was evidently an elderly wise lady, in so far as one could tell by her voice and speech. I introduced myself and told her that I was with Judy at the time and had *seen* her condition. 'It is her decision not to return to school,' I said, 'and I agree with that. I have talked with her father, and he has requested me to ask you not to put any sort of pressure on Judy to return to school.' The headmistress was silent for a while, and then said: 'Please write all this to me, and we shall not expect Judy to attend school any more.'

I scrutinized Judy's face carefully. There was no sly sense of triumph in her expression; only now she put her hands and wrists under her shirt. I had spent nearly two hours with her and was exhausted. I also felt that there was nothing more left to do in this consultation. I deliberately gave her the next appointment after the weekend. I took that risk – I was seeing her on a Thursday afternoon.

When she left, I rang her physician, who had referred her to me, and briefly told him what had transpired. I further arranged with him that on Monday (the next consultation) he should come with Judy and with Judy's father. I told him that what was necessary at this stage was *management* (à la Winnicott) and not psychotherapy, and this I wanted to programme together with them.

On Sunday, Judy rang me, and since she was on the list of 'critical' patients, the housemaid put her through. Judy said that she felt well, so I instantly knew that she was going to make a demand. She paused, and then in the gentlest voice asked: 'Can I bring my girl-friend with me on Monday, when I come?' I said: 'Certainly.' This gave me the opportunity to inform her that her physician and father were also coming. She said that she knew. They had told her. That ended the conversation.

An hour before the consultation on Monday, I began to feel extremely anxious, apprehensive and full of paranoid misgivings, and totally lacking in self-confidence with regard to being able to make a clinically positive encounter with the expected 'mob'. I have always been a one-to-one clinician, and here I felt that I had been bullied by my physician friend into 'group therapy'. I also felt acutely self-critical about not bothering to find out what the 'scandal' referred to. I could have asked the physician, even Judy, or seen the TV news, or the Sunday papers, particularly those that specialize in retailing scandal. Yet I felt that I was right not to have pried. It was not my style of clinical work, and instead of helping me, it would have further incapacitated me. Clinically, I have never found information as such of the slightest use. Alongside, I had such a vivid afterimage of my consultation with Judy, from which I had inferred three things:

1. that the girl I had *seen* was mad, behind all the antics of hysteria she had learnt to manipulate her environment with.

2. that behind the madness there was an ungraspable psychic pain in Judy, which she could neither experience as such nor speak about.

3. that for all her bossing me around to do this, say that, she was an utterly resourceless girl and desperately needy of help.

I felt that it had been sheer madness and arrogance on my part to go any further after the consultation and that I should have advised the physician to refer Judy to a medically qualified analyst.

Whilst I was still sweltering in this subjective and private confusion, the bell rang. Thank God, it was the physician. He had come early and was apologetic about it, but I was relieved. I casually asked him what the 'scandal' referred to. He told me briefly what it was, and it was really degrading and humiliating. I felt very sad for Judy, because she would have to live with it socially for at least six months.

The bell rang, and this time it was Judy and her friend. Judy introduced me to her friend, whom I shall call Linda. Linda was a young woman some twenty-five years old: tall, gauntly handsome, impeccably dressed in a rather eccentric style, with a pleasant voice, and easy to relate to. To start somewhere, I casually asked Judy if she had slept well. She said: 'I had a weird dream, and said to myself, "I must tell this to Khan." But by the time I got out of bed and found a pencil and a piece of paper, I had lost the dream. So I can't tell you anything.' I noted her use of the word 'lost'. Then I chatted with Linda. She had been running a small shop successfully for three years now. Waiting for the father to arrive, and to keep the climate alive, I asked her what made her choose that particular task, because it is very hard work. She told me with a casual and rather self-mocking candour that, after a disastrous love-affair at college at twenty years of age, she had had a breakdown and her parents had sent her with an aunt on a world tour for a year. She had been particularly impressed by South American and Arab cultures. When she returned, she was at a loss as to what to do. She didn't want to return to college. One day she suggested to her father that he might be willing to finance her to open a small shop, and he had said, 'Of course.' So it had all started. I felt deeply relieved by her story, because if I agreed to take Judy into psychotherapeutic care, at least one third of the management side was settled. I would persuade Judy to work half a day with and for Linda.

The bell rang, and at last the father arrived: very polite and shrewd. So now we settled down to the real business. I told him and the physician that unless I could arrange adequate management for Judy, now that she would be idle all day, there would be no question of my taking her into therapeutic care. I deliberately avoided using the concept treatment, because I knew that it would be a long time before we would achieve that mutuality where treatment becomes feasible. First I turned to Linda and bluntly asked her what she felt about Judy working half a day (10:00 to 1:00) with and for her. She was a bit taken aback, paused, and then said: 'Certainly. We get on very well together and I need help.' Judy looked both pleased and relieved. The next issue, I told the father, was that of Judy's education. She must have a private teacher and study for at least three hours a day. He, with a bland cooperativeness, asked me if I knew of someone who could be asked to coach Judy. I told him that some ten years ago I knew a young man whom I used a lot to teach and coach boys and girls for O and A level examinations. I had his address, but didn't know whether he was still living there and doing freelance teaching, or if he had taken a full-time teaching post. The father requested me to try to get in touch with him. I called my secretary and asked her to ring him and, if he was not at that address, to find him. Fortunately, he was at the same address, and at home with the flu.

She said that he was on the phone and asked if I would like to talk to him. I said: 'Yes.' But before I took the phone, I asked both Judy and her father whether I could name the girl I was going to ask him to coach. I was thinking of the 'scandal'. They said: 'Yes.' So I talked with Peter, and briefly told him that I had a young girl in my care whom I wanted him to coach, and gave him the name. I could hear him gasp at the other end. I told him that she needed minimally three hours each day, from 3:00 to 6:00. He asked if he could think it over and ring back in fifteen minutes. He did, and agreed to coach, but said that he had only two hours, from 3:00 to 5:00, and could not start before next Monday. So that was settled. At this point, I agreed to see Judy five times a week at 6:20 p.m. Then suddenly Judy said that she could go to work for Linda and come to me only if Daddy would send his car to take her everywhere. She was not going to travel by bus, tube or taxi. The father agreed all too readily to make a car available to Judy. At this point, I abruptly ended the consultation, giving Judy an appointment for the next day, and we all parted.

It was now clear to me that it would be a miracle if I could make Judy come in her person and speak herself. She was most vulnerable, and so she would for a long time arrive as a *collage*, and not just herself.

Judy arrived punctually for her next session. When she took off her poncho, I noticed her arm was in a sling. As she saw me looking at it, she gaily remarked that, going to bed last night, she had tripped on the stairs and hurt her elbow, but it was nothing serious. From this I inferred that Judy's self-inflicted body injuries were her way of coping with her ungraspable psychic pain and physically localizing it. It was also her way of not sinking into totally depersonalized states. In the next three months, I was to hear a long history of such body injuries from the age of five onwards.

Judy squatted down into the chair. It is important clinically for me to see how a patient uses my clinical space and the furniture available. It tells me more at the start than the patient can possibly speak. Also, the way a patient dresses his/her nudity is very telling for me. The mink coat that she had arrived in for her first consultation was in fact inflicted upon her, as I learnt later, to make her look a little respectable. Judy's normal dress was track boots, tight jeans, a shirt or floppy sweater, and her favourite football club's long socks. From this it was clear that as yet Judy had not differentiated herself into an adolescent girl. She was still a boy-girl being. Her clothes could be worn just as reasonably by a boy of her age.

As I had expected, Judy chitter-chattered about this and that. She had a really witty way of describing people and events, but she talked about and around herself, and not from and of herself. She said that she had enjoyed working with Linda in the morning, but had felt very down (her phrase) all afternoon. There was nobody at home except the staff, and it was her favourite maid's day off. She asked me whether or not her teacher could come in for at least an hour this week. I told her that I had been in touch with him and he really couldn't start before next Monday. I suggested that she should ask Linda to let her work full days this week. She said that she would. Then she told me that since the 'scandal' had become public, she had stayed at home and seen no friends, except Linda. She added, with a sly look in her eyes: 'I cannot eat either, unless Daddy is there. He makes me eat. I just nibble food all day.' Here I returned my first interpretative question: 'How often do you steal?' I really had no clue as to why I asked that. She blatantly answered: 'Not often, and only from one shop. But they earn a lot from us, and I steal only small things, like pencils, rubbers, envelopes, fake jewellery, beads, etcetera.' I dropped the subject, but noted that her present symptoms were anorexia, stealing and phobia.

Fortunately, Linda was only too glad to have Judy work full time that week, because she had her 'sale' next week and all the objects had to be repriced. Otherwise nothing of importance was said or learnt that week. That weekend, Judy was going with her father to their country house, and she felt very happy about that, because she could ride there. She loved horses.

As I thought about the sessions in the first week, what struck me most was that Judy was in fact a very alert, sensitive, healthy person, with a madness inside her, which circumstances over the past years had dislocated into hysterical antics and manipulativeness. She was basically honest, but had been taught to lie by both the parents, and now she herself could no longer tell when she was lying and when she was telling the truth. I felt disappointed with my own contributions during the week, but I had decided to be reticent and watch.

From the first month of her treatment, Judy worked with Linda regularly and had made a very good relationship with her teacher. He found her a very sensitive, attentive and cooperative student. So all that was well. The problems needing urgent management were eating and sleeping. I got around the eating problem by asking Linda to take Judy out to lunch and make sure that she had a good meal each day. I had her father's word that he would pay for both of them. The problem of sleep was more difficult to manage, since Judy herself never, as yet, had said to me that she didn't sleep well. Instead of asking her, I decided to discuss this with her physician, since he had taken care of her since she was a baby. He told me Judy had great trouble going to sleep, but he could not give her any sleeping tablets because he feared that she might take an overdose. She had three years ago stolen all the tablets from her parents' medicine cupboard, and swallowed them, and had to be taken to hospital to be cleaned out. But he promised he would try to arrange with one of the ladies in the house to give her a tablet each night. In fact, I knew that Judy's inability to sleep had a deeper cause and that she would not take the tablets, and she actually did refuse. This convinced me that she was afraid of having a bad dream and I let the matter drop.

The only other important item was that Judy stole twice during this month. Each time it was when something about the 'scandal' appeared in the papers. This gave me insight into one function of stealing for Judy. It was that the stolen object was a private unknowable secret that she could live with. Shortly she was to tell me when stealing had started. Otherwise Judy came, Judy chattered, Judy left. I was quite content that she was at least working in the shop and studying with intense diligence. The subjects she had chosen were English Literature, Spanish and Geography. Linda spoke Spanish fluently.

It was in the second month that things began to happen. One Tuesday Judy arrived, sat up in the chair, and said to me: 'I didn't know I was coming here because I am ill. I have just been gossiping, and it is costing Dad a mint.' I asked her who had said that she was ill. She replied: 'My doctor, my father, and even Linda. I come here so that you can get me well. But I don't know what to speak about. And you don't help. Why don't you ask me questions?' I responded: 'All right, tell me when your sleeping problem started.' A sudden fury flashed in her eyes and she asked me defiantly: 'Who told you that. I sleep very well. Only these days I have to wake up at 8:00 and I can never go to sleep till nearly six. So I don't get enough sleep.' And she sank into a raging sullen silence for the rest of the session. I didn't try to fob off her rage. At the end, she got up and left. Next day, when I was expecting her, I was rung and told that Judy was not well and wouldn't be coming tonight, but would come tomorrow. In the evening her teacher rang to say Judy had sent him away, saying that she was ill and would work tomorrow. When Judy returned on Thursday, she squatted in the chair, without taking off her poncho, but her sullenness was not raging but sad. She did not speak a word, nor did I. The same happened the next session, which was Friday. But as she was leaving she said: 'I am going to the country house for the weekend for the last time.' And she went.

As I thought about the week's happenings, I didn't feel any regret that I might have made a gaff in asking about her sleeping problem. Instead, I felt relieved. I was sure that the period of chitter-chatter had ended and now I would be encountering the ill Judy, and not the one who had come with the alibi of the 'scandal'. I had no notion as to what form her illness would take or how it would express itself. I felt fearful all the same, and again had that feeling of apprehension and inadequacy that I had after the first consultation. One thing I had learnt about Judy from this episode was that she was acutely paranoid behind her jolly facade. Her acute touchiness was one ruse to evade a flagrantly paranoid response.

There were other clues to her psychopathology and her ruses (I deliberately use this word rather than the concept of defence mechanism) for coping with it that I had gathered from the chitter-chatter period. I had little doubt that her insomnia was a way of avoiding dreaming, especially a dream that could vividly project some event of the past that she had dissociated and/or repressed from her conscious day-to-day identity of being Judy. The most palpable and yet unspeakable psychic pain in her was masked by a myriad of little demands and stealing. This derived, I had surmised, from the traumatic and tantalizing deprivation of maternal love and care. Her father's over-indulgence later had helped her to screen this psychic pain. But all her injuries, accidental or self-inflicted, were the physical 'objective correlatives' (to borrow a phrase from T. S. Eliot, 1918) for this psychic pain, as was soon to become all too awesomely clear. I knew little about the actual events of her early familial life. I had only vague clues as to why and how she had become the Judy she was exhibiting at present. She had a vociferously intrusive relative, who kept ringing me to tell 'all', but I had militantly refused to see her. I didn't want to know anything that Judy couldn't tell or speak.

When Judy returned from her weekend in the country (the last visit to her country house), she arrived punctually, and was neither depressed nor sullen and rejective, but just sat very still and sad. After a while she began to cry, and managed somehow to say: 'Now I have lost everything except Dad. Tim is dead, and the country house has been sold.' I could feel her loss and its pain. But what was more frightening was that I had no clue as to which route Judy would take for self-sustenance. She loved riding and wouldn't be able to ride now. She disliked living in London and the school she had been attending in London, because she felt physically lubberly, gauche in manners and uncouth in speech even though, as I have said earlier, Judy had a real feeling for language. But it was part of her protest to go on strike about moving out of her bucolic environment into the sophisticated London set, where the girls of her class were mannered and full of social connivances. In spite of all her ruses, lying, and other ways of masking her psychic pain and madness, Judy was an authentic person with a will of her own. For example, she had refused to wear the fancy school uniform, and stayed in her jeans and a jumper or shirt.

I had noted that when she had said, 'I have lost everything,' she had not included her mother. Once her mood had settled to quietude, Judy volunteered to *tell* me about herself. She started by talking about Tim, her pony. Her father had given Tim to her for her fifth birthday. During the rest of the week I heard all about her relation to Tim. She told me how the butler once caught her sneaking out of the country house with pillow and blanket to sleep in Tim's stable. She had been sleeping in the stable for a week or so. Her father got to hear of it and, such was his indulgent generosity of affection for his daughter that he had a stable made as an extension of the house itself. He already knew how lonely and traumatized Judy was. In Winnicottian metaphor, one could say that Tim was Judy's transitional object. She wrote stories *for* him and drew pictures of him with verses, as she grew more capable maturationally. Tim died from a gastric ailment when Judy was twelve. Gradually, I got to know Tim as a person in Judy's life, and it showed me what a profound capacity this girl had for compassion and care. The surprising thing was that the more she talked about Tim, the less phobic she became, and she started to go out with her father and Linda, to theatres and restaurants. She was also eating and sleeping more.

Then one night, she had a dream that frightened her so much that she rang me at 2:00 a.m. to tell it. The dream was:

> She is walking in the street. Suddenly she hears a voice shouting, 'Look out or you will fall in the pit.' She looks up and sees her mother with her typical sardonic smile, standing in front of her.

On the phone, I simply said to her that now that she had been able to dream this awful dream, she would be able to sleep fearlessly and we would discuss the dream when she came to her session. She felt satisfied with that. I myself wasn't sure whether she had seen a dream, had a hypnogogic image, or pure hallucination. When she came to her session, she didn't mention the dream, and I found her chitter-chattering again. I suspended drawing her attention to the dream all that week. Then one accident happened. Over the weekend, she had what she stated as a 'flaming row with my bloody nosey relative', whom I have mentioned before. It was over dressing to go out. This relative wanted her to dress up, to be worthy of the guests and host, and she wanted to stay in her jeans and poncho. It ended by her throwing a glass of red wine, in front of her father, and the relative retired, screaming that her best evening dress had been ruined. Her father had passively and quietly watched the whole drama. Now the relatively refused to go, and the father went happily with his daughter dressed in jeans and poncho. He couldn't care a damn, so long as she felt at ease and was in life.

During Monday's session, after recounting the episode with her relative, she suddenly stopped and said: 'I want to talk about me and my mum.' Personally, I felt it was a bit premature for her to start telling me about her relationship with her mother. We had covered a lot of ground talking about Tim, and I would have liked to have had at least another week of that, to stabilize her mood and trust in me. I felt the episode with her relative had somehow distracted her into a triumphant manic mood. But I had no option but to let her talk about what she wished. It is my clinical experience that a patient can give very significant material to us, but in the wrong mood, and often it stays as inert information, and we, the patient and analyst, fail to transmute it into new affective psychic experience.

The most frustrating thing about recounting clinical work is that the small details that in fact make the destiny of the patient as a person and also dictate the destiny of the clinical process, often cannot be told for reasons of professional privacy. This is more true in Judy's case than in any other that I have ever written. She talked a lot about her relationship with her mother, and I shall abstract the crucial themes, but not retail actual events, except a few. I trust that the reader will use his or her own good will and imagination to reconstruct what is left unwritten.

As I have indicated already, Judy had shifted into a manic mood when she started to tell her 'story', because it was told without affect or any communicative quality. The essential facts were that her mother was an outrageously hysterical woman and Judy had never seen the parents mutual or happy, even in a formal way. The essence of her mother's affective relating with her was neither rejection nor caring, nor even ambivalence, but *tantalization.* In her sober good moods, when her husband was away, which was often, she would indulge Judy without bothering to find out in the slightest what Judy liked or wished. For example, Judy told me that from all the stuff that was hers, toys, dresses, etcetera, she had brought only Tim's gear (saddle, blanket, etcetera, and her riding boots). The rest she had given to the village people around their country house. She knew her mother's gifts were a way of bribing her for the episodes when she would be quite wildly physically violent and beat her daughter in a rage, which rarely had anything to do with Judy's behaviour, but was the overflow of some row with her husband. She once hit Judy so hard with a stick that it fractured her arm. Judy was eight at the time. Over the weekends when her father was present, the house was always cluttered. I use this word instead of crowded, because Judy related to no one but Tim, Dad and the butler. She had very precociously begun to realize that her nanny was an accomplice to her mother. It was when Judy was nine years of age that her mother, in a drunken state, began to tell Judy secrets. Judy knew of them already. She told all this and other events in a rather manic, impersonal manner, as if they had happened to someone else. Listening to her narrative, which was mixed with gossip from her daily life, I felt that very early on, Judy had been driven mad by her mother and had learnt to live with her madness in her country life. Only the demands of a sophisticated school in London and her father's social life put a strain on her, which was incompatible with her stance of madness, and gradually during the past three years, she had learnt all the manipulative ruses of a true hysteric and hid herself behind them. In fact, she had succeeded so well that she was no longer in touch with her mad self, which was truly Judy. She exploited her environment negatively, to her disadvantage as a person. It was very much like a caricature of her mother's character. And her father's indulgent affection was now no longer nourishing to her, because she exploited it with a cunning devious vengefulness to be a nuisance to her relatives, who tried to tame her into a groomed, sophisticated girl in the style of her social status.

It was in this ambience that a girl-friend of hers from childhood returned to London after five years abroad. She had been Judy's 'chum' (her phrase) since she was three. The girl who returned was now a very jet-set type, and Judy took to her with manic passion. She worked at Linda's, studied with her teacher, and then would disappear with her friend, who was in town only for a month, to some discotheque or elsewhere, and stay away all night sometimes, returning just to change to go to work.

Unfortunately, her father was away on business for two weeks and her 'nosey relative' kept a very exact record of Judy's goings-on. The nosey relative rang me one evening and bullied my butler to put her through to me. With an arrogant malicious note of triumph in her voice, she told me how Judy had been staying out very late all night and was not taking her 'pills' regularly. So she had arranged with her gynaecologist to insert an IUD as a preventative, and Judy was going to see the gynaecologist tomorrow. I warned her that sometimes the body of a girl does not accept the IUD, and in Judy's case, there was a real danger that all her illness could express itself through somatic symptoms. But she wouldn't listen. I asked to speak to Judy, but she said that Judy had already gone somewhere, and put the phone down. I immediately got in touch with the physician, who even called at their house and was sent off with the information that everyone had gone out to dinner and would not return until very late. He rang me, and we sent the relative a telegram, jointly signed, stating that we were against her plan, and advising her to postpone it until the father returned, which would be on Friday night. We added that if Judy was pregnant, or was going to get pregnant, that couldn't be stopped tonight. And once her father returned, we could take the necessary medical measures to protect her from any accidents.

It was all to no avail. Judy had gone to the gynaecologist and the insertion of the IUD had been physically traumatic for her. When she came to her session, she was white as a sheet and in considerable pain. She asked for tea and I got it for her. I asked her why she had not refused and rung me, but she was mute. I noted the similarity of passivity with which this wilful girl as a child had impersonally suffered and obeyed her mother, and now her bossy relative. Since her pain grew worse, I sent her home and phoned the doctor to ask him to call on her at his earliest free moment, which he did. I had absolutely no doubt that now Judy's madness would find a somatic idiom and might even lead to a psychotic breakdown. The first thing next morning, the physician rang me and said that Judy's father had rung him at 3:00 a.m., that she had been taken in an ambulance to the hospital, and another gynaecologist had been called in to remove the IUD.

From here onwards, a nightmare started, the like of which I had not experienced in thirty or so years of clinical work. To helplessly watch Judy's hidden madness, which was compatible with living, turn first into the most agonizing physical pain and symptoms, and later into psychotic states of paranoid delusions, hallucinations and utter delapidation of her person, was most painful for me. Not having been hardened to human suffering, physical and psychic, due to lack of medical education, this phase of her illness was as traumatic for me as it was destructive of Judy the person.

Briefly, the events took this course: the IUD was removed, but the gynaecologist had made a real mess of her uterus. Judy was in hospital, and nothing cured the infection or alleviated her pain except pethidine which, being an addictive drug, had to be dosed carefully. So Judy lived in relentless physical pain. Then she started to have paranoid delusions about the matron, and one night ran out of the hospital. Fortunately, a police car was passing by and she was brought back. The father asked for consultation with me, the new gynaecologist and the physician. It was mutually agreed that Judy should be nursed at home. So Judy returned home very ill and was nursed at home. Judy's physical condition oscillated, but her mental condition changed to a patently schizophrenic paranoid state. She would not eat or talk. I called on her every evening after dinner for an hour, and so did the physician. We often found her either in a comatose state and mute, or in a state of hallucinosis. In the latter state, she would mutter in a garbled language. I shall recount one such hallucination: I had been sitting quietly by her bedside for half an hour, when I saw Judy stretch out her arm and embrace an 'object', muttering, 'Darling Tim, Mum has hit and cut your lip. Poor Tim. I am going to make it all right.' And she sank back into her comatose muteness. I recalled seeing a scar on Judy's lower lip the very first time I had seen her.

After a month of progressive deterioration and hallucinations, in one of which she set fire to her night-dress, shouting, 'The house (naming the country house in fact) is on fire,' the physician and I had a consultation with her father and advised him to let us call in a psychiatrist who specialized in physical methods of treatment of schizophrenic hallucinatory states. He agreed and Judy was taken to hospital. She was treated by physical psychiatric methods, and her mental condition improved miraculously, in so far as she had no more hallucinations or paranoid delusions. The father was very relieved. I had not seen Judy during this hospitalization, my reason being not to interfere with the possibility of transference to her psychiatrist.

On her return home, Judy immediately asked to see me. Her father rang me, and I cancelled my patients and immediately went over. The girl I saw was now quietly herself and mad. I had no doubt of that, but it made me have some hope again for her. She asked to talk to me alone, so the father and the nurse left the room. Very gently she asked me to arrange with her father to allow her to leave home and to go and live elsewhere, in the countryside. I promised her that I would do my best to arrange that for her. She was strangely, passively alert and awake, and said that the three weeks in hospital had not been very bad. She made a faint complaint about the food. Otherwise she recalled little.

I talked with the father and the physician, as well as the psychiatrist, and put forward a very strong case for Judy to be sent to some country house where the family atmosphere was congenial and acceptable to Judy. The father agreed instantly. The question was, which family, and how far from London.

In the two weeks following, Judy gradually became able to walk around and eat with the family. She even asked to have lessons again. The teacher reported that although she was utterly cooperative, she took in nothing. At this point, an event happened that resolved all our management problems. An aunt of hers who had a horse ranch in Argentina arrived out of the blue. Judy was fascinated by her aunt's account of the ranch and the people she employed. Thus it was decided that Judy should go with her aunt to the ranch in Argentina, and Judy left in a week.

That was some three years ago. She wrote to me regularly, short letters every six weeks or so, with a photograph of a pony, a foal or a horse. I always answered promptly. Then, some four months ago, I heard nothing from her. I tried to get in touch with her father, but he was abroad. So I sent a telegram to her aunt, asking news of Judy. She rang me and said that whilst training a horse, Judy had fallen and broken her arm. But it had healed well, and she was writing to me. This made me immediately fearful that Judy was again sinking into a psychotic state. I received a letter from Judy a week later, telling me of the accident and assuring me that she had suffered little pain and was riding again. At the end of the letter she wrote, and I quote her: 'A young foal has been talking to me, but I can't understand him. If there are any books on horse language, please send them air mail. Dad will pay.'

I knew for sure now that Judy had moved out of her mad state and was getting deluded and hallucinated. I sent a letter, saying I was glad to hear her news and was searching hard to find some books about horse language. In a few days her father returned, and I rang him and asked him to call me. I also called the physician and the psychiatrist. When we met, I read them Judy's letter and told them of my apprehensions about Judy relapsing into psychotic states again. The father volunteered to ring this aunt and tell her that if she should find Judy behaving oddly in any way, she must immediately ring him, and he would fly over and fetch her.

Some six weeks have passed since then. I have not heard from Judy, but I ask myself as I prepare to receive her in whatever condition she arrives, what I shall do this time. Would I be able, with the help of her physician and psychiatrist, to re-establish her in the privacy of her madness, which is compatible with living, or will the encrustations of mental derangement be irreversible now? But of one thing I am sure: I cannot expect her to free associate or speak her madness, because she would not know how to speak – what, how, to whom!

Judy chooses a vocation: an odyssey!

Some two months later, one Saturday afternoon, the phone rang. I answered it: it was Judy! She said: 'I am in London – can I please see you today? I have a major decision to make and I need your help.' I told her that I could see her at 1:30 that afternoon. As I awaited Judy's arrival, three things kept tugging at my mind:

1. Judy's voice was so reticently articulate, unlike the Judy who used to blurt out things or who was mute.

2. I had never heard Judy use the word 'please' before. All her demands were expressed through symptoms, hence she never felt responsible for what was provided for her.

3. She had never admitted her 'need for help', which is quite different from a 'demand'. To accept 'need for help' implies that one is not autonomously omnipotent, and acknowledges both the separateness and the resourcefulness of the *other* to be able to help one.

Of course, by now she had lived some three years and more abroad, in a culture and setting that could not be more different from her environment of childhood and puberty. She also had to learn a new language. But I, in fact, knew nothing about her life during these three years, even though she had written laconic cards or notes regularly.

About one thing I had made up my mind: no matter in what psychic condition I found her, I would not initiate or insinuate, from my side, her asking for a book about 'horse-language'. I would try to meet her on her terms, as she would choose to present herself. Furthermore, I was determined not to refer to her grave illnesses in the past, should she now decide to obviate them from her present identity as a person. I knew all this would entail an enormous discipline of deliberate *un*-knowing on my part, but I was convinced that if I was to help Judy, I had to accept her as an as-if person in her own right, different from the *sick* girl. I was a little disconcerted by the precipitate way that she had left Argentina and arrived in London. I had known this type of impulsiveness in her before, but I decided to give her the benefit of the doubt in this respect as well.

Judy arrived punctually and greeted me with affection. One thing I had not thought of, that the girl of eighteen-plus, working hard on a ranch, would be different in physique from the puppy-fat girl with cropped hair and tight jeans who had left three years earlier. So it took me a little while to get used to her new physicality: she was slim, with long hair, and was discreetly dressed – almost pretty, certainly with a touch of the exotic. Her eyes were strikingly different: she did not have that wild stare or opaque and absent hazed look. Instead her eyes were quietly vigilant and alert. Her voice had also changed. She spoke in a quiet, pleasant and lively way. When she had taken off her coat and placed it neatly with her bag by her side, along with a portfolio she had brought, she was no longer the 'Judy, age fifteen' who would arrive and scatter herself all over the room. Her total *presence* had a different quality to it: she was discreetly trusting and relating. Her gestures also were consentient with her voice and what she was speaking. Of course, she noticed me 'watching' her and remarked with a wry smirk: 'I have changed, as you can see. And I have not been ill in any way in three years, except for fracturing my arm.' I accepted her comment without reacting to it or commenting about the change.

I know it is not usual for analysts to describe the physicality of a patient in such detail. But clinically, to me, the sight of a person – the tone of voice, gestures and general deportment – speak more at the start than their 'prepared' telling and verbal narrative would for a long while. Judy launched straight off with the issue that she had come to discuss. It had all begun a year or so before, when a girl called Luciana had come to their ranch to buy horses. Luciana was a young woman of twenty-seven years or so. She and Judy felt an instant rapport with each other, and she invited Judy to dinner the following week. Judy went, and found that Luciana ran a sort of commune in a large house. She had some twenty persons from fifteen to thirty years of age living in her 'care'. They were all drop-outs, from colleges or jobs, of mixed nationalities and breeds. Some had been drug addicts. All this had deeply impressed Judy. She made up her mind to befriend Luciana. But during her first visit, she had asked no questions and had stayed a shade muted and left early. Then she invited Luciana to lunch and found out about her.

Luciana had lost her mother when she was five years old. She had been brought up by foster parents, who were friends of her father. The father had moved to Europe and did not keep in touch with his daughter. Luciana had a typically turbulent, chaotic and drugged puberty and adolescence. (I am telling this because I knew of Judy's excessive reparative drive and its antics.) Then when she was twenty-one, Luciana was told that she had inherited a huge fortune and was now quite independent. Fortunately, around this time, she met a man much older than herself, who became very interested in her welfare. He had lived in Nepal for five years when young and learnt a lot about Zen Buddhism and its practices. He visited Nepal and India every year and asked Luciana to visit with him. There were no intimate relations between them. Luciana, who had been thrown out of three universities and was in a mess, suddenly decided to go with him. She stayed five years in various Ashrams (like monasteries) and learnt Hindi, Nepali and Sanskrit. When she returned, she decided to open this 'commune', and she explained to Judy how the commune was run. Everybody had a task of their choosing, responsibility towards others, and no one could stay for more than three years. She fed them, but they took care of the house and garden, and they cooked. She also instructed them in 'meditation'.

According to Judy, she was absolutely fascinated by Luciana's life-story, especially its authenticity, both of the chaos and then the discipline and the dedication. She asked Luciana to teach her Hindi and started to attend some of her 'meditation' sessions on Fridays. Gradually, a plan and a purpose began to crystallize itself in Judy. But what decided her was the foal who 'talked to her' and whom she could not understand.

The trouble with the foal was that, at the age of eight months, he still only drank milk and refused fodder and bran, so he was not growing up very well. One day Judy mentioned it to Luciana, who agreed to 'meet' the foal. According to Judy, Luciana was able to 'understand' the 'horse language' and to talk it also. In three months, the foal was eating normally. It was this event that decided Judy to leave Argentina and go to India or Nepal for Zen cum yoga apprenticeship. Luciana had given her quite a lot of information about Ashrams and their methods of 'apprenticing', and Judy had brought some of the literature with her to show me. She had, in fact, already chosen an Ashram in India to go to, if she was accepted.

Of course, whilst I had listened to her, my mind was buzzing with reverberations from endless facets of her ill states, as well as when she had her healthy patches, but I said nothing. After some two hours she paused, looked at me intently, and asked: 'What do you think of my plan, as I have told it to you so far?' I told her, candidly, that it sounded like a splendid programme, but I could not advise her without consulting her father, and asked her how much she had shared her intentions with him. 'Very little,' she answered, 'but I knew you would like to discuss it together with us. So he is waiting for me to ring him, and he will come over.'

Judy rang her father, and waiting for his arrival gave us both a pause. Judy had been speaking, almost nonstop, for nearly two hours. She asked if she could look around the consultation room, and I said: 'Of course!'

I was only too relieved for this respite, to think things over, before I talked with the father and gave my advice. I was gravely concerned and uncertain on many counts. Primarily: was Judy looking for an Ashram in India, or an asylum where her psychotic states could be private to her? Although I have said that 'Judy, age fifteen' was totally unaware of how demanding a person she was and disavowed her *need* of care and others, she was also a profoundly sensitive and precociously over-perceptive person, and 'knew' what a terrible strain her illness had been on her father. I wondered further whether her father's over-readiness to agree to whatever I advised was his way of avoiding a long bout of 'sick-psychotic' Judy at home, completely disrupting and paralysing his private life and, in a certain measure, his professional life as well. Judy in India was safely out of the way, and the burden of that decision and responsibility lay on me.

There were other bits and pieces, casually recounted by Judy, that I had noted mentally. For example, the foal not eating reminded me of Judy's anorectic states during her illness, when she would only take liquids in small doses. Was she fearing another attack of anorexia and hoping to find a mystical cure for it in India? Also, I could not forget that, when I had first seen Judy, she had attempted suicide by cutting both her wrists. So, was she going to India to perish anonymously? Also, from her account of her relationships, except for the year of friendship with Luciana, I could not make out any stable object-relationship with anyone. She merely lived with her aunt and busied herself with work with the horses, cleaning saddlery, etcetera. The folk in the employment of her aunt found her very sympathetic and unsnooty, but largely she lived by herself – I could not say even with herself.

Yet when I weighed all the negatives, I still felt, as I had when she was ill before, that Judy was not dreading a psychotic breakdown and escaping to India. I felt deeply that, in Argentina, not having to play the sophisticated girl, and working and mixing with humble folk, had given Judy a sense of herself and her *difference* from others. By *difference*, I am not implying social status, but psychic states of being. I felt equally sure that she had outlived the creative usefulness of her aunt's ranch and now wanted truly to find herself and a way to speak and actualize it. Thus I was decided as to what I would advise her father.

The father arrived within half an hour. One look at him and I felt reassured that he was both relieved and delighted to find Judy in good physical health and psychically present in her person and being. We three sat and chattered for a while. Then Judy asked me: 'Please tell Daddy what I want and why!' I told her that she could do it better herself, but if she wished me to, I certainly would, but in my own style, and she must correct me where she felt that I was misrepresenting her.

I started back to front, as it were. I told the father that, like him, I was delighted to find Judy in such good health, physically and psychically; that in my opinion, Judy had exhausted, for herself, the creative potential of life at her aunt's ranch, and now she needed to be autonomous and not 'in-care', to try her own ways of finding how to be herself in her future and live it both purposefully and creatively with others; that her wish was to go to an Ashram in India and do a complete 'apprenticeship' in Zen cum yoga styles of meditation, achieving self-awareness and learning some crafts. I emphasized that to try to get Judy to take examinations in London and to go to some university would not only be futile, but I feared greatly that she could collapse back into her illnesses. I added further that the social life of London would make Judy ill – or that at least that was my opinion. I told him that he could ask for a second opinion, and it would not offend me in any way.

The father had listened to me very carefully and sympathetically. He asked me whether he could express equally openly his misgivings in front of Judy. I asked Judy, and she said: 'Yes!' The father told me what I already knew, that he had been to India on business many times and had some good friends there; that out of curiosity he had visited a few Ashrams, and they varied from the true and serious and apprenticing ones to mere charlatanism for druggists. So how does one know, sitting in London, where Judy should go? I answered him that I was aware of this hazard, as Judy was herself; that she had known and befriended a girl in Argentina who had spent five years in India in various Ashrams. I added that Judy does not want to drift from Ashram to Ashram, but to undertake vigorous apprenticeship at one particular Ashram, of which she had the name and address; that I knew of this Ashram, and some very good friends of mine finance its maintenance, but it has a seven-year apprenticeship and it is not easy to get into. I could use my influence, if he agreed, and ring my friends and find out more. It was too late to ring India that day, so I would be in touch with him and Judy the following day when I got through. I gave him their name, address and telephone number, and asked him to try also, to mention my name and find out what was possible.

The second concern that the father had, he found difficult to tell in front of Judy. (I had a fairly good idea of what it was.) So, after a lot of hesitation, he asked me: 'What happens if Judy has a serious *relapse* in the Ashram in India?' I was ready for this question. First I made a mental note that he had not used the phrase, 'relapse into her previous illnesses'. I respected that! I told him that ailments of Judy's type, and even that word, I added, misrepresents what I wish to say, are really growing pains of the self and the soul, which take an individual time to personalize and speak; that Judy, in my opinion, had never been psychiatrically ill *herself*, as I had said at the time to him, the physician and the psychiatrist. She had 'learnt' the usage of symptomatology, however, and we were all compelled to *act* on that, and we had. Today Judy had come through, by her own efforts, and to grow further, she needed a new, different and disciplined environment, where she could both be apprenticed and be private. She had chosen her route, and we all, including Judy, had to take the risk and sponsor her. I asked him whether he had seen or read T. S. Eliot's play, *The Cocktail Party* (1950). He said: 'Both.' So I got out a copy of the play and quoted him what Reilly (the 'psychiatrist') says to Celia (the 'patient'):

> There *is* another way, if you have the courage.
> The first I could describe in familiar terms
> Because you have seen it, as we all have seen it,
> Illustrated, more or less, in lives of those about us.
> The second is unknown, and so requires faith –
> The kind of faith that issues from despair.
> The destination cannot be described;
> You will know very little until you get there;
> You will journey blind. But the way leads towards possession
> Of what you have sought for in the wrong place.

He was really moved by this, and what he called my 'candour, and taking the risk'. I had not minced my words. The father got up at this point and said: 'I am sure Judy has more to say to you, that is, if you have time.' I said: 'Yes, I have!' And he left, thanking me for being always so available.

After he left, Judy was silent for a while. Then she remarked:

'Thank God this room has not changed much except for a few new objects and more books!' I realized how Judy's life had been traumatized at every critical stage by change either of environment or familial personages. This assured me further about her *rightness* in choosing an Ashram with the longest training. Seven years would be the longest period Judy would be spending in a consistent, ongoing human ambience and a 'holding-structure'.

Judy continued her narrative: 'Do you know what was the most important discovery I made at the ranch?' 'Tell me,' I said. 'After I had been at the ranch for three months or so and got to know all the ranch-hands (her phrase), I suddenly realized one day that I could tell the "soulful" persons from the "minded" people (her phrases). And it was by watching the difference between the horses who were looked after by the "soulful" persons and those cared for by the "minded" ones. When presented to my aunt for regular inspection, the horses and the saddlery of the "minded" ranch-hands were always cleaner and smarter, and the horses looked better trained than those of the "soulful" ones. Gradually I realized that the horses of the "minded" people were more restive and unrelating than those of the "soulful" ones. So I began to watch carefully how each ranch-hand behaved. The "minded" ranch-hands were quick with their grooming, harsh in training the horses, and smarted up the saddlery without really working at it. The "soulful" people seemed lazy and absent-minded, but in fact they cared about the animals, groomed them thoroughly, and were proud of them. The "minded" ones were good at putting up a show, but cut corners, whereas the "soulful" persons were often clumsy, and though more proud inside, felt intimidated by the "minded" people. By this time I was getting to know their families also, and I could tell "soulful" children from the "minded" ones. The latter did well at school and were ambitious and eager to please us. Whereas the "soulful" children lagged behind at school, were often bullied by the "minded" ones, and made to do all sorts of chores for them. I asked my aunt if I could give lessons on Sundays for two hours to the "soulful" children. The difficulty was that the majority of the "soulful" children were coloured or of mixed blood and spoke no English, and my Spanish was not good enough yet. But there was a bright young coloured ranch-hand who spoke both Spanish and English and could write them too. My aunt was only too pleased with this plan, because I would not go to any house on Sundays for lunch or dinner, nor join in if others came to my aunt's house. The venture was such a success that, when I left, the aunt agreed that the youth should take on the job of being full-time teacher at her school for children, and give up being a ranch-hand.'

I was utterly exhausted by now, yet I felt that the consultation hadn't reached its 'critical point'. So I waited, with my face in my hands, as is my style when listening, facing a patient. First, I don't like watching a patient with a pretend-blankness of neutrality, nor being stared at myself. Secondly, I can peep through the chinks of my fingers when I *need* to *look* at the patient. Now Judy volunteered to tell me her real intention and secret. She said: 'You know that at twenty-seven I am going to inherit a mint. So when I return from the Ashram, I am going to buy a country house with large grounds where I can build many out-houses. I won't have one large house, like Luciana's, because I would have no privacy then. And I will have a sort of Ashram where I will take ten or twelve children who do poorly at school, from the ages of five to ten, and some twenty adolescents, from the ages of fifteen to twenty, who lose jobs or drop out of school, and apprentice them. I shall learn to make pottery and to weave at the Ashram so that I can teach skills.'

Suddenly she stopped and I looked full-face at her. Yes, there was the same look of ungraspable anxiety in her eyes that I had seen during her illnesses. So I said: 'What is the matter, Judy?' She burst into tears and asked: 'Do you really think I will make it at the Ashram?' I paused, and then answered: 'If you have made it at the ranch, you will at the Ashram. Only remember that you have chosen a vocation, which is an odyssey. Judy, there is no substitute for time. Don't ask too much of yourself, and let them help you learn slowly, and you will make it. You have both the will and the necessary assets.' She smiled. I knew that she had no doubt that she would make it, yet she *needed* my *affirmation*, but not any reassurance from me – there is a difference.

It took a few days before I could contact my friends in India. They were also phoned by her father, and they assured him that she would be welcome to stay with them pending her admittance to the Ashram. They had heard of her father. There were only a few days left to Christmas (1980), and Judy wanted to leave before Christmas. Her father consulted me, and I said that he should let her leave.

At the end of the consultation, which had lasted some five hours, as she got up to leave, Judy bashfully pulled out a wrapped packet from her portfolio and gave it to me as a gift. I opened it. It was a leather-bound *cahier* of drawings by her 'soulful' children. I asked her what she would like to have from me. She said that she would like some verses from a poem of my liking, which she could take to the Ashram. 'But please write in your own hand,' she added. I chose to write the following verses for her, from Cavafy's 'Ithaka' (1911):

> As you set out for Ithaka
> hope your road is a long one,
> full of adventure, full of discovery.
> Laistrygonians, Cyclops,
> angry Poseidon – don't be afraid of them:
> you'll never find things like that on your way
> as long as you keep your thoughts raised high,
> as long as a rare excitement
> stirs your spirit and your body.
> Laistrygonians, Cyclops,
> wild Poseidon – you won't encounter them
> unless you bring them along inside your soul,
> unless your soul sets them up in front of you.

Speech, the Psychoanalytic Method and Madness

Homo sapiens, according to *Encyclopaedia Britannica* (1974), 'is distinguished from other animals and from earlier hominid species by . . . his construction and use of tools, and his ability to make use of symbols such as language and writing.' Under the caption 'Language', it states:

> For an adequate understanding of human language it is necessary to keep in mind the absolute primacy of speech. In societies in which literacy is all but universal and language teaching at school begins with reading and writing in the mother tongue, one is apt to think of language as a writing system that may be pronounced. In point of fact, language is a system of spoken communication that may be represented in various ways in writing. Man has almost certainly been in some sense a speaking animal from early in the emergence of Homo sapiens as a recognizably distinct species . . . As far as the production of speech sounds is concerned, all human beings are physiologically alike. People have differently shaped faces, as much as they differ in other aspects of bodily build, but it has been shown time and again that a child learns to speak the language of those who bring him up from infancy. In most cases these are his biological parents, especially his mother, but one's first language is ac-

> quired from environment and learning, not from physiological inheritance. Adopted infants, whatever their race or physical type and whatever the language of their actual parents, acquire the language of the adoptive parents who raise them just as if they had been their own children. (Compare Burke 1966, Ducrot and Todorov 1972, and Smith 1978.)

From these quotations, two things become quite clear. One, that speech is very intimately connected with growth, nurture and object-relating from infancy onwards. Two, that language is a specialized and sophisticated development of speech, especially when written. In fact, no more than ten percent of the living homo sapiens, if that, can write or read language. Be that as it may, for the purposes of this article, I shall restrict myself to three usages of speech in the clinical analytic situation: talking, telling and speaking.

How an hysteric, Anna O., with a touch of genius, compelled her physician, Joseph Breuer, to listen to her 'talking cure' in the early eighties of the nineteenth century, has been recorded as it happened clinically, by Breuer himself (see Freud 1895*d*), and its traumatic vicissitudes afterwards for the patient have been discussed by Jones (1953), Freeman (1972), and, with greater accuracy, by Clark (1980). Jones (1953) attributes Freud's interest in hysteria and psychopathology to his 'experience with Charcot' (p. 75; cf. Freud 1925*d*). This is certainly a shade misleading, because when Breuer, in November 1882 (cf. Clark, p. 101), had unburdened himself of the story of his treatment of Anna O. to Freud, it deeply impressed Freud. He even tried to get Charcot interested in it, but to no avail. Later on, in a moment of overgenerosity, during his Clark lectures in the United States, Freud (1910*a*) was to attribute to Breuer the origin of psychoanalysis:

> If it is a merit to have brought psycho-analysis into being, that merit is not mine. I had no share in its earliest beginnings. I was a student and working for my final examinations at the time when another Viennese physician, Dr Josef Breuer, first (in 1880–82) made use of this procedure on a girl who was suffering from hysteria.

It was Anna O. who had invented the phrases 'talking cure' and 'chimney sweeping', and made him a devoted accomplice to her 'self-catharsis' (if I may use that phrase). Breuer, in fact, had contributed little to the therapeutic process except his availability and presence (cf. Ellenberger 1970).

It was left to Freud's genius to transform 'talking' into 'telling' in the clinical situation. And it is this that constitutes the essence of Freud's analytic method. Freud did not achieve it in a sudden flash of insight, however – he laboured hard with all the current methods of psychotherapeutics and suffered all the agonies of his self-analysis before he could claim, in retrospect: 'From the date of *The Interpretation of Dreams* (1900*a*), psycho-analysis had a two-fold significance. It was not only a new method of treating the neuroses but it was also a new psychology; it claimed the attention not only of nerve-specialists but also of all those who were students of a mental science.' For an exhaustive account of Freud's travails before he established his psychoanalytic method one has to read the Freud-Fliess correspondence (1950*a*), Jones (1953), Robert (1964), Grinstein (1968), Anzieu's monumental study *L'Auto-analyse de Freud et la Découverte de la Psychanalyse* (1975) and Clark (1980).

In 1904, Freud was to give us his first definitive statement of psychoanalysis as a method of treatment in his paper, 'Freud's Psycho-Analytic Method' (1904*a*). For some strange reason, James Strachey changed the title to 'Freud's Psycho-Analytic Procedure', without explaining why.

If Anna O. had initiated the 'talking cure' with Breuer in 1882, some seven years later another hysteric, Frau Emmy Von N., whom Freud took into treatment in 1889, one day changed 'talking' to 'telling'. In Freud's (1895*d*) own words:

> I requested her to remember tomorrow. She then said in a definitely grumbling tone that I was not to keep on asking her where this and that came from, but to let her *tell* (my italics) me what she had to say. I fell in with this . . . (p. 63)

This is certainly the first incident of what Freud was later to turn into the method of 'free association', but there was a long route to travel yet. It was with Fräulein Elizabeth Von R., whose treatment he started in 1892, that Freud gave up the use of hypnosis, and he himself called it 'the first full-length analysis of a hysteria'.

Yet it was only through his self-analysis, conducted largely through interpretation of his own dreams, that Freud arrived at his analytic method (1904*a*). What was novel to the new method was 'an art of interpretation which takes on the task of, as it were, excavating the pure metal of the repressed thoughts from the ore of the unintentional ideas'. And here Freud emphasizes how 'the task of treatment is to remove amnesia . . . all repressions must be undone . . . the task consists in making the unconscious accessible to consciousness, which is done by over-coming the resistances.' And Freud adds: '. . . the aim of the treatment will never be anything else but the *practical* recovery of the patient, the restoration of his ability to lead an active life and his capacity for enjoyment.' This indeed is a very different therapeutic undertaking from the one Freud (1895*d*) had stated at the end of 'Psychotherapy of Hysteria', where he wrote: 'No doubt fate would find it easier than I do to relieve you of your illness. But you will be able to convince yourself that much will be gained if we succeed in transforming your hysterical misery into common unhappiness.'

It is interesting to note what for Freud were 'various qualifications . . . required of anyone who is to be beneficially affected by psycho-analysis':

> To begin with, he must be capable of a psychically normal condition; during periods of confusion or melancholic depression nothing can be accomplished even in cases of hysteria. Furthermore, a certain measure of natural intelligence and ethical development are to be required of him; if the physician has to deal with a worthless character, he soon loses the interest which makes it possible for him to enter profoundly into the patient's mental life.

He concludes by stating: 'Freud requires long periods, six months to three years, for an effective treatment.' It is rather strange that Freud does not discuss the role of transference in the analytic process and method in this article. But in the postscript to 'Fragment of an Analysis of a Case of Hysteria' (1905*e*), Freud gives a very lucid and detailed definition and account of transference and its role in the therapeutic work. This theme and that of countertransference are further discussed in his later papers on psychoanalytic technique.

It was one of Freud's singular assets that he did not wander away from his chosen task: 'My life has been aimed at one goal only: to infer or to guess how the mental apparatus is constructed and what forces interplay and counteract in it' (Jones 1953). Freud himself stated his lack of passion for saving suffering humanity, and as Jones (1953) rightly states: '. . . from the beginning of his life to the end Freud was never satisfied with emotional solutions only. He had a veritable passion to *understand*.'

In the four decades since Freud's death, the whole climate of analytic research and clinical work has radically changed. Freud had invented a setting and a method where a person could tell his problems and be understood. Today *telling* doesn't seem to be enough. The patients who come to us are as amorphous in their symptomatology as they are unknowing of what they need or want to tell. Hence the emphasis has shifted from knowing how the 'mental apparatus is constructed' to trying to comprehend the patient as a person. Holland (1977) gives a very concise account of the changes that have taken place in psychoanalytic theorizing and practices, as well as the factional proliferation of the basic Freudian psychoanalytic method.

This leads to my last point, which concerns my 'case-history': how do we assess madness and clinically enable a person to contain it, to live from it and with it? And by madness I do not mean psychoses or psychotic states. The *need* of the mad is not so much to know as to *be* and *speak*! I run into a conceptual difficulty here. Although a lot has been written about madness in the past two decades – Foucault (1965) and Szasz (1971), to mention only two books – one is hard put to find a definition of madness that clearly demarcates it as being *different* from other psychic and psychiatric states, such as the neuroses, perversions and psychoses. According to Foucault (1965), madness in the Middle Ages in Europe was treated quite differently, to the point of being almost a privileged state. Then Foucault states categorically: 'Indeed, from the fifteenth century on, the face of madness has haunted the imagination of Western man.' After giving a very extensive account of how the mad were gradually driven out of their familial and social settings into vagabondage, then into leprosariums, and eventually were 'imprisoned' in the nosological medical/psychiatric categories of insanity, psychoses, melancholia, etcetera, Foucault concludes: 'Psychoanalysis can unravel some of the forms of madness; it remains a stranger to the sovereign enterprise of unreason. It can neither liberate nor transcribe, nor most certainly explain what is essential in this enterprise.' In his later book (1976), Foucault argues: 'About the middle of the seventeenth century, a sudden change took place: the world of madness was to become the world of exclusion.' The reason Foucault gives for this 'exclusion' is a socioeconomic one:

> In the bourgeois world then being constituted, the major vice, the cardinal sin in that world of trade, had been defined; it was no longer, as in the Middle Ages, pride or greed, but sloth. The common category that grouped together all those interned in

these institutions was their inability to participate in the production, circulation, or accumulation of wealth (whether or not through any fault of their own). The exclusion to which they were subjected goes hand in hand with that inability to work, and it indicates the appearance in the modern world of a caesura that had not previously existed. Internment, therefore, was linked, in its origin and in its fundamental meaning, with this restructuring of social space.

This phenomenon was doubly important for the constitution of the contemporary experience of madness. Firstly, because madness, which had for so long been overt and unrestricted, which had for so long been present on the horizon, disappeared. It entered a phase of silence from which it was not to emerge for a long time; it was deprived of its language; and although one continued to speak of it, it became impossible for it to speak of itself. Impossible at least until Freud, who was the first to open up once again the possibility for reason and unreason to communicate in the danger of a common language, ever ready to break down and disintegrate into the inaccessible. On the other hand, madness, in internment, had forged strange new kinships. This space of exclusion, which had grouped together, with the mad, sufferers from venereal diseases, libertines, and innumerable major or petty criminals, brought about a sort of obscure assimilation; and madness forged a relationship with moral and social guilt that it is still perhaps not ready to break. We should not be surprised that, since the eighteenth century, a link should have been discovered between madness and all *crimes passionels*; that, since the nineteenth century, madness should have become the heir of crimes that find it in their reason for being and their reason for not being crimes; that, in the twentieth century, madness should have discovered at the center of itself a primitive nucleus of guilt and aggression. All this is not the gradual discovery of the true nature of madness, but simply the sedimentation of what the history of the West has made of it for the last three hundred years. Madness is much more *historical* than is usually believed, and much *younger* too.

I have quoted Foucault extensively, because it is precisely the need to 'speak' itself that constitutes the essence of the mad person's self-experience, as I have tried to show in the 'case-history' of Judy. How we are going to provide 'holding-structures' for the potentially mad, for them not to take on the *given* languages of psychoses or drug addictions, is perhaps the most urgent psychotherapeutic task facing us today. Lévi-Strauss (1962), discussing his concept of the 'savage mind', states his aim:

> . . . in this book it is neither the mind of savages nor that of primitive or archaic humanity, but rather mind in its *untamed states* [my italics] as distinct from the mind cultivated or domesticated for the purposes of yielding a return . . . The exceptional features of this mind which we call savage and which Comte described as spontaneous, relate principally to the extensive nature of the ends it assigns itself. It claims at once to analyse and to synthesize, to go to its furthest limits in both directions, while at the same time remaining capable of mediating between the two poles.

For an account of how some 'primitive' societies deal with this problem, see Pouillon (1970).

David Cooper (1978) states: 'We have, I believe, to distinguish between Reason and Knowledge. Reason and Unreason are both ways of knowing. Madness is a way of knowing, another mode of empirical exploration of both the "inner" and "outer" worlds.' I think that it was precisely such needs that first brought on the illnesses of Judy, because her environment could not *provide* her with the idiom with which she could *speak* herself. Later, through *placement* (Winnicott 1956) in a new environment, which did not make the counter-demands to her own needs, and through her personal efforts, she was able to find what her *difference* was from others and ask for the possibilities, socially and through apprenticeship, to cultivate her own style of being and living with and amongst others, purposefully, but also privately and creatively.

5
From Secretiveness to Shared Living

A vast psychoanalytic literature exists today prescribing how to help a patient make use of the analytic situation and process. On the one hand is the Kleinian approach, insisting that the earlier an analyst interprets and exposes the archaic unconscious fantasy systems of a patient and the corresponding anxieties, the sooner the patient is able to get into analytic process (cf. Segal 1964, Meltzer 1967). On the other hand, there is the classical approach of gradually analysing the defence systems of a patient, conscious and preconscious, to establish a working alliance (cf. Greenson 1967, Sandler, Dare and Holder 1973).

In the British Psycho-Analytical Society, where I have been reared, there is a third tradition: namely that of Winnicott and Balint. Winnicott (1965) had emphasized the necessity of *management* in the regressed and borderline cases, before interpretations can be mutatively effective. Balint (1968) had recommended the creation of an unobtrusive clinical ambience to establish a climate of trust with the patient.

In the clinical work that I shall report now, my emphasis will be how I, as an analyst, *accommodate to* the quirks and the needs of a patient before true interpretative analytic work begins to materialize. Here my style of clinical handling is influenced more by witnessing Winnicott's therapeutic consultations with children over some two decades than by his work with adults.

Clinical Material

It is one of the ambiguous privileges of being a nonmedical psychoanalyst in England that no patient can self-refer himself to me. Either a physician or a psychiatrist refers a patient to me when he thinks the person concerned can gain from psychoanalytic treatment. One great advantage of this is that we, the lay analysts, do not have to take a case-history. We have no choice but to start an analysis straight away, or refuse it, unencumbered by a debris of organized facts and rehearsed events by the patient. We can wait for the person to tell or not tell his facts before he can find that mutuality of trust and privacy that is the essence of the psychoanalytic method.

A distinguished physician had rung me to inquire whether I had a vacancy and could take into analysis a very bright young man. I agreed to it. He asked when Jonathan could come for his first session. I gave the date and time. He asked Jonathan, who was with him in his Consultation Room at the time, and it was all arranged. The physician then asked me whether I wanted to be sent detailed notes, and I said: 'No, please!' However, he insisted on telling me, with Jonathan's permission and demand, that the prospective patient was a youth of twenty-four, of foreign origin, who had made a fabulous success during the past three years in his profession of choice, both economically and socially. But he was in one hell of a mess in himself and in his personal life, and needed urgent care and treatment analytically. He had been in and out of psychotherapy with analysts and psychiatrists since the age of nine years! Furthermore, the physician added, 'I am allowed to tell you that now he is dangerously near to getting hooked on drugs, but he is a youth of true integrity and honesty.' I accepted all that as a frame of reference. I did state one condition to the physician concerned, namely, that he must stand by me all the way, twenty-four hours each day, because the acute and critical moments he will have to handle medically, and not fail to meet the *demand* of that need, no matter how hysterically and deliberately engineered by the patient, and whatever the hour. I further added that this meant that of the total strain and stress of this treatment, the physician shall have to carry seventy percent and I, thirty percent. He agreed to it, and I must categorically confess that I could not have seen this case to its conclusion if this physician had failed the person of the patient even once – which he never did.

Now I shall report from the first three sessions. For his first session, Jonathan arrived forty minutes late. He was apologetic: 'I am sorry, Sir, but my car did not arrive in time.' I noticed his use of the word 'Sir'. It was most atypical and unusual, both for his culture and his generation. But he had spoken it with a sincerity of respect towards an elder and that I could not disregard. Jonathan was not nervous, he was fidgety. He asked me: 'Do I lie down or can I sit and talk?' I responded that most persons find it more private to speak about themselves lying down! He took off his coat and lay down on the couch. I watched his compliance and could not help registering that he did not know what to do with his hands or where to place them once he lay down on the couch. In less than a minute, he was standing and asking whether he could smoke a cigarette. He shuffled through and searched his coat and his trouser pockets, and then somewhat sheepishly, but with a distinct note of arrogance, said: 'May I borrow a cigarette, Sir – my chauffeur has forgotten to give me some.' I smiled with irony and said: 'In that case you must sack the chauffeur!' He sat down in the chair and relaxed. He changed the subject and asked: 'Have you read all these books?' I replied that cultured persons do not read books, they live with them. He changed the subject again, and said: 'I rang my mother last night and she tells me you are very famous.' I deadpanned that and told him it was generous of him to let his mother know he was again going to be in treatment, because she must have been very worried. For the first time a curiously earnest look flickered across his face. Of course, I had realized that he had felt insecure and paranoid enough to check on me, but I did not say so. Then he asked anxiously, 'Will you take me into treatment?' and I replied, 'I cannot tell that today, since I hardly know you, but I am willing to take you into analytic *care*.' On that note the first session ended.

I shall drift away from the clinical material here to make a few comments. Some twenty-six years ago, towards the end of my two years of supervision of my first clinical case as a student, Miss Freud had once remarked, and I quote it as I remember it and not exactly as Miss Freud had said it: 'It is important to think about a session afterwards afresh, and not only remember what was actually said in that session by both the parties concerned. Only thus will you build up a personal "card-index" in your head for future reference!' I shall now use the phrase the 'after-image' for what Miss Freud had insinuated as a necessary task of thinking back about what had clinically transpired. And I never fail to examine and take notes on this 'after-image' after a first session and all critical sessions with a patient.

Now to return to Jonathan and the 'after-image' of my first clinical encounter with him. I had already surmised that he was incapable of reaching out for unsponsored help, because his physician had made the appointment for him. He had arrived forty minutes late with a snobbish excuse, and had learnt the tricks of aristocracy, which is nonexistent in his country of birth and nurture, but he was handling them very clumsily. But what had surprised me most in the 'after-image' was his relation to his body, especially the inquietude of his hands. He had very subtly touched something all the time: his face, the cigarettes, the chair, his tie and the like. I deduced that as a child he must have suffered from compulsive tics, and recalled Winnicott once remarking about tics: 'Tics are a child's way of making sure he *exists* as well as the world around him, by touching all the time. We can say by looking at a person that he exists, but he doesn't know it for himself, necessarily!' I had also noted that Jonathan's mannerisms of speech and behaviour were those of a puppet. And I was really aghast when I recalled what he looked like: a shabby golliwog impersonating a human being! His hair dishevelled, his expensive clothes messy! He was bizarre indeed! But he knew his way in life! I also realized he had told me nothing about himself and shared nothing.

For his second session Jonathan turned up punctually. He was dressed this time in typical Hippy style: jeans, a tight sweater and an open-neck shirt with a glaring scarf round his neck. He had cigarettes and sat in the chair and told me he had been *through* many 'head-shrinkers' since he was nine. I noticed his cheekiness and let him be. He gave me a rather long list of very celebrated people he had encountered and mixed with since his last session. Suddenly he asked me: 'Does it bore you, Mr Khan?' I waited while he itched, pinched and scratched himself everywhere, and then said: 'No, but it does not impress me!' Then he astonished me with a question: 'Do you think, Mr Khan, I am sick?' I answered immediately: 'I don't think so, but you are all loused up!' He laughed and told me how his Negress Nanny used to pick lice out of his hair, and it used to annoy his mother very much, because there were no lice in his hair. Before I could say anything he asked whether he could use my phone. I said: 'Yes!' He talked to someone and I left the room. He remarked: 'Please, Mr Khan, you don't have to leave the room.' I told him: 'I don't have to, but I shall, because I respect privacy.' When I returned he was silent for a while and then told me his reasons for seeking analysis. According to him, he was the 'whizz kid' of the Pop Jet Set in London, and everyone invited him and sought him out, and he didn't know what to say and felt ridiculous; hence he always took some beautiful model girl with him. Here I asked my first question: 'How many children did your parents breed?' He said he was one of the only twins; he had a twin sister. Then he praised a painting on my walls. After this he shuffled around and asked how long his analysis would last. I said I couldn't tell. He told me of his last therapist and what a fool he had made of him. I told him that he wouldn't succeed in that respect with me. He sat fidgeting a little longer and then said he must leave as he had an appointment with his solicitor. The session had lasted thirty-five minutes.

Jonathan did not turn up for his next session. His physician rang me when I was expecting him and said Jonathan was very sorry he had confused the appointments, but he needed to see his physician more urgently than me and would keep his next appointment. I accommodated to that and he did turn up.

I felt sure that Jonathan had vividly and genuinely demonstrated to me his style of functioning in life and coping with a diffuse and chronic ailment in himself in these first three sessions. He had also made clear his incapacity to fit or use the *prescribed* analytic process. He was a youth who had real talent and had made his way in life by using it. I had to respect that and accommodate to *his dosage* of the therapeutic relationship and process to himself. All too often, reading the contemporary analytic literature, I get the impression that diagnosing and interpreting psychopathology in our patients is our clinical variant of morality. We pretend not to judge, and yet our interpretative language is normatic and demands standards of psychic health, while it makes out to be helping the patient to recover from his ill-health. Of course, it was not lost on me that Jonathan had reacted to his first two encounters with me with panic and paranoid anxiety, and had taken flight into hyperactive manic proliferation of his professional activities on the one hand, and dispersion of his being into others – his colleagues, friends, parents, and his physician – on the other. Hence, his physician had sedated him, shrewdly realizing what had happened. There is now a myth of pure psychoanalysis that actualizes only and exclusively through the transference and the analytic process. We, the analysts, are the only ones that believe in this myth and persist in perpetrating it. In lived lives, we and our work call upon others who do all the dirty work for us and carry its strain from our patients, be it their families, friends or physicians. I had sensed a certain authenticity of resourcelessness in Jonathan and realized that he was manipulative but not devious, cunning but not dishonest. I also felt I had to work for him to find his trust in me and discover his being in his own person. Given the support of his physician, I felt sure I could help Jonathan be his own person. On this conviction I decided to continue with his analysis, realizing the risks entailed, both for myself and largely for his physician, who would have to account for any lethal mishaps during our mutual care of Jonathan. Suicides rarely work when intended, but accidents are the surest route to suicide, and Jonathan drove supercharged cars recklessly.

I hope I have not given you the mistaken notion that I had any illusions that Jonathan's care and treatment were going to be easy. For a year and more he kept up the same pattern: arriving late or leaving early or disappearing abroad for professional reasons. But during this year I got to know all Jonathan's manoeuvres in private and professional life. All the same, I was beginning to get discouraged and felt I was achieving nothing for Jonathan and should give up. Only his physician's insistence that I was helping Jonathan kept me going.

Then a fortuitous happening changed the whole climate and nature of therapeutic work with Jonathan. One day he arrived beaming, carrying a beautifully wrapped parcel. He asked me: 'Will you accept a gift, Mr Khan?' I hesitated because I had learnt that Jonathan was a compulsively generous person and his gifts were his technique of negating gratitude or belonging. I hedged by asking: 'Depends on what it is.' He squashed that, parrying me by saying: 'Please open it and find out.' I did, and it was a magnificent backgammon board. He asked me whether I knew how to play it and I said: 'No.' 'Then let me teach you; only last night I won over 1,500 pounds playing against one of the best players in London!' There was a joyously naughty gleam in his eyes when he said that. Then he added: 'I will play you ten games to teach you how the game works and then we play for real.' I accommodated to that. While Jonathan was setting up the board to play, myriad ideas and apprehensions scampered through my head. Was he intent on asserting his omnipotence and humiliating me? Was he trying to subvert the whole analytic process by this ruse? Then I recalled that only a few weeks earlier, when he was bemoaning his incapacity to converse with people, I had interpreted that he always tried to astonish or dominate with what he spoke, and did not realize that conversation in ordinary social intercourse is playing. Now he had brought me a game. I had the potential space to change his gamesmanship into playing. I took that chance, recalling Prince Hamlet's device: 'The Play is the thing wherein I shall catch the conscience of the King!'

In the session in which Jonathan had taught me to play, I noticed two significant facts. He had played only two games and then sat and told me in a coherent narrative how he had won the game last night. He had not bounced from one thing to another, as he always had before. Secondly, he had stayed the full length of the session for the first time. The rhythm of relating that evolved was somewhat as follows. Jonathan now arrived punctually and would either talk first and then ask to play, or if he was wrought up and nervous, play first and then talk. But he was beginning to talk about himself, even though tangentially. Of course, he slaughtered me in each game and collected his ten pence per game. In one session I took the opportunity and said: 'You realize, Jonathan, you do not play, you slaughter!' This had a curiously significant effect on him, and he told me how he used to drive his mother, his Nanny and his therapist crazy when he was about eleven years of age. He would build complex structures from Meccano sets, and just as they would begin to get excited, he would complete whatever he was doing and would smash it all up.

From this point onwards, it was possible to show him that he had missed the experience of playing in childhood and had instead taken to asserting his will.

Gradually the backgammon games diminished over a period of some three months. But during this time, I learnt a lot about his childhood.

Before I relate that, I must describe one of the last games we played. I was winning, and suddenly he introduced a new rule of which I knew nothing and of course he won. Then he rather sheepishly asked: 'Do you think that was dishonest?' I said bluntly, 'No, it was not dishonest,' since he had also given me a book on how to play backgammon, and if I had read it, I would have known the rule; but that he was *secretive* for sure, and that worried me, because it was out of character with his general behaviour. For the first time, Jonathan began to cry in a session.

Now I shall report the last phase of Jonathan's treatment, which lasted roughly six months. Jonathan asked me whether he could attend three times a week instead of five, and I accepted that because I felt it meant he had grown out of attachment towards dependency and relating in the clinical setting. During the backgammon games, I had learnt a lot about his childhood. His parents had divorced when he was four years of age, and he was shuttled from grandparents, to living with his mother, to visiting his father – all of whom lived in different cities. Leaving each one always caused him enormous anxiety and terror. His father was very fond of him, but because of his own business preoccupations, he had little personal time to spare, and Jonathan was handed over to his staff to be spoiled and indulged. He was a bedwetter up until the age of eleven and could make no use of psychotherapy, to which he had been submitted from the age of nine. In his private life, he was a very compliant, shy child, riddled with tics. Now it was possible to show him how all his pinching and scratching of his face and body, as well as of objects, was really the same phenomenon as tics, and it was his technique of making sure that the world around him did not disappear.

Jonathan was a person of acute intelligence, and I was myself surprised, once he began to change, at how he grew rapidly into an adult youth. He no longer spent his private time ringing everyone all over the world and became very self-sustaining. Towards the end of his treatment he was able to start a relationship with a woman, which was mutual and nourishing for him. This was also the first time in his life that he had a home of his own and a private life. He had always lived vagrantly, drifting from friend to friend. In his relationship to me, he also began to be able to use the couch and could tolerate my absence from his sight, and therefore be private with himself in my presence. Unfortunately, his treatment had to end for external reasons, as he had to leave the country. He still comes every three to four months for a few sessions and has maintained his growth.

Discussion

I have deliberately eschewed giving a detailed account of the complex psychopathology of this patient, which we had analysed quite thoroughly. Here my intention is to show how the potential space of the secret for a child, where he can build up and sustain a private tradition of the maturing and growing Self (cf. Khan 1974), can become distorted into secretiveness. The function of secretiveness is not only to protect the Self from impingements that the growing but vulnerable ego cannot cope with, but also to protect the significant care-taking persons in the child's familial environment. Jonathan was exposed to, and witnessed, events and conversations in the lives of his grandparents, father and mother, which he had been exhorted by each party concerned not to tell and share with others. This splitting of familial coherence of experience he had, at adolescence, turned into his technique of living. As Winnicott (1960*b*) has remarked: 'In psycho-analysis as we know it there is no trauma that is outside the individual's omnipotence. Everything comes under ego-control, and thus becomes related to secondary processes.' Jonathan's life-style shows clearly how his ego had brought under its control the cumulative trauma of being made an accomplice to the secretiveness in his family. But this achievement had turned him into beserk extroverted vagrancy of existing and robbed him of that potential space within which a person can grow in secret and privacy with himself.

This brings me to my second point, namely, the clinical tolerance of nonrelating by such patients in the clinical situation and the transference. Our bias is to interpret such nonrelating either as resistance or hostile refutation of the analyst as a persecutory figure. That can often be true, but to interpret it is to make a patient feel culpable for a basic incapacity in himself. In this area of work with such patients, I find a concept of Winnicott's most helpful. Describing an infant's way of relating to the spatula in the consultation situation, Winnicott (1941) describes 'a phase of hesitance' that intervenes between the infant's attraction to the spatula and his final acceptance of it. I believe that what we take for resistance in such patients is, in fact, 'a phase of hesitance' that must be clinically allowed for and accepted as such.

The last point I wish to make is that Freud's concept of free association entails the capacity in the patient to play. We cannot demand this capacity as a *given* in such patients. We have to enable them to be able to play with their fantasies and inner world experiences before they can free associate. Once that capacity is reached, then analysis proper can start, and then, as Dr Lacan (1953) says, '. . . when he (the patient) can speak to you of himself, the analysis will be terminated.' I would add to it that then the patient can also begin to live from the potential space of the secret and his privacy with himself, as well as sharing life with others.

6
Secret as Potential Space

> Be silent!
> of Nothing,
> ever,
> to anyone –
> there
> in the embers
> time
> is singing.
>
> *Osip Mandel'shtam*

In our clinical work, sometimes, it is more important to sustain a person in living than to rid him of his illness. Winnicott (1967) summed this up in his statement, '. . . absence of psycho-neurotic illness may be health, but it is not life' (p. 100).

The demand for *life*, and if that is not possible, for *not living*, is made upon us by the patient and is not a bias of our restitutive omnipotence as therapists. When a patient makes this demand upon us, we have every right to *refuse* it, but not to confuse it. The patient is willing to stay ill and suffer the consequences so long as he or she is *living* or *not living*. If we try to subvert his life by a cure, he either escapes us or gives up his right to be alive and ill and enters into a complicity with us that we mistake for 'treatment alliance'. Gilles Deleuze (1973), in spite of his mocking acerbity, raises an important issue. He argues that Melanie Klein establishes a contract with her patients in which the patients bring their intense experiences of living and she translates these into fantasies for them. He argues that Winnicott takes the psychoanalytic process to that limit where this contract is no longer viable. It becomes more than a mere question of translating the vécu into fantasies or interpreting it. With Winnicott, that point is reached when one has to share with the patient his experience. Deleuze asks whether this is a question of sympathy, empathy or identification. He concludes: 'What we feel is rather the necessity of a relationship which is neither legal, contractual or institutional.'

Of course the philosophers are always wiser and more just than we are; they are not harassed by the ordinary daily humiliations of having to fail a person in his demands. The *word* is by its very nature inexhaustibly munificent and more understanding than the *act*. Yet Deleuze is right: 'Il faut y aller, il faut partager son état.' But to share and partake of another's predicament implies time and space. What is the nature of *this* time and space with such persons?

Philosophically to comprehend and share 'des états vécus' of a dead genius like Nietzsche, whom Deleuze so insightfully writes about in the context from which I quote him, is one thing; to make oneself available for *use* (to cite Winnicott's concept) to the *living* Nietzsche was another matter altogether. None succeeded.

On 4 January 1889, Nietzsche wrote to George Brandes from Turin: 'To my friend Georg! Once you discovered me, it was no great feat to find me: the difficulty now is to lose me . . . the crucified' (1889, p. 345).

If Deleuze were to make the retort that we analysts are all too adept at *losing* those who do not fit our machinery of cure, it would be hard to refute him. Still I believe it is becoming clinically possible for us to meet the *need* of such persons who insist on *living* outside contractual or institutional relationships.

During the course of any psychoanalytic treatment, we witness a patient inhabiting and fluctuating through many spaces – inside/outside, subjective/objective – and we share these with him. The total analytic situation meets the various demands of the patient in his different states through three modalities: the analytic process, the analytic relation (transference) and the analytic setting. The analytic process actualizes through interpretation and deals with the hidden meaning (Freud), the absent meaning (Green) and the potential meaning (Khan) of the patient's communications. It is here that the analyst is par excellence the 'supplementary ego' (Heimann 1956) of the patient. The transference relationship organizes that affectivity in the patient that enables him to project the roles of significant figures from his past onto the analyst in the here and now of the analytic situation. In recent decades two more functions have been added to the analyst's role in the transference relationship, namely, those of *holding* (Winnicott) and *containing* (Bion). The use of the analytic setting by the patient has come under scrutiny only recently, largely through the researches of Winnicott and Balint.

In classical analysis a patient's capacity to use the analytic setting was taken for granted and most of the analytic literature is devoted to discussions of a patient's use or abuse of the analytic process and the transference relationship. The researches of Winnicott (1955), Balint

(1968) and Milner (1969) have progressively sensitized us to the fact that a patient in certain states of distress and disturbance may be able to use only the analytic space, while he finds himself incapable of using the analytic process or the transference relationship.

In my clinical experience patients use the analytic space in two distinct ways: as concrete space to be in and as potential space where they sustain moods and larval psychic experiences that their ego-capacities cannot yet actualize. I am borrowing the concept of *potential space* from Winnicott (1967). In his paper, 'The Location of Cultural Experience', he states:

> From the beginning the baby has maximally intense experiences in the potential space between the subjective object and the object objectively perceived, between me-extensions and the not-me. This potential space is at the interplay between there being nothing but me and there being objects and phenomena outside omnipotent control.
>
> Every baby has his or her own favourable or unfavourable experience here. Dependence is maximal. The potential space happens only in relation to a feeling of confidence on the part of the baby, that is, confidence related to the dependability of the mother-figure or environmental elements, confidence being the evidence of dependability that is becoming introjected (p. 100).

Winnicott himself has not examined the analytic setting in terms of this hypothesis. Yet it seems to me that his squiggle-game consultations give us a vivid account of how a child uses paper as potential space in order to be privately alone with Winnicott. And this potential space of the paper is a *shared* space where both Winnicott and the child *mutually act* towards that 'significant moment' when the experience of the child can be interpreted to the child (cf. Winnicott 1970).

The most interesting clinical example of how a patient creates a secret potential space is given to us by Marion Milner (1969) in her book *The Hands of the Living God*. Milner recounts how her patient, Susan, had made a drawing the night before her first consultation. The patient had not mentioned or shown this drawing to Milner during some ten years of analysis. In her discussion of Susan's drawings, Milner does not elaborate upon the necessity for Susan, at first, to draw in secret privacy outside the analytic setting. In contrast to Winnicott's squiggle-game drawings *with* the children, Susan, when she had first started to draw, could share her drawings with

Milner only *after* the event. Susan's use of the potential space of the paper is an essential part of her 'self-cure', to use Milner's phrase. Something from the total analytic experience is suspended by Susan, to be actualized later in the potential space of the paper. I am borrowing from André Green's (1973) new slant on Freud's concept of deferred action. Green postulates:

> One major capacity of the psychic structure is the capacity to cut off, to suspend an experience, while it is still going on. This is not for the purpose of observing the experience as in the conscious mental functioning, but to shut off the awareness of it in order to recreate it, in one's own way later on. It is important to see that this cutting off or inner splitting is a precondition for the establishment of further links by association. We should distinguish the moment of the experience and the moment in which it becomes meaningful.

It seems to me that for Susan, at first, the *experience* of herself in the analytic situation became meaningful only as a *secret* – the secret of her drawing in her own isolate privacy. The potential space of the paper captures and articulates this *secret*. I shall now give some clinical material to show how a very young girl created a *secret* and used it as the potential space where she could continue to be, quite apart from her inner life or familial existence in the outside world.

A colleague had asked me to see a young woman urgently because, according to him, she was having a psychotic breakdown. This patient, whom I shall call Caroline, arrived in a most confused and agitated state. All she could tell me in the first consultation was how her husband had jilted her in a most brutal and humiliating manner a week earlier. He had now left her to live with another woman. She kept repeating, 'He has destroyed me!' and her crying was both intense and incessant. I was struck by her utter incapacity to relate to me. She had hardly looked at me once during some two hours of consultation, even though she was sitting facing me. I had been told by the referring consultant that she was a doctor and for the past week had been unable to work. Alongside this acute feeling that she could not relate to me, there grew in me across the time of the consultation a sentient conviction that Caroline felt safe and viable in the space of my Consultation Room. It was this latter conviction that persuaded me to say to Caroline that I was willing to take her into analytic treatment if she so wished. Caroline accepted my offer with a blank absence of response.

Caroline turned up for her sessions five times a week with a punctuality that was almost frightening. This absence of resistance left me clueless as to what was happening to her, inside or outside analysis. Her mood-swings were dangerously volatile. Fortunately I had been able to find a physician of great ability to look after Caroline medically. It would have been impossible for me to hold Caroline in analysis or in life without the medicating care provided by my physician colleague. Caroline was not a silent patient. She either cried vehemently, moaning 'My husband has destroyed me', or she would arrive in a manic state and talk wildly about everything and everybody in her environment but herself. After some three months of analysis, I knew no more about who Caroline was than I had after the first consultation.

It was very tempting to interpret her absence or, to use André Green's more telling phrase, her suspension of experience in the analytic setting as resistance, either from anxiety or hostile suspiciousness. There was a distinct flavour of secretiveness to all her behaviour in analysis and I chose to respect it, both as her right and as her privacy.

Then one day Caroline had an accident. She had not noticed the traffic lights changing, and she banged her car into another one in front of her. A most courteous gentleman had emerged from the other car to look into the damage done. Caroline was so resourceless in the situation that he offered to meet her for lunch the next day and arrange matters. He was much taken by her. Caroline is a plump and pleasant looking girl of some twenty-seven years of age, and there is an ebullient helplessness in her general way of being that is rather attractive. Within a week Caroline was living in the care of her new friend in his house. This was indeed a great relief and respite, both for her physician and for me. Her mood-swings had been so excessive that we had started to think seriously of hospitalizing her. The newfound friend made this unnecessary. He was deeply devoted to her and had the patience of Job with her mad antics. The moment Caroline started this relationship, quite a different person emerged from her being.

Caroline had been married for some six years and lived most docilely with an outrageously cruel and delinquent young husband. Now she began to act out and test the love and care of her friend with a vehement vengefulness. She mistrusted his motives and was violently rageful. She put him into the most embarrassing social situations. Fortunately for everyone concerned, her friend had an inexhaustible capacity to contain and tolerate her nuisances. In analysis her cry now changed from 'I have been destroyed by my husband' to 'I have lost myself somewhere in my life.' It is not my intention to discuss this phase of her treatment here. Gradually Caroline began to personalize into a coherent being and her moods became related to her actions.

It was at this stage, when she had been in treatment for some nine months, that she arrived one day for her session and, before lying down, paused and said to me: 'I know now what is the matter with me! I have hidden myself.' She lay down and continued: 'I have never told you what I did at three and a half years of age.' She recounted how one day she had taken two silver candlesticks from her mother's dining room and buried them in the garden. There had been a lot of searching around for them. Police had been called and eventually the insurance had paid up the price. They were an expensive item. She had a sense of all that was going on in the house about the candlesticks but had said nothing. Some five months after this event the parents had moved to a new house in a different city. The whole episode had been forgotten. Then one day when she was nine years of age, during vacations, her parents had returned with her for a visit to the old house, of which they were very fond. The new occupants of the house were friends of theirs. When everyone was having tea, Caroline had gone into the garden, dug out the candlesticks and returned them to her parents. She concluded her account laughingly: 'Real hell broke loose and my father gave me a big thrashing.'

In the weeks following this communication, Caroline was able to give a detailed account of the familial circumstances surrounding her act. When Caroline was three her mother had given birth to premature twins and had suffered from toxaemia of pregnancy. The whole climate in the home had changed. A nurse had been employed to look after the twins, who were both girls. The mother had sunk into a severe depression and was for years incapable of taking an active part in the running of the family. The parents hadn't even taken vacations until their visit to the old house the summer the mother had started to work again. It was then that the patient had dug up the candlesticks and given them back to her parents.

From the very beginning of her treatment, I had from choice allowed Caroline the privacy of her antics, inside and outside analysis. There was a definite risk involved, which I felt it was her need and demand that I take, by providing clinical coverage and holding (in terms of time and space) so that she could *transcribe* whatever she was reaching after in her chaotic and bewildered way. What further aggravated this situation was Caroline's incapacity to work during this phase; she had to give up her job and hence she was stranded with herself all day long. Her friend went to work early and returned late in the evening. Because of her confused mental state, I could get no true picture of her daily existence. Not only was each session an isolated *happening*, with no before and after, but it was also a clutter of bizarre bits and pieces of her random perceptions and volatile affects. Yet I had this sure feeling that Caroline was making a very private *use* of the analytic space and, gradually, even of me as a person. But she kept it all strictly to herself.

Once she told me about the candlestick episode, everything changed in her manner of talking in analysis. She had taken some three sessions to tell all the story. This was the first time Caroline was able to sustain continuity of theme from one session to the next. What was even more important was that I began to have some inkling of her way of *using* me. I interpreted to her that, by burying the candlesticks, she had found a way of *absenting* herself from the changed and traumatizing familial environment. I deliberately used the word *absenting* rather than *hiding*. Here I was exploiting a concept of André Green's (1973). I interpreted that the candlesticks symbolized all the good nourishing experiences of her infancy and early childhood from good-enough mothering. She then split off these experiences and *absented* them from the ongoing life of the family, in which she felt precarious and could merely exist, and which threatened to destroy even the goodness of her past relation with her mother. There was a distinct precocity in her capacity to use such a self-protective manoeuvre at this early age. The burying of the candlesticks created a secret where she could continue in suspended animation a part of her that she could no longer live and share with her parents, especially the mother. The *secret* encapsulated her own *absent* self.

Caroline responded to my interpretation by telling me of repetitive psychosomatic illnesses between the ages of five and nine. These illnesses had kept her away from school. She said that she never missed going to school during these illnesses, even though she was an active, sportive and gregarious child. She added: 'I had to withdraw every now and then, and be with myself it seems.' To which I said: 'To be with yourself and with your secret at the same time.'

When we were working in this area of her creating a secret where she could suspend a part of herself, Caroline asked me: 'Why have you never interpreted that over the past two months? Almost every Friday I have forgotten something in the waiting room, or don't you know of it?' I told her that I knew of it all right, since my staff had always informed me, and I had instructed them to return whatever item it was to her on Monday when she would return to analysis. She quizzed me: 'Why didn't you tell me?' And I answered: 'Because you never told me yourself and I respected your secret play with the waiting room and my staff.' She became pensive and started to cry quietly. I think it was the first time I had seen Caroline cry in a session, with an affect that was related to what was being said or experienced. After a while I interpreted to her that I had registered the fact that she had started to leave things behind during the phase in which she had become very suspicious that her man-friend was trying to control her life; that I had understood it to mean that she was using the space of the waiting room to leave behind, over the weekend, some object that stood for a very private bit of herself. Thus a bit of her was safely there for her to collect on Monday, and she also saved her friend from whatever anger or rage might erupt from this part of her; that now, knowing about the candlestick episode, I would say that she was using my waiting room as she had used the garden in her childhood, to find a place where she could leave a bit of herself in secret. The reason, I added, that she had not used the Consultation Room was that I might have noticed the 'left object' straight away and she would have had to take it with her; if I had found it later, I would have sabotaged her secret by interpreting it. She couldn't take that risk.

From this point onwards her mode of communicating in the sessions changed. I was surprised to witness in her a joyous capacity to recall and narrate, with a sparkling vividness, experiences from all areas and phases of her life. I am not concerned with that material here. Briefly, the story as it emerged was that she had some four buoyant carefree years from nine to thirteen years of age. Then the twins had fallen ill with a crippling illness that took years to remedy. During this period Caroline became a devoted ally of her mother in the nursing of her sisters. Just as that was ending, she met her future husband and *capitulated* (her phrase) to him. He was truly evil and she became his willing victim. She had given up all hope of a personal life shared with someone. This had ended with his brutal jilting of her, and her breakdown.

My argument here is that a person can *hide* himself into symptoms or he can *absent* himself into a secret. Here, the secret provides a potential space where an absence is sustained in suspended animation. Like the antisocial tendency (Winnicott 1956), the secret carries a hope that one day the person will be able to emerge out of it, be found and met, and thus become a whole person, sharing life with others. I am grateful to Pontalis for drawing my attention to a passage in Freud's letter to Fliess (6 December 1896):

> As you know, I am working on the assumption that our psychical mechanism has come about by a process of stratification: the material present in the shape of memory-traces is from time to time subjected to a rearrangement in accordance with fresh circumstances – is, as it were, transcribed. Thus what is essentially new in my theory is the thesis that memory is present not once but several times over, that it is registered in various species of 'signs' (Freud 1950*a*).

What has been even more enlightening for me towards an understanding of the function of a secret is the commentary on this letter by Laplanche and Pontalis (1973):

> This idea might lead one to the view that all phenomena met with in psycho-analysis are placed under the sign of retroactivity, or even of retroactive *illusion*. This is what Jung means when he talks of retrospective phantasies: according to Jung, the adult reinterprets his past in his phantasies, which constitute so many symbolic expressions of his current problems. On this view reinterpretation is a way for the subject to escape from the present 'demands of reality' into an imaginary past.
>
> Seen from another angle, the idea of deferred action may also suggest a conception of temporality which was brought to the fore by philosophers and later adopted by the various tendencies of existential psycho-analysis: consciousness constitutes its own past, constantly subjecting its meaning to revision in conformity with its 'project' (p. 112).

This discussion helps me to understand retrospectively a certain quality that characterized Caroline's behaviour before she told me of her secret. Her way of talking randomly often struck me as rather mad. I could interpret all sorts of fantasies into it, but, in fact, it was meaningless. There was no retroactive elaboration, psychically or symbolically, of any experience. Now I can begin to see how Caroline's secret had helped her consciousness *escape* its own past.

Caroline lived in the instant here and now of explosive affects and random behaviour. I can see now that what is hidden inside or repressed lends itself to endless rearrangements and even retroactive *illusion*. But what is absented into a secret stays out of reach for any sort of further elaboration. Hence I now consider erroneous my remark that the candlesticks *symbolized* the early good relationship to her mother. What was important for Caroline was the *act* of burying them and not any symbolic meaning they may have had. This *act* concretized and encapsulated into a secret the point at which her growth in *mutuality* with her mother had been disrupted. The potential space of the secret imprisoned that fact and kept it frozen. But it also disabled Caroline from being able to elaborate or correct it in terms of new experience. The location of a secret of this type in psychic topography is neither inside nor outside a person. A person cannot say, 'I have a secret inside me.' They are the secret, yet their ongoing life does not partake of it. In analysis what Caroline could report was either the bric-a-brac of daily existence or nothing. And to have treated her incapacity as resistance would have engendered only reactive guilt in her. This is a very specific issue with such patients: their tendency towards compliance makes them over-receptive to any interpretation that makes them feel guilty. Hence my quote from Deleuze, who rightly protests the translation of lived life into mere fantasies. Such interpretation of fantasies creates a pseudo-psychic reality to which the patient gets addicted. This leads to those interminable deep analyses which we often hear about these days.

Clinically, it is only if we succeed in gradually creating an atmosphere of *mutuality* with these patients that they can share their secret with us. This sharing of the secret amounts to that 'experience of mutuality' (Winnicott 1970) that is the essence of the mother's capacity to adapt to the baby's need. What had enabled Caroline to share her secret was my capacity to contain and hold all the confusion and risk her behaviour perpetrated inside and outside analysis over the first eight months, as well as my capacity to allow her to *use* the waiting room in a private way for the weekend gap in analysis.

Lastly, I want to suggest that the creation of a secret creates a *gap* (Green 1973) in the person's psyche, which they reactively screen with all sorts of bizarre events, intrapsychic or interpersonal. We as clinicians are then required to discriminate between the true experience of such persons and their reactive behaviour. In Deleuze's phrase, these patients have to be enabled to *share* their experience with us, not merely report on it in terms of fantasies or through symptomatic gestures. What was important for Caroline when she left things behind, such as her umbrella or a packet of chocolates or a book, was the *act* of leaving them. It was this *act* that I held for her and unobtrusively shared until she was ready to share it mutually.

I have tried to give a clinical example of how a child absented herself into a secret when her ongoing life with her mother broke down and how she gradually linked up with it in her analysis. Secret is only one way of encapsulating such experiences. Pseudologia fantastica often provides similar potential space to a person. And sometimes during analysis even repetitively forgotten dreams have this function.

I have found in Carl Jung's autobiography *Memories, Dreams, Reflections* an interesting corroboration of my hypothesis that the secret can provide a space in which the threatened ongoing life of a child can be sustained intact. Jung recounts how in his childhood, when he started to associate with his 'rustic schoolmates', he found that they alienated him from himself. The years from seven to nine were full of turbulent inner crisis for Jung. Then at the age of ten 'my disunion with myself and uncertainty in the world at large led to an action which at the time was quite incomprehensible to me.' Jung carved a manikin on two inches of his ruler, wrapped it in wool, placed a stone by it and put all these in a case which he hid in 'the forbidden attic' of his house. He wrote letters to the manikin in a secret language and from time to time he would clamber into the loft unnoticed to leave them there with the manikin. Jung (1963) concludes his narrative:

> The meaning of these actions, or how I might explain them, never worried me. I contented myself with the feeling of newly-won security, and was satisfied to possess something that no-one knew and no-one could get at. It was an inviolable secret which must never be betrayed, for the safety of my life depended on it. Why that was so I did not ask myself. It simply was so.
>
> This possession of a secret had a very powerful formative influence on my character: I consider it the essential factor of my boyhood (pp. 34–5).

7
The Empty-Headed

Peindre, non la chose, mais l'effet qu'elle produit.
Mallarmé

What are all the fish that lie gasping on the strand?
Yeats

La preuve première d'existence, c'est d'occuper l'espace.
Le Corbusier

'You hinder me more than you help me,' said Mercier.
'I'm not trying to help you,' said Camier. 'I'm trying to help myself.'
'Then all is well,' said Mercier.
Samuel Beckett

The ravine is deep
but where it closes briefly
blossoms the same fear.
anonymous Haiku

In the beginning, there is the *act* and the *gesture*. Fantasies, thoughts, dreams, playing and imaginings follow afterwards. Psychic reality is an *après coup*! *Acts* and *gestures* initiate it, dictate its fatedness and destiny.

A colleague was on the phone, insisting that she speak to me urgently about some patient. It was past 8:00 p.m. The clinical day had come and been! For some reason, I agreed to receive the call. My colleague, a female analyst, was direct in her demands. She knew, she said, that I did not like to be disturbed in my private time by professional calls, but she was in a quandary. She needed my advice. A young girl-patient of hers had wrecked her Consultation Room. She was always an eruptive character, but this time she had pushed things to the limit. My colleague felt that she could no longer 'hold' her in private analytic care. This was not the first time this had happened. The patient had been hospitalized before, on her own demand, after unmanageable behaviour in the sessions and at home, but to no avail.

The analyst did not want to hospitalize her again and asked if I would please see the girl and give my opinion. I asked how old the patient was. She was some twenty-three years of age, came from a well-off, good family, and was highly intelligent, anorectic and episodically very antisocial in conduct – intentionally so! 'She is not a promising character,' I said. The analyst said: 'No! She is very gifted, and I think you could *hold* and help her.' I thanked her for her confidence in me, and asked: 'When do you want me to see her?' 'Tonight,' she said, 'if possible! They say you work at all hours! If you cannot, then I will have to hospitalize her tonight because her mother won't be able to cope with her in her present mood and state.' I said: 'All right, I'll see her at 11:00 p.m. Who will bring her?' 'The mother will,' she said. That ended the conversation. The patient was in the room, listening, when her analyst rang me, so I felt that things were clear and explicit, at least at one level. I never search my mind when I make such outlandish clinical decisions. I simply wait for the next *happening*. This event took place more than fifteen years ago, but even then I was convinced of the futility of prevaricating considerations about a person's *analysability*. One accepts, or one refuses – that is all there is to it.

I was waiting in my Consultation Room for the girl to arrive. This is not my usual style. I prefer to let a person sit a while in the waiting room, and then personally to escort him to the Consultation Room. The time/space that this allows me for observation has always been most indicative of a person's style and character. But I had decided to be in the Consultation Room, knowing that the girl was in a disturbed state and might start creating a mess while waiting. So when she rang the bell, most punctually, the houseboy showed her to the Consultation Room, where I greeted her. She grunted, looking away. She was pent-up and anxious. She refused my gesture of offering her a chair and stood with her back to the wall, her hands folded behind her. She stared around like a caged animal. I watched. She was not quite the 'person' I was expecting to meet. For an anorectic, she was fat and hefty. She was tall and rather Indian in looks. She was almost beautiful, but at the time, looked messy, wearing her expensive clothes vengefully, like a tramp's rags.

After an uncomfortable pause, she stated, rather than asked: 'Has *Calamity* talked to you again?'

'Who is *Calamity*?' I asked.

'My analyst, who has made me come to see you. She says you *will* help me.' I was rather amused and relieved by her pet name for her analyst. It showed that she had not only a sense of wit but also a capacity for affection. Even more revealing, it showed that she was *self-aware* but projected onto others what she perceived and/or experienced in herself. *Calamity* was standing on two feet, right in front of me. I made no comment, but noted this for future use. She said again, a little put out: 'Has *Calamity* rung again?'

'No! Why should she?'

'Well, she knows everything, so why hasn't she told you more? I won't tell anything.'

'I have no curiosity to find out anything,' I said. She looked noticeably nonplussed. After a while, she threatened: 'I am going to wreck this room, too. It has too many books and things.' She looked menacing and I felt she meant what she said. So I said to her: 'Before you try any of your antics, please come and let us shake hands.' She hesitated, did not move, but put out her right hand. I stood up, went over, and took hold of her hand firmly.

'Please try and squeeze my hand,' I demanded.

'I won't!'

'In that case, I will squeeze yours!' She looked undecided for a moment, and then taunted me: 'You won't!' I started to squeeze her hand, harder and harder. Within a minute, she was crumpled on the floor, shouting: 'Let go! Let go! You are hurting me!'

'I mean to,' I responded. There was a knock at the Consultation Room door. 'Come in,' I said, and I let go of her hand. Hearing her shouting, the houseboy had come, fearing there was trouble. She stood up. I told him it was all right and he went away. She was pretty shaken. I sat back in my chair and said firmly but gently to her: 'You see, you cannot wreck my Consultation Room; not only am I physically stronger and more agile than you, but I have staff to provide me with coverage. I don't need hospitals.' She stared vacantly at the floor.

'You can't make me speak, anyway!'

'I have no such wish or intention,' I said.

'Ring *Calamity*, she'll tell you!'

'It's rather late to ring now.'

'I ring her at all hours. She always answers.'

'Well, I never ring anyone after 8:00 p.m.,' I said.

'I will,' she said.

'If you so wish!' I suddenly realized that the telephone was next to my writing table. I warned her: 'Make sure you don't knock anything over or I'll really louse you up.' She rang! Her analyst answered. The girl was lost for words.

'What do I say to her?' she asked me.

'How do I know!' She said something, and then asked me to come over because her analyst wanted to speak with me. I agreed. Her analyst said: 'She wants me to come with her tomorrow, if she is even to try working with you.' I said: 'As you want!' The three of us arranged to meet the next day at 5:00 p.m. She mocked me: 'Don't you have any other patients? *Calamity* can never change her patients' times; that's why I sometimes see her late at night.' I parried, rather cynically: 'Perhaps my patients are more accommodating.' She started to leave. I felt that it had all gone her way. I wanted to trip her up a little in her omnipotent manipulativeness. So I asked her: 'Has your mother driven you here?'

'Yes, she is waiting in the car.'

'Please go and fetch her. I want to talk to her before meeting you and your analyst tomorrow. The houseboy will accompany you.' She agreed without any fuss. So, I thought, her defiance was just bluff from resourcelessness.

She returned with her mother – an elegant, well-groomed woman, with a soft voice. She sat down whilst her daughter stood as before. I could sense that the mother had talked with the analyst and was hoping, if not intending, that I would take her daughter into analysis. To ease the situation I said to her: 'From your accent, it sounds as if you have not grown up in England.'

'All my life I have lived abroad,' she said, 'until my husband died ten years ago.' Another silence. I helped her out again: 'I have had a good look at your daughter and hope to know more from her analyst tomorrow. In the meantime, will you kindly tell me some simple facts about where and how you live.' The mother told me that they lived in a large modern flat in which her daughter had a room of her own. Since they had no living-in staff, there were only the two of them living in the flat, but she had a large family and frequently had many relatives staying. I asked her what she did with her time. 'I visit friends and relatives!' she replied.

'And your daughter?'

'She does odd-jobs from time to time but hasn't been well for the past five years so has stopped studying.' I told the mother quite bluntly that if I agreed to take her daughter into my *therapeutic care*, I would ask for an environmental management routine mutually agreed amongst the three of us. I had deliberately used the phrase 'therapeutic care' rather than 'treatment' or 'analysis'. The mother did not quite understand what I meant, so I explained: 'I shall schedule your daughter's way of daily living, that is, when I know her better and if she will give me that chance. I would then recommend what she should do further. I won't accept her just "being a patient" as a way of life.' The mother said: 'I will do anything you ask, but she is very difficult to handle.'

'I am sure of that,' I said, 'but I have been brought up to tame *creatures* like her.' I deliberately used the word 'creature' to provoke her daughter. I noticed that she did not react, so I told the mother that was enough for tonight. I would ring her the following night and let her know what I had decided, after meeting with her daughter and the analyst. They left politely. Once again, I asked the houseboy to escort them to their car. I did not want any 'scenes' outside. The girl had been too compliant so far! Just as she was leaving, I caught a look of panic and terror in her eyes.

The whole first encounter had taken only some forty minutes. My general reaction to it was one of being 'intrigued' by this *creature* and her antics. Before I quote from the 'notes' I took that night, I must state parenthetically that I have been tutored by my training analyst, John Rickman, and two supervisors, Miss Anna Freud and Donald Winnicott, to jot down the life-events reported by the patient in the first consultation, the patient's presenting symptoms and my personal impressions. I was also advised to keep note, later on, of 'significant' dreams and events in and out of analysis, as well as some record of what I say myself. John Rickman had always insisted that what one could not write down from a session on one side of a five-by-ten card was not worth writing, because somehow *that* session had scattered in all directions. Fortunately, neither Miss Freud nor Winnicott liked being 'read to' from lengthy notes. As to my readiness to see the girl's mother, I reckon that this derives from years of therapeutic work with children, especially under Winnicott's supportive and guiding care. Since I have never worked in or with any institutional structures, I have always had to see parents, friends and relatives of my cases personally. Even if I could use 'social workers', I do not think that my temperament and style would fit in with that regime of clinical work.

To return to 'the girl': I am aware that I never used her name, even in my notes, except when I first wrote down her name and address. Only much later did I start to call her by her Christian name. I quote verbatim some of what I wrote after our first encounter:

> She may not be a person but she certainly has a soul. Whatever that means . . . a lot of her outrageous conduct and gibing results from incapacity to relate and communicate with herself and the others . . . all extravagant *neediness* and instant demands are symptoms of a lack of her resources vis-à-vis her needs, desires and wishes . . . A lot of what she presents/flaunts as her 'derangement' is only partially hers; a lot of it is impingements that have accumulated, which she can neither render into personalized psychic experience, nor shed as irrelevant (should I be saying: she can't use the psychic mechanism of repression effectively!) . . . Is too concerned with the well-being of others, can't manage it and then messes it up . . . Has been obviously reared properly, richly and lovingly. By whom? is the question . . . Whether I can help her will depend on the quality and character of her relating and abuse of her last analyst! . . . Personally, I like her as a young girl with a palpable potential for health and creative living . . . we are both wilful characters – that would be the real snag for each of us! . . . She has made herself into an *absurd creature* à la Camus! no past, no language, no passions. Only muted rage, absence, and looking-on! Little meaning to her self-experience as yet. Compels others to *provide* meaning! (cf. Khan 1972*a*, 1972*b*; Winnicott 1972*b*)

The girl arrived punctually for our next meeting, *with* her analyst. She must have waited downstairs for her, since they had travelled separately from different places. Her mother had driven her, again. Her compelling urgency to 'control' her environment was obvious. I found myself somewhat unsure of which tactics and strategies to deploy. It was a completely new experience for me to see/consult a 'patient' with her analyst. I had never done it before, nor has it happened since.

I recognized the analyst but we kept a semblance of anonymity. The girl challenged it immediately: 'You know each other, so why are you pretending you don't!' Her analyst, who was comfortably seated, smiled affably. I looked at the girl sternly – and meant it, too! She stood as before: hands folded behind her, upright against the wall, silent. She snarled: '*Calamity*, tell him everything. He must know. He is very conceited and thinks he can *manage* me. That is his favourite word.' I told her analyst that I had no wish to pry into how the analysis had been conducted or how it had fared. I only needed to know about some *events*, since 'that girl' said that she had no memory and could not tell anything. The girl chimed in: '*Calamity* is my memory. She can tell you everything. She knows it all.' Her analyst responded very calmly: 'Yes, she finds it very hard to tell anything and cannot tolerate any interpretation.' I took this as a signal. She went on to tell me that the girl was roughly twenty-three years old and had been in analysis with her five times a week for some three and a half years. It had been a turbulent period for the girl, and at one point she found living with her mother and family visitors so exhausting that she wanted to be hospitalized. The analyst had sent her to a hospital, where she had stayed for nearly a year. She came for her analysis regularly, but sometimes the analyst had to visit her in hospital. Though the girl never 'misbehaved' with the hospital staff and was very caring of other patients, she invariably played havoc when she was visited by her analyst. My colleague told me further that the girl was born and brought up in a foreign country and had a happy familial childhood. Her special relationship during that period was with her native nanny, who had always met her needs and demands instantly. She was the youngest of four children. When the girl was eight years old, her father had moved all the children to London for their education. Within three years he had died suddenly. They were a very affluent and cultured family and, until his death, had lived in a large mansion in London. Afterwards, the mother decided to move into a modern flat, got rid of the servants, and went rather manic, doing curious odd jobs to keep herself busy and travelling a lot. She also started analysis herself. The girl had gone to a good school and was doing well. She did not react overtly to her father's death, which the analyst felt was one of the key problems. She did miss her nanny, who had to be left behind, a great deal. She had started well at school but around age fifteen, when her menstruation was delayed, she started to be *ill* and could not work at school. Her mother was very compliant and let her have her way. The mother was in analysis herself at the time, so when her daughter's symptoms and behaviour at home became unmanageable, she found a female therapist for her. This turned out to be rather traumatic for the girl. First, the therapist fell ill and handed her over to her husband, who was also a psychotherapist (medical). Then the girl got very involved in her analysts' divorce. She had started to become delinquent, in many respects, and her eating problems worsened. She would either starve herself to a skeleton or stuff herself and become fat, and she was outrageously aggressive to her mother. She started doing odd-jobs and it was in such a state that she had been referred to her present analyst. At this point the girl shouted: 'Why don't you tell him the truth, *Calamity*. They made a real mess of me, between the two of them. Didn't they? You said so, yourself.' I interposed and said to the girl: 'What happened then is of little consequence today.' Then I turned to the analyst and asked her to tell me briefly what had *happened* in and during the girl's analysis with her.

My colleague told me that the girl had started her analytic treatment when she was just over nineteen years of age, so that she had been in treatment for some three and a half years. She had not been an easy patient because she could not talk about herself; she could only *act* when anxious or depressed; that at one stage, the girl had found living with her mother insufferable and had demanded to be hospitalized. My colleague, who was a medical analyst, felt the girl's need was real and her demand justified, so she had her hospitalized. The girl stayed in that mental hospital for nearly a year and got on very well with the staff and the patients. She came regularly five times a week for her sessions, but when she was too depressed, the analyst would visit her, and the girl invariably made a scene. During her stay in hospital, she started to study again for her examinations and succeeded in doing a short course in professional childcare. But since leaving hospital, she had become more and more unmanageable in conduct, both at home and in the sessions. Her wrecking the analyst's Consultation Room was the limit and compelled the analyst to contact me.

I said that I had sufficient information to make up my mind. The girl got into a panic at this point and was about to assault her analyst physically. I said: 'No violence here, or you know what I'll do.' She burst into tears and pleaded with her analyst: '*Calamity*, is he going to take me on or not. They say he is very arrogant and hard to get.' Her analyst looked at me quietly and inquiringly. I had been deeply impressed by the way my colleague had reported about the girl and also by her manner of handling the 'crises' with her patient, which I could guess must have been frequent, very messy and outrageously exhibitionistic, involving as many persons as possible. Yet I felt the analyst had never let go of her determination to help this girl gain some *insight* into her problems and personality. She had gone to extreme limits to *accommodate* to the patient's needs, by way of 'management' à la Winnicott, but had never 'managed' the running of her daily life or tried to take over from her mother the responsibilities that truly belonged to the mother. I found this mixture of professional reticence and adequate provision of *actual* care most commendable.

There had been a long awkward pause, and I knew that the girl would 'explode' if I didn't *act*. I say *act* because words for this girl were actions. Addressing her analyst, I stated quite explicitly: 'Yes, I am willing to take her into my therapeutic care if you will continue to provide medical coverage (since I am a nonmedical analyst) and to see her when she *needs* to see you, *at your convenience*.' I emphasized that last phrase. The girl glowered at me: 'I am not going to accept any conditions.'

'That brings us to the real issue,' I quietly replied. 'Please let me have my say and you will have all the time to accept or refuse. There is no question of professional complicity between your analyst and me. Hence I am refusing to take over totally from your analyst.'

In order to have my say, I talked into the *in-between* space that was there, the girl standing and the analyst sitting. I find that how, where and at what/whom one looks during a consultation is just as, if not more, important as what one says. I had learnt this from watching Winnicott in his therapeutic consultations with children. He had such a talent for being unobtrusively present and not encumbering the freedom of the child's play or doodling with *expectant* looking or a *knowing* gaze. Of course, whilst listening to my colleague, I had been working out a tentative strategy of therapeutic endeavour with this girl and the best way to present it to her. I knew by now that she was as 'demanding' as she was intolerant of any demands made on her, especially in her own interest. From the little I had been told of her stay in the mental hospital and her successful completion of the childcare course, I had inferred that she could care for others if *some* others would *care* for her, that is, take her into total care. Furthermore, I was convinced that the most *therapeutic agent* so far had been the *space* of the mental hospital, which was so different from her shared familial space with her mother.

I started by saying that I did not consider this girl to be as *ill* as her therapeutic history would mislead one to believe. She was a *displaced* person, and *unrouted*, by which I meant that since leaving school, she had had little direction or purpose and few relationships in life and had been sustained by a variety of 'therapeutic as-if relationships'. I was impressed, however, by the fact that all 'new beginnings', as Dr Balint would say, in the past two years had started when she was in the *space* of the mental hospital. Hence the first question was: how do we arrange home-space for her to live from privately and functionally? The girl mocked me: 'You'd better think up another! We are more crowded by visitors than a hotel.' I told her that this was not her worry; I would arrange things with her mother.

Then I addressed the girl directly, person to person: 'You have said that you know I am a "hard" and "demanding" analyst. I don't know what you have heard about me but this much I can tell you: you cannot expect either the quality or the quantity of availability, compassion and patience from me that you have been used to with your analyst. Furthermore, I will not accept you living from hand to mouth, as it were. When we get to know each other better, I shall advise you what to study, where and how much.' She snarled: 'You can't make me work! *Calamity*! You have told him nothing about how I have no control over what I get up to and do.' I reassured her that there was little need for me to be told that just yet. So she screamed: 'What will you be asking me to do?' I paused, and replied: 'Three things, in this order of priority: one, you come to your sessions regularly at the appointed time, five times a week. Each time, if you can't take staying, you can leave, but without fuss. There is no obligation on either side to suffer a full fifty minutes routine.'

'But my mother can't wait for me all the time,' she hurled back at me, 'not knowing when I'll get fed up and bolt.'

'There won't be any need for her to wait,' I said. 'This is a large, well-staffed flat. If you can't stay in the Consultation Room, you can always go to the secretary's room, so long as you don't disturb her in her work, to sit and read there; or you can sit with the houseboy in the kitchen and have tea or coffee – but he won't gossip, so don't try it.' She seemed to accept this and asked what was the second thing I expected of her: 'You know I won't speak or lie down.'

'I am not expecting you to! The second thing is: you get private tuition for one hour each day, seven days a week.'

'Seven days,' she yelled. '*Calamity*, what is he up to?'

'Yes, seven days a week,' I repeated, 'because I want your day to have a minimal *structure*, other than your coming to sessions.' She sulked and waited.

'The third thing is: whatever your usual style and habits of dining are, at least three times a week you dine with your mother, alone or with your sister – no other family guests.'

She laughed with ridicule: 'I will see how you get Ma to stay at home three nights!'

At this point I turned to her analyst and said: 'I have heard you and you have heard me. I am going to give her a regular hour, five times a week, from next Monday (it was then Thursday). I hope you can still see her tomorrow. However, I do want to make clear that my offering to take her on in no way constitutes an obligation on her part to accept it. I don't want to play the game of "victim-victimizer" with her, as she has done with everyone else. So if from personal wish, fear and wilfulness, she decides not to come, just let my secretary know. If I don't hear – I addressed the girl – I shall expect you at such and such an hour on Monday.'

On this note we parted. I was exhausted, having had no clue as to how it would fare amongst the three of us and which way it would go. Its success was largely due to the sagacious calm of my colleague, who was in fact junior to me in clinical experience and professional standing. She had dignity, poise and courtesy. I have always remembered this clinical encounter with a certain pleasure and gratitude.

It is always in the after-image that I get things into perspective. When I try to recall from memory my after-thoughts in this case, I draw a blank. When I consult my notes, taken immediately afterwards, I find the following jottings, without any attempt to write an account of this rare, *only once* event in my clinical experience:

> Thank God it is over! What I have taken on I haven't the foggiest notion of. But then I never do!
>
> *Her analyst:*
> What an extraordinary person: combining such 'distanced' devotion and care, without intimacy of concern, and so adamantly intent upon fostering *insight*! How our training conditions us to that!
>
> *The girl:*
> Bizarre creature. Could *become* any person: a pervert's accomplice; a junky; a professional therapist; a responsible wife and mother! Has keen intellect and is sharp of wit. Real problem: has no *framed space* to live from – external or internal!
>
> Is manic and pervertedly cultivates excited states till they run her: it is the question of the tail wagging the dog! Highly eruptive – but these actions should not be mistaken for passion, rage or sexual needs!

Her outrageousness is her only ruse for presenting a semblance of having some identity.

She is autonomous, and cussedly so! But knows little of independence!

Overcare in childhood by nanny, I guess, has led to this absurd equation in her: seeking to provide *care* to others and demanding *total* care for herself. A barter, not relating!

If mourning for her father is absent, she has no resources to meet her mother's 'mad' ways of coping with her loss and responsibilities.

When resourceless, she *acts* to provoke care; she can't ask for help.

Her eating! – just as no sense of space around her, little sense of space *within* her.

Cannot tolerate herself! Yet, has this *telling* quality of presence, stillness and gazing!!

Is waiting to internalize what she has only *registered* so far. Can I build a 'psychic apparatus' for her? How?

Her *ungraspable* anxiety! So sentient. So *non*-psychic! This is what *compels* her to act outrageously.

Although these afterthoughts did not help me gain much insight into this girl's predicament, they at least decided me on three scores of clinical action: first, to establish firmly from the start that *my clinical space* was different in what it offered and in how it was to be used from all other spaces that she had experienced; secondly, to emphasize the importance of her *behavioural conduct* within and outside the clinical space rather than explore the psychic contents or the whys and wherefores of her relationships; and thirdly, to establish and sustain *clinical relating* between us rather than foster any type of *relationship*, transferential or otherwise. Although I am writing this some fifteen years after the events occurred, I have still not found an adequate way of defining for myself the difference between *relating* and a *relationship*. I have tried to explain it to myself in terms of Rickman's (1951) one-body, two-body theory and Winnicott's (1969) concept of the *use* of an object, but they do not help me much in stating the difference that I know and experience. I can offer only a few tentative remarks. *Relating* should not be mistaken for an aloof and impersonal clinical attitude to the person in therapeutic care. It has more to do with *dosing* the quantity of affectivity and keeping a certain psychic distance; and, even more, it has to do with time. *Relating* is limited to each encounter and its continuity accrues cumulatively from such encounters over time; whereas, at least for me, a *relationship* can start immediately and there is no vigilant anticipatory caution about how it will develop into mutuality. *Relating* has less mutuality but more *intent rapport* at the time. It is also 'framed' more consciously, at least by me, in terms of my personal responses and reactions. I feel that a *relationship* implies some sort of surrender from both parties. In *relating*, each retains a separateness and distance, which allows more room for playing.

To return to the girl: she arrived punctually at the appointed time on Monday and was escorted to the Consultation Room, where I was waiting for her. She took up exactly the same position in the same place. I noticed that she was wearing an almost full-length overcoat and her face looked rather lean and gaunt. She was silent. 'It is quite warm in this room, so you can take off your overcoat,' I said.

'I can't,' she answered, looking embarrassed. There was an awkward silence. Then angrily she hurled: 'It is not my fault. All yesterday we had family, for lunch and dinner. I got mad at Ma in the end and ran away at midnight and drove around till 7:00 a.m. Then I overslept and Ma woke me up. So I have had no time to put on any clothes and am only wearing my nightdress.'

I looked at her carefully while she spoke. There was nothing salacious in her turning up in her nightdress and a long overcoat. Yet I felt it epitomized myriad things for her, of which I knew nothing. So I decided to act on 'the first score'. I told her gently but firmly that she had successfully sabotaged any possible work I could do with her that day by her mode of dress. Unless she could accept that my clinical space was different from her bedroom, I could not function in any positive way. So we had better stop the session there and then and she should come properly dressed tomorrow. I deliberately abstained from inquiring what she had been up to, driving around for some seven hours at night. She was unexpectedly quiet and unremonstrative. After a pause she said: 'I don't think Ma will be outside waiting for me.' I replied that the houseboy would see her to a taxi.

'I haven't brought my bag, so I have no money.'

'He will lend you the money.' I rang the bell and the houseboy knocked at the door. As she was about to leave, she turned around and asked: 'Are you really going to find me a teacher?'

'Yes,' I said. 'I have already talked to someone. I'll discuss it with your mother tonight. Please tell her that I shall be ringing just after 8:00 p.m.'

As arranged, I rang her mother around 8:00 p.m. the same day and requested her to call her daughter to the other phone, which she did. I told the mother that unless she changed her style of housing so many relatives, I would have to *place* her daughter in some residential set-up, which I would rather not do because people pick up all sorts of new tricks from others in such places. As it was, her daughter had enough for us to cope with. The mother was most eager to assure me that there would be no more weekends like the last one and she would eat with her daughter three nights a week. I then asked her to ring me immediately, no matter what the hour, if her daughter ran out in the car at night. I had instructed my staff to receive and convey to me any messages from her, at all hours. I explained that I would prefer the police to 'detain' her daughter because she was disturbed rather than arrest her on vagrancy or criminal charges. In the latter case there would be little that I could do, but I did have access to police to provide custodial care in such cases. The mother agreed and was most grateful. Lastly, I told her that I had contacted a very experienced teacher who specialized in tutoring persons in her daughter's situation. For the time being, he could teach only three times a week, for two hours each time, but he wanted to decide with her, in my presence. So if they both agreed, I could ask him to come on Thursday during her session. They both agreed to this arrangement.

I know that there is little that is unusual or dramatic in what I have reported so far. All my colleagues have handled such situations hundreds of times. Yet though we read a lot in the literature about the 'working alliance', transference and management, very little is written about the way an analyst actually initiates and regulates the character and conduct of his therapeutic endeavour. We talk generally of 'the fundamental rule' and a patient's capacity or incapacity (resistance) to meet it. But in real clinical experience, things work out very differently with each person, whatever one's usual style of work.

The girl, the prospective teacher and I did meet and it was arranged that he would teach her maths, English and history, three times a week. He would increase the number of lessons when he had more time available. Thus the *setting* was more or less minimally arranged. Now I shall report from certain crucial stages of this treatment, which lasted for over five years, those details that are relevant to the theme of this article, which concerns a person searching for respite from internal stimuli or externally provoked impingements that do not allow him the space and time to be himself, *blank*, and from there to dream, think, relate, play and work. Instead, he experiences a void, an empty-headedness, futility of all mental functioning, and an unassuagable psychic pain (cf. Winnicott 1935, 1971*a*; Giovacchini 1972*a*; Pontalis 1977).

So far, I have detailed what was entailed in the management of this girl's 'placement' in her own home. I am taking this concept from Winnicott (1956) who, in discussing antisocial tendencies in a boy whose treatment he had to terminate because of the havoc he created at the clinic, wrote: 'It can easily be seen that the treatment for this boy should have been not psycho-analysis but placement. Psycho-analysis only made sense if added after placement.'

I had deliberately acted on this principle. The amazing thing for all of us – the mother, her last analyst and myself – was that the girl not only accepted this managed 'placement', with all its rules and restrictions, but actively participated in it. I have always wondered why! The only reason I can offer is the *timing* of it. She was now *ready* for it, whereas she had not been ready for it at fifteen when she first fell ill. Unfortunately, her management had been further messed up by the private circumstances of her psychotherapists. I am emphasizing this point of timing because I feel that we underrate the importance of a person's readiness and availability of himself to himself for analysis to be meaningful. It is not always the severity of a patient's illness that decides what use he will make of analysis. Pontalis (1981) has discussed this issue in a novel context, that of the negative therapeutic reaction. When the girl had started with her previous analyst, she was begrudging, and vengefully and militantly suspicious of everyone. She could no longer experience her *feelings* in their true context, nor could she *think* her own thoughts. Her analyst had done a heroic job of keeping her alive and in life. I do not write this lightly. So I inherited a valuable tradition of psychotherapeutic care of the girl and I could cash in on it. We read very little of how a person is handed over by one analyst to another. I kept her last analyst informed throughout her treatment.

To return to the girl: what I have written above should not be misunderstood as my underrating how difficult and complex her psychotherapy was going to be. It had its expected load of crises, but at no point did I feel that she was not determined to make a success of our work together, given all her handicaps. I repeat that I never considered her *sick* at the root, so much as *immature*. Immaturity is rarely used as a diagnostic concept. Only Winnicott, to my knowledge, has considered it a serious clinical or personality problem (cf. Winnicott 1945, 1958*a*, 1962). At the core of immaturity is a *state of unintegration*, which instead of being assembled through the maturational and developmental processes into what a person calls 'me', becomes dissociated and gradually all sorts of bizarre symptoms, intrapsychic and characterological, get encrusted upon it. All these antics of survival from inner confusions and external stresses constitute a 'self-cure'. This 'self-cure' was going to be the hardest thing to undo.

The first task was to make the girl recognize and realize that her 'madness', her 'being crazy' – as she would state her condition in different moods – her being *empty-headed*, were all masks protecting something she valued deeply in herself, to which she herself had lost the clues. It is not difficult to interpret symptoms or behavioural disorder but how does one interpret 'something' to a person, of which that person has no memory, indeed, *can* have no memory.

Things had fared better than we expected. She worked hard at her studies but was very lonely. I knew how much agony there was in the girl but there was little that I could say or do to help her as yet. After her first examination, she reported a dream of the previous night. It was her first dream since starting her treatment with me. In the dream she had woken up feeling that she was in my Consultation Room and thus must have slept there on the couch. In the sessions, in fact, she was still standing up. She had often remarked how she woke up every morning with the strange feeling that the place around her was not the one in which she had gone to sleep; that it took her a while to recognize her room again. She had been terrified of going 'empty-headed' into the examination and not being able to understand the questions. In fact, she told me, she had found the examination paper easy. She asked me about the dream. I simply said that she felt safer waking in my environment than at home because I knew how much it mattered to her to do well. For her, it was not just a question of passing the exam. She had to give of her best and could not anticipate how that would work out in the actual situation. Here I reminded her how often she remarked jovially that her Ma could never feel for herself what was happening to her; she had to be told. This strange *absence* of empathy in her mother was the cause of many rages. She agreed that it felt a good dream to her and made her feel more hopeful about doing her paper that day.

I felt that she was asking for more interpretation. She had six more papers to take. I decided to take the risk and go one step further. I said to her that even though in her own dream she woke up in my *space* (the Consultation Room), she refused herself the amenities available to her there.

'Like what?' she asked.

'You could have dreamt that the houseboy had woken you up with a cup of tea.' I knew that waking up was a real problem for her because she lost her psyche-soma coherence in sleep.

She laughed and said: 'You certainly have a strange way of analysing. *Calamity* would have interpreted it in terms of sexual fantasies and whatnot.'

I told her that could well be true also. But what struck me was that though she had found the trust and confidence to use my *space* in her own private way, something in her did not let her *thrive* in it. I advisedly used the verb 'thrive' and went on to say that this was the real hazard for her in taking these examinations. She might *refuse* to make the most of what she knew. She picked instantly on the verb 'refuse'.

'I promise you I mean to do my best.'

I told her that I was sure of that but, as she knew only too well, quite often what she intended to do and what she ended up doing were very different. I attributed the reason for this discrepancy to her extreme dread of *fallibility*. When she asked me to explain further, I said that fallibility means the fear of making an error; that in spite of her overt tradition of mess-making, there was in her a much more taxing and demanding tradition of perfectibility, which she had collected from two cultures – that of her nanny and that of her parents. From what she had told me so far of her life at the school, it was clear that she was rarely in rivalry or competition with her fellow girl students but, more, was checking herself against what she expected of herself. What she described as 'freezing' in sports was the same thing that I was trying to draw her attention to now – that is, that the terror of fallibility in her pre-empted the initiative to try. I went on to link it with her not letting herself thrive, as I had interpreted it in the context of her dream. Later I shall be detailing further the crippling role of her very exigent ego-ideal structures, which became both imperative and absolute the more she was dissociated from the relationships of her childhood out of which they had grown – for example, the quality of care and attention that her nanny provided for her and the stability of a large family held together by the presence of her father and his authority. She herself was not even aware of these structures. One could only infer their presence from the negativity in her behaviour, once her illness started, and she became more and more isolated and alienated in herself.

She seemed to be taking this in, which rather surprised me, because normally when I started to speak, I saw that glazed look in her eyes, which was a sure sign that she was registering but not actually listening to what was being said to her. I felt that she had shifted in her stance of relating to and refusing me. From speaking parallel to each other, as it were, we had now moved to a camaraderie of converse. She was pleased with the way she had managed her exam. As she put it, her curiosity had been *tickled* by the two words I had used in interpreting her dream, namely, 'thriving' and 'fallibility'. She asked: 'Is it because of what you call my dread of fallibility that I have to be *contrary* with people I really care for? I am so full of remorse later, when I let them down, that I start off with a mess.' I noted that she used the word 'remorse' rather than 'guilt'.

'Perhaps after the summer vacations I shall try "the couch".'

We parted for the first long break in her treatment on that note of goodwill.

When I returned from my vacations, a letter from the girl's mother was awaiting me. She said that her daughter had asked her to write to me to tell her news; she felt too shy to write herself. The girl had not only passed in all the subjects but had got a few distinctions. What was more, she had been accepted at the university in London of her choice, for the subjects she had selected. This was good news indeed because one of her acute dreads was that she might find a place in some university outside London and would then have to choose between having analysis and waiting another year, or quitting analysis. I immediately wrote to the mother, thanking her for sharing the news with me and for her unfailing trust and goodwill during all the past months. Knowing the girl was bound to read the letter, I added a sting by way of a casual after-thought: 'Now starts our real task. Let us hope we can all continue to give of our best efforts.' I had deliberately put the emphasis on trying rather than achieving.

The girl returned punctually and had remembered her intention to 'try the couch', but she asked for a week's postponement of that, until after she started attending her college. I agreed to this. I have already reported on two features of her clinical experience – namely, dread of surrender to resourceless dependence and the *necessity of failure* (Khan 1972*a*) – and on an aspect of her character, the nature and role of grudge (see Chapter 3). Here my choice of material is different. Also, the memory of a patient's analysis never remains a static *fact* in one's mind – if it ever is or becomes a *fact*. It changes in time, through experiences with other patients and in our own life, and either dwindles away or gains in its spread and significations. Only a few patients have the latter reality for us. The girl was one of these few for me.

I was very struck by her *new* corporeal presence. She had slimmed into a most shapely figure, which was different from her stuffed-fat or skeletal-starved oscillations during the past decade. She had really worked hard at presenting herself to the new human milieu at college. I knew that she had great misapprehensions on many counts. Terrorizing herself was an ego-perversity with her. She asked bashfully: 'Have you received a letter from Ma?'

I rather mischievously answered: 'Yes, and have you read my reply to her?'

She laughed! 'You and Ma get on so well together; and you both like fixing things!'

I let this pass. Also, I had taken great care not to congratulate her on any count. If she was outrageously intolerant of the slightest criticism from others, she was even less capable of receiving and accepting praise. Praise to her meant only one thing: a tyrannical demand to do even better. That it was all of her own imagining was as yet beyond her psychic means to accept. Limits and boundaries were a provocation to transgress, rather than containers à la Bion (1967). I was later to read Pontalis' (1977) sensitive and fresh approach to these problems. The movement from *jeu* to *je* was certainly never linear with her. It was explosive, intermittent, chaotic. Pontalis (1977) writes in his Preface to the French edition of Winnicott's *Playing and Reality*: 'The potential space evoked in *Playing and Reality* – and which is already present in the reading – makes us aware of a reality which we usually perceive *out of lack*.'

I think, in this context, that we can extend Pontalis' astute remark and say that a case-history is the perception and completion of one's encounter with the patient as a person, *out of lack*, which must be there in every clinical encounter. Hence the style in which I have written this article. Also, it is not the last time I shall be writing about this girl and I know that, each time, it will be a different 'me' writing about a different 'girl'. Pontalis (1977) neatly states: '. . . analysis requires that both participants search together.' This can never achieve the honorific status of a *fact*. Each party involved experiences and remembers this 'search *together*' differently. One is amazed in doing the second analysis of a person who has been 'written up' by his previous analyst as a 'case-history' how different is the patient's recall of what happened to what the analyst has reported. Hence in recounting my clinical work with this girl, I have deliberately not used the concept 'case-history' and have opted for 'clinical encounters'. In the girl's experiences, as I shall shortly report, 'the movement from *jeu* to *je*' encountered the basic problems of living and dying.

To return to the girl: contrary to all her dreads, she found herself *instantly* popular, both with her fellow students and the lecturers. She was older than almost all her fellow students. I have deliberately underlined *instantly* because I regarded her popularity not as an achievement but as the result of a compulsion. Things must happen instantly, immediately. She had no *trust* in time and process. She was soon well-established in her new milieu and her ruse for achieving this is worth telling. She became everyone's *confidante*. I interpreted this as a vicarious mode of establishing her identity through the *other*. I went a step deeper and said: 'As in your dream, in which you wake up in this Consultation Room but refuse to be nourished, at college you are doing the same – instead of making friends and relating, you are 'stuffing' yourself with your fellow students' material.' She was in a manic state of exultation and pooh-poohed my interpretation as my envy of her capacity to listen to others and help them. She went so far as to say: 'I do a better job of listening to others than you do.'

I gibed back: 'Anyone can be a wastepaper basket!' I wanted to avert, somehow, her crashing into sudden dismay and disillusionment. I knew how psychically precarious and fragile she still was.

Things took their own course. She was working hard at preparing her first essay of the term. She read fanatically; she wrote it. The day that she was to hand it in to her professor, she rang me at 8:00 a.m. She was in a total panic. She said that she must see me before she gave in her essay – she had dreamt her 'recurring dream' that night. I fitted her into my schedule. She arrived trembling and lay down, opened her bag, and handed me a ten-by-five white card, saying:

'I have written my dream for you. It has always been the same. You were right in thinking that I would "crash".' (I had never said that to her!) 'I know now I won't make it at the college. After dreaming this "recurring dream", I always fall ill: I can do nothing.'

While she was talking away, I read the dream. I reproduce it here exactly as she had written it:

> *Recurring dream on this theme:* The two budgies (blue/frail and green/robust, had not been fed enough by me. I'd run out of bird-seed and had not fed them for some days. When I opened the door of the room where they were flying freely, they would flutter around weakly and then remain motionless, dead (especially the blue bird).

She paused and asked: 'How do you interpret it?'

Before I could say a word, she 'spat' out: '*Calamity* always interpreted this recurring dream to be expressing suicidal wishes, or death wishes against my mother and siblings.'

I said: 'Well, that could be true! But first please tell me what the phrase "on this theme" refers to.' She said that it referred to her illness, her anorexia. It was after she had dreamt this dream the first time, when she was fifteen years old, that she had stopped eating and her illness had started. She repeated: 'I am going to fall ill again. Please do something. Help me.'

I was sure that she was right in her fears that she could fall ill again. I tried to play for time and quieten her down a bit. She was explosive with panic. I asked her: 'Have you finished your essay?' She opened her bag and handed me a neatly typed manuscript of some fifteen pages. 'That is a help,' I said. 'You don't run out of seed, except for your budgies!'

'But is the dream destructive wish-fulfilment?' she asked. 'I have never been sure since fifteen whether I want to live or die or whether I am living or dead.' She started to cry.

'That is certainly what the dream is about,' I said – 'living and dying. What is not clear to me is why you recurringly dream this theme, when you are conscious of it each day. This is what makes me wonder whether you dream this dream, or whether it is a repetitive story you tell yourself.'

'*Calamity* never questioned it was a dream,' she remonstrated. 'Why do you?'

'As I read your text,' I replied, 'I find it lacking in absurdity as well as a certain hallucinatory quality. And in my experience, all dreams have these qualities in some measure. Your dreamtext is too literary and too reasoned. Be that as it may, tell me about your experience of dreaming it last night.'

'It is always the same: I feel remorse and sadness for the budgies.'

I noticed that she had used the word 'remorse' again and had not mentioned her concern or guilt. I shifted in my approach to the dream and said: 'This recurring dream has one thing in common with the first dream you told me.'

'What is that?' she nearly yelled.

'Just as you don't thrive in my Consultation-Room-Space, your budgies don't thrive in your dream-cage-space.'

'I can't see any connection. You have to do better than that. I can't go to college in this state.'

We both paused. I felt that I was failing her, so I tried another approach. I asked her: 'Supposing one of your "friends" at college confided this dream to you, as they sometimes do. What would you say?' This challenged her. I had felt her drooping palpably.

'First,' she said, 'I would accept it as a dream. Then I would ask myself: "What is the latent dreamwish!"' This amused me and I decided to *play* with her remark.

'So you did read Freud's *Introductory Lectures* during the vacations.'

'Yes, I did! But so have you. Why don't you tell me what you think is the latent dream wish?'

'Well,' I said, 'I will tell you what I think *of* the "recurring dream". It recurs because it *hides* something successfully. And it hides *it* not by keeping it latent but by making it obvious. What it shows is your envy of the birds "flying freely" at first. They start to "flutter around weakly and then remain motionless, dead" while you are looking at them. I don't think running out of bird-seed and not "feeding them for some days" is the essential part of the dream, but is patched on to it to make the situation plausible in itself. You take responsibility on the wrong count.' She did not question my interpretation but, like me, changed her tactics and asked: 'Why do you think I dreamt it again last night?'

'You had finished writing and typing your essay. I think you are convinced that it is good and your professor will like it. You are frightened of the envy of your fellow students. You are terrified that they will no longer "feed" you with their confidences. You are afraid of losing the status you have established for yourself through being their *confidante*.'

After a pause, she said: 'You do talk some rubbish. I'd better rush or I'll be late for my professor.' As she was leaving, she turned around and said: 'Thank you for changing my time.'

I was no more convinced than she was by my interpretation, but it had done the trick! She had gone to college; she had taken the risk. I had interpreted her fear of her friends' envy, rather than her terror that the essay might not be as good as she was convinced it was, because I wanted to get some psychic distance between her and her 'recurring dream'. While reading it, my first impression was that she was too identified with the dream, only then I did not know what to make of it. Today I would not hesitate to use Pontalis' concept of the dreamobject and interpret that the *sickness* of the dream derives from the fact that she as a person and she as a dreamobject (caged birds) occupy the same dreamspace. The dreamer and the dream are one! This lack of psychic distance is what makes her seek empty-headedness, because she cannot differentiate her thoughts from her thinking-self. But I am writing this with hindsight, some ten years later. At the time, I was searching for ways and means to enable her to experience *making* her dream a *psychic event*, which was a personal creation and yet at one remove from her, intrapsychically.

In the weeks and months that followed this session, she put the 'recurring dream' aside, as it were. Other life experiences occupied her attention more urgently and insistently. I can best designate them by the concept of *corporeality*. She was becoming progressively more aware of her young womanhood and its needs. I have used the word *corporeality* rather than *sexuality* because I think that there is a very significant difference! Sexuality becomes an attribute (component) of the body-ego once it reaches a certain maturational stage in development. Corporeality precedes this and gradually encompasses it. But that is a theme I hope to discuss another time. Here, it is sufficient to say that she fared well through the first year of college, got engaged and passed the first-year examinations most creditably. Now I shall report a dream from the period when she started the last term at college, before taking her final examinations.

Before my discussion of the girl's third dream, with which I shall end this narrative, I should briefly tell a little more about her life situation at the time:

1. She had got engaged, as I have mentioned, and after her examinations she was to get married and move into a flat with her husband. I need only say this much about him, that he was a very

decent person, devoted to her and no match for her – hence no rivalry! But he was also a scholar and a student and was a few years older than she.

2. Although it was an 'arranged' marriage as was the custom of her family, she and her fiancé had gradually evolved, since their engagement, a genuinely trusting, caring and considerate relationship. It was not a passionate love-match, which was just as well. We all – the girl, her mother, I and her previous analyst – knew that and accepted it as such.

3. In the past months, since dreaming her 'recurring dream', she had really participated in the analysis. We had done some extremely interesting work in understanding her 'corporeal identifications' with her mother's desolate and 'mad' state after her father's sudden death and how she had empathized with her mother's predicament but could *contribute* little towards her well-being. The mother had been traumatized out of her 'head', to use the girl's phrase, by her husband's death. He was quite a figure, and with him behind her she had been most effective in caring for him and her children, as well as the rest of the family. When he died, she was utterly lost and, instead of grieving, took to maniacal overcare of her children and acted quite crazily. She would not think of remarrying, even though she was quite young. The girl's maniacal mess-making was both a parody and a vengeful imitation of her mother's behaviour. This had 'loused up', to use her phrase, her personalizing into her new emergent corporeality as a menstrual girl, and her womanhood. But I am not going to go into that here.

4. Since her engagement, roughly *nine* months before the dream that I shall report, I had cut down the frequency of her sessions from five to three times a week, after the summer break. It was by consent from all parties concerned – the girl, her mother and her previous analyst. I had made no mystery of the fact that I was doing it to allow more personal time and space to her and her fiancé. In my judgement, she was ready to take on more responsibility for independent 'shared' living with another person. She had lived too *attached* and protected and it had served her well. Now she must risk and venture otherwise. She had accepted it heartily and *participated* most positively in all spaces of her living and relating.

It was in this climate, when she had started the last term at college before her final examinations, that she arrived one day looking thunderously 'dark' and furious. She 'spat' out: 'I am not going to lie down today. I have had the "recurring dream" again, but it was different.' Pause. 'No, I am not going to tell it to you. I have other things to tell you first.'

I quietly said: 'I can wait!'

'You'd better!' she snarled, and then collected herself to begrudge and berate me for some half an hour in a most proper, jeering and vehement way. I later wrote down the gist of her accusations, as follows:

'I am crazy. Ma knows it. *Calamity* knows it. You know it. And I know it. I came to you crazy and empty-headed, and what have you done? Nothing! I am still just as crazy and empty-headed; Oh yes! You and Ma have done a great job of conning everyone, including me!'

I deliberately sat back, allowing her tirade more space, and listened with a mixture of mock-impatience and true compassion. When she failed to get a rise out of me by her first sally of grudges, she changed her tactics and continued:

'I am not only crazy. I am mad. And that poor fool, who is going to marry me, thinks I am so clever and intelligent. Yes, my head is stuffed with all the nonsense I have had to read. But I don't understand a thing. I am empty-headed. I tell you, I still can't think. I can't even try what that head of yours does all the time! Do you ever stop thinking? Never! Everyone says how clever and well-read you are. Stuff and nonsense. You can't help it. You are just as *sick* as I am, only in a different way.'

When she couldn't get me to banter back, she changed tactics again. She was crying and laughing while talking, in a way that I knew meant she was feeling desperate. She snarled: 'You haven't asked me to tell you the dream. You don't care a damn, do you?'

I said: 'You know I have no curiosity about my patients. When you are ready and feel like it, you will tell and share your dream. You can't undream it.'

'But I'll forget it. That is another thing. I forget everything. Nothing stays in that head of mine. She paused. Is it true what they say about you: that you have read all of psychoanalysis and remember everything?'

'Not at all,' I answered. 'But most of what there is of it is in English. I have a different problem from yours: I can't forget. That is the devil of it.'

'Oh don't feel sorry for yourself. What a ham you are! I know all your tricks. You are determined to cool me down and have it your way and Ma's. But I am telling you, I am going to louse up everything –

my exams, my "marriage". Do you know what? Ma is already making guest-lists and has asked me twice whether you will be attending the marriage.'

'What marriage?' I asked, with calculated mockery.

'Mine, of course – who else's? Or are you palming off some of your other analysands too? When you *decide* you have done your honourable bit (she said the word "honourable" with acid mockery), then you let others take over. But I shall teach you a lesson. I am going to louse it all up – good and proper.'

'Thank god you are learning to respect the necessity of style,' I said.

She blew her top: 'Why can't you ever take me seriously, as you do your other analysands. Do you know I have made friends with quite a few of your analysands, past and present. They are all "cracked" on you (her favourite jargon of spite!). Yes, why can't you take me seriously.'

'Had I taken you what you call "seriously", you would have "loused up" this analysis too and we wouldn't be talking together today.'

'How pleased you are with yourself – aren't you. And so is Ma with you. And so is *Calamity*.' She roared with maniacal laughter. 'If only she knew how you analyse, she would have a fit. She is so square and earnest but she is honest. She let me be crazy and make my messes – but not you! I had to work hard, pass examinations. You and Ma even got me engaged, but I am going to louse it all up. I am not going to oblige you: pass my exams, get married and start popping out brats – like Ma! You know she had university education too. Look at what she has done with it. Nothing! Yes, I am going to louse it up.' She paused. 'Soon you will be telling me it is time to end today. Well, I will tell you my dream of last night: it was the same cage, but it was totally empty. No birds, or bird-seed or bird-droppings in it – just a clean and empty cage. Like my head, you are going to tell me.'

I quietly asked: 'Were you in the dream?'

'No, this time I didn't see or feel that I was in the dream. I saw only the clean empty cage.'

I paused, and then said: 'It is certainly a new and different dream. You are growing up, you know, young woman' (the first time I had addressed her like that).

Her eyes glinted a bit: 'You really think that it is a positive dream?' Pause. She started to cry gently now. 'You are just saying that so that I will leave. But I am not leaving today.'

'You know that you can always rest in the secretary's room. You have done it before. And I meant what I said: it is a different dream and it has wit to it too. I mean its imagery has wit!'

'What do you mean?'

'You have been saying you are empty-headed. Another way of saying that or being crazy is to say *witless*. And that is what the dream pictorializes, renders into an image. You are right in your interpretation of it: the empty clean cage and your empty head are the same. Only now you can *dream* about our empty head. That is the difference. It entails psychic capacity to create such imagery and metaphors of one's feelings and sense of self.'

'You are never lost for words, are you? Well, you did try, even if it makes no sense. So I'll leave now. Don't forget the dream please. You will tell me more about it. There is much more to it, isn't there. It is not a silly dream, is it?'

'No – not at all!' I said. 'I shall think about it. You know it always takes me time to catch up with you.'

She left.

Yes, it did always take me time to catch up with the girl. She had a way of 'blocking' my thinking. She was too *present* in my space. Whenever she left, I would immediately know the 'right interpretation'. Later, I would learn to find a way of interpreting the 'afterthoughts' at the right time. Sometimes I had to wait for weeks to find the opportunity to give 'my interpretation'. I understood this to mean that it was another way of her making me 'hold' her. After all, she had started by telling me that *Calamity* was her memory. I changed the *function* of memorizing her from remembering material to 'psychic holding' of her when I was absent in reality. I had casually interpreted this to her.

I have given this detailed account of the bantering and rather ruthless exchange between the girl and myself to give some idea of how, with this girl, I learnt to use words and language (*les mots, les paroles et la langage*) as a *space* where speaking, listening and looking were: *playing* with wit (a sort of verbal squiggling); *sharing* of mutual effort (what Pontalis calls 'participation'); and *discourse* (which is more than just an exchange of material and interpretations).

It is my clinical experience that patients have poor prognoses if they lack the capacity to use *wit* in verbal participation in the clinical process. Similarly, I find that children are really *sick* if their drawings lack *wit*, and there is not much one can do to make them thrive psychically or affectively. If this girl had not been capable of using *wit* in her speaking, berating, begrudging and sharing, the clinical process would have collapsed and there would have been no participant mutuality of clinical camaraderie, play and discourse. Having said this, I shall now end by telling what I *made* of the dream from my side.

Huffing and puffing, the girl arrived a little late for her next session. She lay down and rattled off: 'You would interpret that I have acted out my resistance and anger by being late, but my car wouldn't start. I had to take a taxi.'

'Not at all! On the contrary,' I said. 'You have endorsed the basic wish in the dream.'

'What is that?'

'Impatience, that is, intolerance of time!' I replied. 'You are menstruating?'

'Yes,' she said. 'You knew it, so why do you ask.'

'Just so that we can agree! It is now almost exactly nine months since you became engaged. If you had not had the examinations to take this year and had acted nature-wise, you would be/should be pregnant by now.' She sat up and roared with laughter, saying: 'You are so funny! You know everything! I made love, at first, then I thought afterwards: "Supposing the pill doesn't work and I get pregnant. That would put Khan's nose out of joint all right. He will never agree to an abortion and so it would louse up my studies." '

I said: 'But you haven't got pregnant. That is the asset of being able to dream. It stops one acting out. But in your dream, in fact, you jump time. You have already finished with the examinations; you have had two children. There are no more baby messes and no more maternal choring. You are free, at last, to do what you wish. The empty-headedness, for you, is an ideal state of being. It is a blank state to start from positively. It is devoutly sought after by you and equally dreaded. So even though the latent dreamwish changes, on waking you plonk your apprehensions on it. The question is real enough. After your studies, marriage and having children, what do you wish to do?'

She didn't hesitate for a moment. 'I want to be a psychoanalyst.'

'You can forget about that,' I said. 'It is most regrettable that they won't accept you because you have "hospitalization" in your "history".'

'Are they really as stupid and stuck-up as everybody says they are?

You were nutty enough, how did you get through?'

'The climate was different then and I was heavily sponsored by the British analysts and Miss Freud.'

'You have been very lucky all your life, haven't you?' she asked rather ruefully.

'Yes,' I said, 'but don't give up. There are ways of training and doing the same work. It is the work that you want and *need* to do, isn't it?'

'Yes! Will you sponsor me? You have influence everywhere.'

'Yes, I will, once you have settled down in marriage and have a child.'

'I will be too old then to train.'

'No,' I said; 'I promise you that I will get you proper training.'

'Will you train me?' she asked impatiently.

'No, I am afraid not.'

'I knew that. I know you very well, you know. I knew you had it all planned in your head. What will you do?'

'Well, we have to wait and see, but first things first. I shall see you through until you are expecting a baby. I will continue to provide you "coverage" but stop your analysis. You must take total shared and mutual responsibility, with your husband, for having and rearing the baby. When the time comes, I'll find you an analyst or you may find one yourself. Anyway, I will sponsor the training.'

'No one will refuse you?'

'No, they won't. I rarely make unreasonable demands.'

After this rather dramatic session, the clinical work sank back into its normal rhythm and, with the mental vocabulary available to each of us, we were able to work through in considerable detail what empty-headedness entailed for her. I shall conclude by itemizing some of our inferences about it. I am stating it so tentatively because much of the material that I could only grasp vaguely at the time has become clearer to me from the researches of the past decade. I owe a great deal of this insightful *après-coup* to the researches of my French colleagues and French thinkers who have been writing on the theme of language and thinking in particular – from Professor Levi-Strauss to Michel Foucault.

To complete the story of the girl: she stayed in analysis for almost another year and a half. During this time she passed her exams brilliantly, got married and made a home of her own. When she became pregnant, we terminated her analysis by mutual consent.

After she had her first child, she was accepted for training in psychotherapy and trained with another analyst of her own choice.

Empty-headedness! What did it mean to this girl? What did it do for her? How did it function in her? How had this state of being originated? Why was it so paradoxical in character: a profound wish-fulfilment, as one dream symbolized it, and a question of living and dying, in another?

In the total epistemology of her self-experience, one could postulate a triangle, of which the three apices were: empty-headedness; search for perfectibility; and terror of fallibility.

The space of this triangle was largely occupied by two affects: 'white panic' and remorse! These were aggravated in her by 'confusion of tongues', to use Ferenczi's (1933) concept in a different way, between 'corporeality' and thinking (cf. Merleau-Ponty's concept of *le corps vécu*). She *exorcized* these affects through the 'confessional' of mess-making! For her, *acts* confessed more tangibly than words. Also, *acts* could stay 'outside' psychic reality, as 'not-me' phenomena! (cf. Ricoeur 1967).

Empty-headed meant *un*-thought or, to put it more accurately but clumsily, one could say: below or beyond *thinking*! She had thoughts. In fact, they never stopped. Hence at one point I have a scribbled note that reads:

> Asks why the birds fly and then flutter to death?
> I answer: Thoughts never stop; only thinking does.
> Mania is a killer. It knows no limits.

A non-interpretation for sure!

Another scribbled note towards the end of her analysis reads:

> Moaned of her empty-head. And the anguish-agony that she experiences about it. Then panicked: I will die of an empty-head. I say: not if one goes by your two dreams. The birds die because they are in a caged space; and you stand resourceless and resourceful. In the clean empty space everything is perpetual. She says: recently I have started a new white panic – what if one never dies! Lives on and on for ever. Like the mountains?

What made this girl oscillate so steeply from childish, impatient, demanding behaviour to true profundity of thought? I have still not worked that out, just as I cannot account for the acute anguish-agony she experienced. She compelled me to think about the difference between aetiological interpretative reconstructions and ontological phenomenology. Neither can replace the other. These two approaches need to be supplemented further by all the recent researches into the use of language for myth-making, discourse and self-relating Analysts can no longer account for their work only with the 'vocabulary' of Freud's metapsychology. Such patients demand that we enlarge the scope of our 'vocabulary' to meet their needs in clinical converse and participation. We can no longer complacently sweep under the metapsychological carpet, with the broom of our 'vocabulary', *the unrest of thinking* in clinical psychoanalysis.

8
The Evil Hand

> Cette manie bizarre de faire le mal pour le seul plaisir de la faire est une des passions de l'homme la moins comprise et par conséquent la moins analysée et que j'oserais cependant croire possible de faire rentrer dans la classe commune des délires de son imagination.
>
> *de Sade*

Clinical Material

The patient who arrived, referred by a physician I did not know, turned out to be a tall man, suave of manner, elegantly dressed, and politely reticent in speech. For me, clinically, the physical self-presentation of a patient in the first consultation is as – if not more – important as the first 'rehearsed' self-reportage. I noticed when he had sat down that he had a somewhat crumpled, damaged right hand, which he had tried neither to hide nor flaunt. So I concluded that he had come to terms with it, whatever its cause. After a brief pause, he remarked: 'I am an evil man and there is no cure of that.'

I was taken aback by this self-diagnosis because in some twenty years of practice I had never heard a person or a patient say that about himself. Fumbling to make a move from my side, I responded: 'Perhaps not, but we can try to explore a little, should you so wish, what has led you to such a damning verdict on yourself.' I chose the adjective 'damning' very carefully. He was silent for a while and then asked me what his physician had told me. I answered, 'Very little,' and added that all I knew from his physician was that he was married, with children, and had a successful job and a contented family life until about three months ago when he had suddenly sunken into acute depression and had not been able to go to work. I added, 'Your physician has told me that you have refused all suggestions of psychotherapeutic help,' and asked him, with a certain wry sense of irony, what or who had coaxed him to come to me. He replied that his wife was a professor and had read some of my work. She had assured him that I would not try to *make* a 'patient' of him nor trick him into having treatment, so he had agreed to *meet* me. I noted his use of the word 'meet' and not 'consult'. At this point I held back one factor of his present condition that the physician had been most worried about, namely, his refusal to eat. At best, he could be persuaded to take liquids or food in liquid form. He had refused hospitalization. From watching him, I could tell that he had lost a lot of weight, because his hand-tailored suit hung limply on him, but I didn't think he was very depressed. I felt that he was both determined and acutely dismayed. The dullness in his eyes and the flat tone of his voice made me infer that some recent experience had disillusioned him traumatically about himself. Hence his diagnosis of himself as 'evil'. But I interpreted none of this to the man who had come to *meet* me. The pauses had been long and the silences private but not resistant. Hence I didn't even attempt to enter into 'therapeutic contest' with him at this stage. He agreed to come again the following week and we parted genially.

I had seen him at midday before my siesta, and as I was thinking about the first encounter between us and dozing off to sleep, I was perturbed by a sudden thought that flickered across my mind: 'If he is so wilful and negatively motivated, how come he hasn't killed himself?' Somehow his crumpled right hand stayed very vividly in my mind. Neither he nor his physician had disclosed what he did, and long clinical experience has taught me that to squeeze information from a person who is not ready to share is not only useless but also damages the possibility of working together in the future. By precipitate interpretation, one can pre-empt the benign therapeutic contest, and the person either shifts from a mood of 'untrust' to aggressive mistrust and leaves, or becomes a 'compliant patient' from which his own self is absent (cf. Winnicott 1960*a*).

The man arrived (I am deliberately not calling him a 'patient' as yet) with the same stance of mood and being. There was a long pause, then he asked: 'What can I tell you?' I decided to accept his disguised challenge and said bluntly: 'I have noticed your damaged right hand. How did you *manage* that!' I had advisedly used the verb 'managed'. He blandly answered: 'I didn't *manage* it; it happened to me.' I noted that he was very sensitive to my use of language and that he had blamed no one – himself or any other – for the damage. This still told me nothing. He left that issue aside and talked a little about his family, especially his concern that his present 'condition' – as he called it – was distressing his children (he had two sons and a daughter) and interfering with their preparation for A and O level examinations. This encounter between us was just as amiable as the first and equally non-committal on both sides. When I thought about it afterwards, I had a strong feeling that he had left me *in suspense*. I took that to be an essential component of his inner psychic life.

Mr X – as I shall call him henceforth – came regularly three times a week for the next three months before the summer break. I am rather surprised how little I recall of what transpired in the sessions and how little there is in my notes from that period. From my notes I quote:

> In the thirteenth session (i.e., a month since he started coming to me) Mr X reported that he has started to work again and asked to change his appointment time. I have accommodated him.

Then some six week later I note:

> Mrs X rang tonight. Was most apologetic about ringing, fearing I may take it as interfering with Mr X's treatment (her word – it has never been used by Mr X or me!). She had rung to tell me what a relief it was that her husband had started to eat proper meals. She had added, rather awkwardly, that she wasn't telling on him but she knows, though he is not a secretive person, that he finds it very hard to speak about himself. I thanked her.

I didn't in any way insinuate to Mr X or try to make him tell me that he had started to eat, as I had not told him that his physician had mentioned his not eating to me, nor had the physician. Also, though I had initiated the damaged hand issue, I had not picked it up since he let it drop. I could easily have done so on many occasions, by translating his overt verbal narrative into the unconscious anxieties and fantasies relating to the damaged hand, but I was convinced that I had to allow him *his* time and readiness to share information about himself.

It was in the last session before the six-week summer break that Mr X started by saying: 'You once inquired how I had *managed* (his tone of voice underlined that verb used by me) to damage my right hand.' Briefly, the story he told me was as follows:

> On a wintry day he was cycling home after lunch at a friend's house in the country. It was a rainy day and the country lane was narrow and slippery. A car honked to warn him and, as he tried to pull nearer the hedge, the cycle skidded and he fell

down; the car crushed the whole of his right arm. The next thing he remembered was waking up in some London hospital, his arm stiff and in plaster. His parents and family were sitting by his bedside. After a week he returned to his country home to live with his family. Things didn't fare well and in the next six months he had four changes of plaster under anaesthetic. He remembered vividly the surgeon whispering to his father in the corridor that there was infection of the bone and fear of gangrene, in which case the arm might have to be amputated. He was taken back home and nothing was told him overtly.

Then a friend of his father who lived in the Swiss Alps had come to visit them and persuaded his father to let him take Mr X (he was then fourteen years old) to his chalet, because he knew a surgeon, personally, who specialized in setting and curing such multiple fractures. The parents agreed and in a few days he found himself in the Swiss Alps and in this surgeon's clinic for three months, having various operations. But at the end of three months, his arm was in bandages only and he returned to his father's friend's home, visiting the clinic every other day for physiotherapy. The surgeon had been very frank with him and told him his arm would heal perfectly, but the damage to the tendons from earlier operations could not be corrected as yet. He had the use of his thumb and his second and third fingers but the other two were stiff and crumpled.

He had told the story in his usual reticent, measured tone and manner. It had taken him more than an hour and a half to tell it and I had allowed for the time since he was the last patient of that term and day. He said he was going away for six weeks with his family and asked for an appointment on return, which I readily gave him.

As I look through my notes on this session, I find that I have written:

Strange how readily I accommodate to this man's needs. Is it because he never states them as demands?

He has spoken so little and talked around himself but not from himself, yet he has never bored me. Why? I have not asked him to 'free associate' or offered him the couch either. In fact, I too have suspended treating him as a patient. I have decided to bide his time and wait for his readiness to share. I have deliberately withheld all interpretations and have made no attempt to 'gather material'.

It is equally important to note that we have quite rigorously established our codes of conduct vis-à-vis each other, without stating them verbally. For example, we move in the same social set and I have seen him and his wife in the foyers of theatres and at cocktail parties but have never exchanged a glance or a word, and neither of us has ever mentioned it in the next session.

There is little doubt that we are testing each other. To what end, I have no clue, either from my side or his. It is quite clear to me, however, that he is enacting, unknowingly, some essential features of his accident and its aftermath.

There is also little doubt that a need to keep me in suspense and waiting is imperative for him at this stage. There is something vengeful about it but I cannot define its character. I sense it but it is quite amiable.

As for his narrative of his accident and its long painful consequences, I am very impressed by the 'cool' way he described it all, without subjectivity and expression, even of pain and discomfort. Just events, and not his response to them: psychic or affective. This dissociation, I think, will turn out to be most important in his character-formation and inner psychic life, if we ever reach that point of shared discovering.

When Mr X returned from his holiday, he was very tanned and looked extremely fit physically. Preparing to re-encounter him, I cannot say that I was sure how I would start or how I would dose my accommodation to him in the therapeutic setting. Fortunately for me, he resolved some of the issues. After a brief comment that he had spent a very good holiday with his family, he asked me how I had spent mine, to which I replied, 'Most restfully.' He paused, and said: 'I am surprised how much I have been dreaming about my cycling accident and the year of various operations on my arm. I could never remember any of the dreams on waking, but the last one I made a deliberate effort to write down.'

As he reached towards his pocket to take out the piece of paper on which he had written the dream, I took the opportunity to manoeuvre the situation towards a more explicitly psychotherapeutic relationship. I casually remarked to him that though I had no objection to him telling me his dreams and talking to me sitting up, in my clinical experience, when a person recalled the psychic area of dreaming, he felt more private and comfortable telling his dreams from the couch. He rather innocently – for a man of his sophistication – inquired: 'Are you asking me to lie on the couch and saying that it will be better for me?' I unhesitatingly said: 'Yes.' He took off his coat and without any further questioning he lay down. The dream that he reported was from the last week of his holiday:

> I am cycling in a country lane – I'm not sure which country – and two young girls overtake me, racing each other. As they pass me, I spank the one nearest me with my right hand, on her bottom.

He then said that he couldn't recall any more of the dream.

Of course, I made a mental note immediately that there were two things in the dream he could no longer do: one was cycling; the other was spanking with the flat of his right hand, which was now too crumpled for spanking, though of course he could hit with it. He paused for a long while, and for the first time since I had started seeing him, I felt that he was fighting in himself and with himself whether or not to tell me something. He was undecided. I did not interpret the dream at this stage and he moved on to talk about starting work the next day (cf. Khan 1972*e*).

Mr X turned up punctually for his next appointment, looking tired, haggard and anxious. At first I thought it might have to do with starting work again but he soon put me right. He told me that he had spent a sleepless and restless night and that this was most unusual for him. His wife had noticed it and remarked about it at breakfast. He had told her that he had had a dream during the holidays, which he had told to me yesterday, but nothing had come out of it. He had then told his wife the dream. He paused.

I felt extremely disconcerted. Had I made a grave error in not doing something about the dream, in not gathering more material? But in this session, a new factor had emerged as a component of Mr X's inner psychic and emotional needs: *to confess*. Now I read his reticence as a self-preservative device against self-damaging, compulsive confession and also as a ruse to make *the other* an unwitting accomplice (cf. Khan 1964). Furthermore, I was now convinced that Mr X had come to me seeking neither insight nor cure but a return to a *state of grace* he had lost. Hence his use of the adjective *evil* to define his identity in his first remark to me. I am aware that it is foreign to the analytic language to discuss the predicament of a 'case' in terms of evil and a state of grace (except for Karl Menninger 1973, and perhaps Fairbairn 1952). Yet these terms do constitute the verity of the private self-experience of some of our patients whom we misguidedly traduce, from lack of any adequate conceptual vocabulary, by our habitual metapsychological jargon and its clinical tactics.

I resolved to stick to my approach and after a short pause Mr X came to my rescue. He said his wife had suggested that he should take the dream up with me again, if telling the dream had upset him so much.

Now I decided to show my hand. I told him that the dream was indeed significant but I had no way, as yet, of deciphering its meaning since I knew so little about him. I added that he had done two things in the dream that he was now incapable of doing, namely, riding a bicycle and smacking with a flat right hand. I said that he could help me more if he told me about his life with his family and his activities before the accident. He replied that during the holidays he had listened to his wife talking to a friend about the psychological necessity, for some writers especially, to keep diaries and journals. The idea had occurred to him that perhaps he should write a brief account of his life and give it to me. It would save us time. I told him that it was much more productive in the clinical situation (I used this concept for the first time) if the person told it from himself, in his own voice and gestures. I really cannot justify, even to myself, why I had added the noun 'gesture'. Evidently he had given it a lot of thought, because he gave a succinct account of his childhood, roughly as follows:

> He was the middle child amongst five, with two elder brothers and two younger sisters. He had grown up in the large country house of his parents, who were both affluent and had high social status. His brothers and sisters were very bright and clever. He recalled himself as a rather dreamy and lazy child who just managed to pass his examinations without much effort. They were a large family, with aunts, cousins and nephews, so the weekends were very convivial. The children played in the large grounds of their country house where they had their tennis court and table-tennis. The parents had married very young and so were active participants in the play and games of their children. His favourite games were tennis and croquet. The parents didn't push him towards intellectual and academic achievements because they considered him a late developer. It was, he said, an idyllic childhood in every respect. He had only one illness that he recalled – tonsillectomy. And what he remem-

bered from it was how the nurses spoilt him with endless supplies of ice-cream to suck and swallow.

We had reached the end of the session, and this time I deliberately made an interpretation. I remarked to him that it had struck me all along how candidly and lucidly he reported about himself, but I was always left feeling that he had not spoken of himself. For example, I added, I knew how much agonizing discomfort he must have suffered due to his operations, but he had left that out of his account, just as in the dream it was a 'back-to-normal' state of affairs. I said further that perhaps if he could collect his memories about how he reacted to his drastically curtailed style of living after the accident, we could go more deeply into his self-experience and *self-cure* (Khan 1970*b*). I emphasized the latter, explaining that it was no mean achievement for him to rehabilitate himself so successfully after such a long period of traumata and the irreversible after-effects he had suffered.

As he was putting on his coat, he remarked rather sardonically: 'For some thirty years now, I have put all that aside, but I shall try my best to recall what I can.'

This was the first session in which I felt that we had got nearer to what ailed him inwardly. I still had no precise clues to it, but I began to suspect that he was a *pervert manqué*. This, in my collating assessment of him, fitted in well with his adjectival use of 'evil' to judge himself. I felt that he had succeeded in living creatively by a sustained mental and wilful dissociation, which had somehow broken down some eight months ago. Now I felt confident that I could both 'hold' him as a person and help him as a 'patient'. The way he had involved his wife, by telling her the dream, I considered to be a very typical tactic on his part; he made *the other* participate rather than sharing from need. It was also his way of staying distant from, and impersonal to, his own inner psychic life (Khan 1979). Since I was not sure from his material about any of these issues, I did not interpret them to him.

After this session, Mr X carried on with his scattered self-narrative for weeks, talking about his daily life and family. I noted that he had still not told me what he did. He had a very subtle way of talking 'anonymously' about himself.

We had reached the mid-term school break for Mr X's children and he asked if he could go for a long weekend with his family, to visit his parents in their country house. He hadn't seen them for nearly a year, as they lived in their Côte d'Azur house most of the year, and it was also his father's birthday. It meant that he would miss two sessions. I am giving these banal details because such considerateness on his part gave me true clues to the quality of his character. As we shall see later, all this would play a big part in his 'depressive breakdown'.

A rather sombre and dejected Mr X returned from his stay with his parents, which he said had been most pleasant for his family. After a long pause, he said:

'I got a chance to ask my mother how I *behaved* [his word] during the long period of my arm operations and therapy. She told me that the car that had run over my arm had not stopped but fortunately another car soon came along. They recognized me and took me to the nearest pub, and from there they rang for an ambulance and contacted my parents, whom they knew. My mother kept on repeating what a brave and cheerful patient I had been all along and she recounted three episodes that might interest you. On waking after the operation, I was not very upset. But when the nurse brought me food, I burst into tears as she tried to feed me, since I couldn't manage with my left hand. Fortunately, my mother was present and took over, and for the rest of my stay in the hospital and in the country house she fed me herself. Personally, I recall none of this except for the discomfort of having to sleep straight because of my arm being in plaster. The second thing she told me, with a certain amusement, was that I refused to be washed by the nurses, and my father persuaded the surgeon to let our butler wash me. The same arrangement was made when I went to Switzerland – the butler accompanied me. I have no memory of that, either. All I can vaguely recall is a sense of humiliation at being so helpless and dependent on others. My mother did tell me that on returning home from the various operations, I began to shy away from my brothers, sisters and cousins because I could no longer participate in their games, and I spent my time either reading or wandering alone in the large garden that spread around our house.'

I noted the link between humiliation, overdependence and refusal to eat but made no comment about it at that stage. I did remark:

'In short, you became progressively more alienated from your family and friends.'

He said, 'Yes, you could put it that way,' and continued:

'It became worse when I went to Switzerland. Though the children of my father's friend could speak English, they usually spoke a peculiar mixture of French and German that I could not understand, so I felt left out. I went for long walks, always accompanied by the butler, lest I should slip or fall and injure my arm again. I was very fond of Tom [the butler] because he never told me not to do this or that. Also the surgeon was very kind and taught me how to eat with a spoon, onto which I could push cut-up food with a strange metallic gadget that I could barely hold with my right hand. Gradually, I became an expert at it and was very glad to have regained 'freedom' [his word] in this sphere. I have still got the gadget. It is, in fact, made of silver. Unfortunately, attempts to train my left hand to write failed completely. I think that it had something to do with my not accepting that I was crippled for good.'

This insight on his part rather surprised me because so far he had talked about himself without any hint of introspection or self-comprehension.

I noted for my future use the factors of alienation, uncommunicability and the use of a gadget as a means of finding some self-reliance and freedom again (Khan 1972*c*). I have always considered that a single major trauma does not affect the character-formation in the same way as what I have called the cumulative trauma, by which I mean the continuation of small traumata curtailing the ego-functioning in childhood or adolescence. These often lead to either character-disturbance or perversions (see Khan 1963*a*, 1964*b*, 1973, 1980).

Now I shall abstract salient features from the clinical work done in the six weeks before Christmas that year.

I first want to delineate the changed nature of our relationship. He became more trusting and digressed from his personal life less and less. I cannot say that he developed a transference in the proper sense of that word; a certain distance and impersonality were patently there in his style of relating. But he spoke less about himself as if he were another person he knew well and more feelingly about his surgeon and a teacher in Switzerland.

Continuing with his narrative, Mr X said that he had four operations, and within six weeks his arm was in bandages and on his right hand two of the twisted fingers were free. Physiotherapy gave little mobility to his hand. Then the surgeon had a new idea: he sent him to an old painter who gave private drawing lessons. He hoped that learning to handle the pencil would gradually retrain the atrophied muscles, and it worked. Mr X took to the teacher and the teacher found him to be a talented pupil. He drew well and as his hand became more supple he could use it more for little tasks in ordinary life, such as eating with his fork in the right hand. He now began to feel 'unimprisoned' and 'unbound' (both his words). He also learnt the language of the children and so was more sociable. (He knew French already, but not of their variety.) But, he emphasized, he had become more reticent and controlled. Before his accident, he was a buoyant and rather hyperactive child. He often found himself browsing a lot, without quite registering what he had read, as if he were 'elsewhere' (his word).

The surgeon decided that he had recovered enough to return to his family for Christmas; no more treatment was necessary, but he still needed care. In the last week of his stay, an event happened that changed his whole life. It took a lot of effort on his part to tell it. Briefly, he told me:

> He was walking to the chalet from his drawing lesson on a sparkling, snowy winter day, when two girls cycled past him, racing each other. They were wearing tight white shorts, sweaters and socks. This sight had excited him in a curiously intense way. On reaching home, he drew his first doodle of a girl on a cycle. During the night he had a startling dream, which he felt had changed the whole course of his life. He had dreamt that two girls in white shorts were racing past him, and with his flat ruler [used for drawing], which he was carrying in his right hand, he playfully smacked the nearest one on the bottom and she turned her head and winked at him. The dream had awakened him and he found that he had had a nocturnal emission – his first. From this dream onwards, he started to doodle cycles and girls on cycles, and a fantasy began to evolve compulsively.

Typically, he had told me about this event in the last session before the three-week Christmas break so there was little I could say. As he was putting on his coat, he remarked: 'I don't think you know what I do, or has my doctor told you?' I replied: 'No!' He smiled and said that he specialized in designing and making furniture and he had his own workshop. He made these to order, or if he designed and made something that was really nice, he would offer it in a limited number to a few shops. He was very successful, 'in spite of the fact that I am rather lazy, and with my handicap, it takes me longer than others to finish the design and make the object.' He said that he would tell me how he became a designer when he returned from holiday. He wished me a happy Christmas and produced a properly wrapped bottle of champagne as a gift. I was quite touched by this sudden explicit friendliness and accepted the gift with zeal, wishing him and his family a merry Christmas.

I did note his timing, however, and his leaving me in suspense about how he became a designer, but this time he did say that he would tell me on return. I understood this to signify that he could now trust in the continuity of our relationship and our working together.

Things changed dramatically after the Christmas break. Mr X returned for his treatment punctually, and in the first session he sat and said quietly that he must first discuss a practical issue. During the Christmas holidays, a friend of his, doing similar work, had brought along a friend from a Far Eastern country who was also in the same sort of profession. This foreigner – of great distinction in his own country – had been very impressed by a few pieces designed, made and carved by Mr X, which he had seen at his friend's house. He asked to visit his workshop, and afterwards he invited Mr X to come as his guest and design in his workshop-factory for a year from September; he would receive payment for anything he designed and made. He also assured Mr X that he could arrange for his wife to finish her PhD in his country and that such exchanges were acceptable to the London University. Mr X said that it would be an ideal opportunity for both of them, since they were free from the care of their children who were all at different colleges and did not live at home. But, he added, his wife had insisted that he should consult me, and she felt that his 'treatment' (his word) should be given first priority. He asked me quite frankly what my opinion was and what I would advise.

I was quite unprepared for all this. I decided to be as candid with him as possible and talk to him as a responsible adult person rather than 'treat' him as a patient. I told him that, clinically, it would leave us very little time and a lot needed to be done yet; ideally, he and I needed at least another two years of treatment. But, I added, it is my clinical experience that in certain cases where the ailment is focalized, one can do a lot – with the cooperation of the patient – in short-term treatment, and leave it to God, living and chance to promote the patient's further healing and personal growth. I said that I fully agreed with him that such chances come rarely, especially at his age, and I could very well sympathize with his need and desire to augment his skills and sensibility through working with colleagues from a very different culture, using quite different techniques. I concluded: 'Let us try to do our best by and for each other until the summer break.' He offered to come five times a week but I refused that, my logic being (if it was logic!) that we could not expedite the treatment through artificial intensification. The *increase*, as I put it, should come from within him and the clinical situation. We agreed to start with this premise as our frame of working alliance.

Mr X lay down and started by asking me to guide him a bit and not let him 'wander off' (his phrase) in irrelevant directions. Little did he realize that his silent *untrust* at the beginning had rendered the therapeutic process and relationship extremely precarious for months, and that if I had exerted any intrusive pressure to gather his material, he would either have left or would have hidden himself into an absence, bringing me merely debris of stale events. I accepted his invitation, without indicating what I have written above, and said to him that perhaps we could best start by his telling me how the dream about the girls on the cycle had 'changed' his whole life. I left out any mention of 'smacking with his ruler', at this point, because I now knew that his masturbatory fantasies would certainly contain 'beating' as an essential component.

Mr X told me the *how* of it, which I abstract as follows:

> So far his education had been geared to studying languages for A level in order to go to some university to study languages and political science and then to try to get into foreign service. After his Swiss dream [as he henceforth referred to it], he felt strangely buoyant and 'awake' [his word].
>
> Instead of browsing or playing chess and monopoly with Tom the butler, he now began to mix more with the host family and their children, and he was preoccupied by a rather strange fantasy. It evolved and changed all the time but the central theme was the same. He felt that it was a pity the dream had come so late because only about ten days remained before his final departure for England to be with his family for Christmas.

Mr X paused with the tension of expectancy and the 'demand' that I should make some interpretation. I noted that two new elements had emerged from the style of his telling me how the Swiss dream had changed him: taunting and tantalizing me to urge him on, by interpretations, to produce more material. It was again a subtle nuance of pitch of voice, gestures and pauses that indicated these elements to me; my account does not specifically show why I felt taunted and tantalized but I cannot tell it a better way. Now to return to Mr X's narrative:

> He and Tom had travelled back to London by train, on the advice of his surgeon, who thought it was safer for his arm since

> aeroplane seats are very close together and he could easily be knocked by other passengers. His surgeon had also advised him to keep wearing the sling and to rest his arm in it when not using it, for at least six more months. The sling would remind him that his arm was not fully healed and that he had to be careful about it, and it would also signal to others to be careful with him. He didn't cherish the prospect of 'advertising' his 'handicapped arm and hand' [his words] to all and sundry but he had complied totally and was to discover in time how wise the advice of the surgeon had been. He had a profound respect and true affection for his surgeon.

I must state that the more Mr X obliquely taunted and tantalized me to interpret, the more cautious I became in the precision and economy of my interpretations. For example, during the first sessions when he was telling me the *how* of his 'change', I made hardly any interpretations and restrained myself to brief casual comments to show him that I was present, listening and en rapport. To continue again with Mr X's narrative:

> The whole family had come to the station to receive him and they were happy beyond belief to find him so fit and to see that his arm was functional. They were surprised indeed that he could use his right hand to write and draw. [This they had known for some months from his cards, on which he would write and make doodles for his parents, brothers and sisters, the nature of the doodle depending on the person to whom he was writing. This sustained familial relating had impressed me as a very positive aspect of his personality.]
>
> When Christmas was over, the question arose of his renewing his education. The surgeon had written to the parents, recommending that he should start school in the autumn of the next year but should have private lessons at home until then. The parents had readily agreed to his suggestion. It was in this context that he insinuated 'the first change' [his phrase] to his parents. Instead of studying languages, geography and history, as he had done before the accident, he asked to be tutored in languages (only two: French and English), mathematics, physics and chemistry. The parents tried very gently to dissuade him, saying that he might find his 'handicap' [as it was called henceforth by the family and himself] would make it very difficult for him to do the experimental work in physics and

chemistry. But since he insisted, they let him have his way.

After Christmas, when his brothers and sisters had started their school again and his parents had gone to work (his mother had started to do voluntary work again), he found himself rather lonely, and except for his private lessons, he didn't know how to occupy himself. He often played chess and monopoly with Tom the butler but that didn't satisfy him. He was not drawing now because he was used to doing it with the teacher.

Quite by accident one day, one of his sisters' bicycles was left out leaning against the wall. He had a sudden impulse to draw it and made a drawing that he felt wasn't bad, for a first effort. [When he showed it to me much later, with other such drawings, I was quite impressed.]

Now drawing bicycles (and later, furniture) became his pastime. He could not do still-life drawings of flowers, etcetera, and had no model for life drawing, except Tom the butler and very occasionally his sisters, when one of them could sit still for an hour or so. His parents were very relieved and delighted to find him using his left hand more effectively and his right handicapped hand more creatively.

Some time during February of that year, a neighbour who was his godfather and a friend of his parents invited him to stay with his family for a weekend. This friend had a farm and he was very adept at doing all the carpentry himself, as a hobby as well as a necessity. During this stay, Mr X carried tools and helped his godfather with little jobs. At the end of the weekend, he asked his godfather whether he could come for a few hours every Saturday to help him and to learn how to use the tools, such as the screwdriver and the electric saw. His godfather and his parents were delighted with his intentions. It was during this stay that Mr X inwardly made the 'final' decision about his professional future. He was now determined not to go to university for academic education but to go to some college where he could learn manual crafts.

At some point I have a note of Mr X remarking: 'You see how that Swiss dream freed me and gave me a vocation. After that dream I started to draw cycles and furniture.' Then he had added tauntingly: 'You haven't said anything about the Swiss dream.'

I see from my notes that I had taken that opportunity to interpret the dream to him as not only giving him freedom but also restoring the belief and confidence that he could use his handicapped hand mischievously and playfully. And I had added, deliberately: 'All craftsmanship and art start from playing.' I had intentionally given an 'ego-interpretation' of the dream, though its sexual implications were obvious to me, because I wanted to establish his self-esteem and support his ego-ideals at that point. I had instead put emphasis on the dreaming experience (cf. Chapter 2) in the 'dream space' (cf. Pontalis 1972). I have often found some of what passes for deep analysis in supervision of candidates and in the literature to be a rather morbid pursuit of our special epistemological expertise. I also suspected that he might be masturbating a lot when drawing the cycles but had waited until he mentioned it first before interpreting the myriad psychic interconnections between his Swiss dream, his masturbatory fantasy (which I had yet to hear) and the cumulative traumata that he had to live through the year following his accident. I also had other reasons for not interpreting precipitately the sexual contents and psychic material of the dream. He had had a depressive breakdown. In such breakdowns and perversions, the super-ego (unconscious or preconscious) plays a mutative role (cf. Freud 1905*d*, 1924*c*). I did not want to aggravate, by assumptive interpretations, the psycho-sexual inner experiences of this patient, about which I knew so little *from him*.

I read in my notes that at the beginning of March that year, Mr X brought to show me, for the first time, one of his 'girly-cycle' drawings (as he was to nickname them, ironically). I myself was very surprised by his finesse, exactitude and acute perceptual observation, and its manual transcription into the drawing of the cycle. The girl on the cycle – seated, bent forward, with buttocks sticking out – was rather shabbily sketched in this drawing. He paused as I scrutinized the drawing and then asked rather tauntingly: 'Well, what do you make of it?'

I joined in the *contest* now, and said: 'That depends on what you tell me.'

He bantered, 'Ask me,' and I said:

'All right – during or after you have made such a fine drawing, what pleasure and satisfaction do you get from it?' and I very pointedly added, 'And what do you *do* with it?'

He blushed. He got my message and from here the whole theme of his masturbation fantasies and practices opened up. I shall summarize it briefly, from his account.

Every clinician knows how hard, if not impossible, it is to convey the rhythm and criss-cross consequentiality of the spoken narrative in the clinical situation, particularly the subtle and often spontaneous, unpremeditated interventions of the analyst (called interpretations) that sponsor and sustain this contest of dialogue, silence, and mere narrative (Khan 1972*d*). All the same, I shall try to give some idea of the atmosphere and character of the analytic work in the eight or so weeks before the Easter break, when we worked through the contents (psychic and sexual) of his masturbatory reveries, 'girly-cycle' drawings and acts of masturbation. It was during this period of working together that I discovered what a varied and rich personality Mr X possessed, how keen was his intellect and aesthetic, and how encompassing was his imagination.

He had lived a benignly 'dissociated' below-par life before his arm accident, followed by a year of invalidism – with physical pain, varying from acute to constant, and the accompanying anxieties and apprehensions about the future of his arm – without complaining about it to anyone. Yet he had registered with singular acuity of perception every experience in himself, as well as the behaviour of others, during this year. All this he had gradually 'sorted out' into four ways of being: (1) his very secret, silent one, which was released by the Swiss dream and 'girly-cycle' masturbatory drawings into full consciousness in himself but was unshared till now; (2) his resolute stance of 'stiff upper lip' regarding the physical pain and the intrapsychic vicissitudes of mood and affectivity sustaining his social and familial relationships; (3) his learning craftsmanship in carpentry; (4) his deeper self, hidden even from himself, which would one day be *him* and integrate the rest into a whole person, Mr X (cf. Khan 1972*c*).

Before I offer some sort of coherent account of Mr X's activities after his return from Switzerland, I must state two things. First, he himself never called his 'girly-cycle' drawing masturbatory; I am using that adjective here to help the reader but I never used it with Mr X, even though we worked out in detail the relation between these drawings and the acts of masturbation. Secondly, when Mr X started to converse more freely and mutually about his drawings, he recalled and recounted a conversation that he had had with his mother on his return, during the Christmas period. He had asked her why she was so impressed by his efforts to use his 'handicapped' hand and to strengthen his left arm and hand. For example, he wrote slowly but with persistence with his right hand and he played croquet with his brothers and sisters, no matter how poorly (which they didn't mind), with his left hand, merely guiding it with slight support from the right hand. His mother had replied that when he was a child, he was vague, lazy and utterly uncompetitive. If he found himself losing in any game, he would give up too soon and try to end it. He never resented the other person winning. Remembering our new terms of working alliance, I took the initiative here – for the first time, so far as I can recall – and gave a 'leading' interpretation. I said that what I understood from what his mother had told him was that he *dismayed* too easily and did not sustain the *effort to improve and master* his relative lack of skill compared to his elder brothers. He protested that he behaved the same way playing monopoly with his younger sisters: once he felt he couldn't win, he readily gave away his game. I answered his protest by saying that it made little difference to what I had said. I added that in his case the accident and the 'hand-handicap', plus the dream, had awakened in him the desire to make an effort and sustain it, with vigour and playful humour. I do not know why I mentioned his humour, but his way of conversing with me had changed so much that I now began to realize he had a rather subtle wit and used language with a certain gracious humour. All these factors had led to his success, which was rather rapid and solid, in the profession of his choice – design and carpentry. But to return to his drawings, I abstract once again – from the random collation of material – the significant data:

> After drawing the bicycle of his sister, over which he had taken weeks, Mr X began to notice a certain mood in himself that would prompt him to draw the cycles. Because of the absence of his family during the day, and in spite of his private lessons and Tom the butler's availability to play games, he found that he had quite a lot of time on his hands, doing nothing. But now he didn't 'wander off' into what his mother had called 'being vague' but felt a strange excitement build up in him. Here, he added a most significant detail, namely, that his first proper drawing of the cycle was after the stay with his godfather [whom he called Uncle James] when he helped him do the required carpentry in his cow-sheds, etcetera.

I made a mental note of how his sexual fantasy (incestuous?!) and his learning to master the 'handicap' of his hand ran parallel, though they were dissociated in his self-awareness. He gave many versions of the early stages of the fantasy. In fact, the fantasy had emerged only when he started to draw a girl seated on the cycle. I never discovered whether he had masturbated while drawing only bicycles. It took him months to arrive at the final version of the fantasy, which afterwards stayed almost the same, with minor variations here and there, right up to his depressive breakdown. The fantasy was:

> He is cycling in a country lane. It is summer, and a beautiful sunlit day. A girl in white shorts on a bicycle overtakes him. He races to catch up with her and a conversation starts. Gradually, he persuades her to visit him one day soon. They agree on that. The girl visits him for lunch on a Monday, when all the family are away. By various clever and tantalizing ruses, he persuades her to see what he makes in his studio. There is a bicycle carved in wood by him. It has wheels that don't move and the seat is noticeably higher than the handlebars. He tells her that he is at college, learning crafts, and it is a hobby of his to make 'cycles' and other wooden objects, in all sizes, for his family and friends.

Of course, Mr X emphasised, it took years for the fantasy to achieve its final version, and that was when he was nineteen and already at college. He now told me how he had initiated the second 'change' in his plans for the future when his parents had asked him what he wanted for his fifteenth birthday (which was at the end of March). He had unhesitatingly said: a carpentry set. The parents has consulted Uncle James and they bought him the best one, with all the necessary tools, some of which were as yet beyond his ability to handle. The set was presented to him on his birthday, and when the fifteen candles on the cake were lit and just as he was about to blow them out, his youngest sister remarked: 'You must have a wish.' He loudly exclaimed his wish: 'I want to go to a college that teaches crafts. I don't want to go to an academic university.' His parents and their friends who had come were rather taken aback, though everyone wished him a happy birthday and nothing was said about his wish for weeks. Then one day his father called him into his study and he found Uncle James there too. They both asked how serious he was about going to a college where crafts were taught rather than to a university. He told them frankly that he had been thinking about it since he realized that he could use his right hand to draw and his surgeon had assured him that his 'handicapped' hand was functional, though crippled, and in time would become more supple and efficient in every way. He told them that he had decided to study physics and chemistry because he would need that knowledge to fulfil his ambition. He also told his father that he had wanted to talk to him about it for weeks but felt shy, because he knew how much concern and money his treatment had cost them and he did not want to worry them again so soon. The father and Uncle James readily agreed to his wishes and Uncle James assured his father that, from what he had seen of the boy's efforts to work with him and help him in carpentry, he felt sure that he had talent and determination.

I too was very surprised by such purposiveness in him at that age, because so far I had heard and known only about his capacity to endure pain and discomfort. Once again I chose the ego-approach to interpret the fantasy and remarked that in it, he recovers his pre-accident capacities to act and that, furthermore, he can share with the girl his achievements with his handicapped hand. This must make him feel 'equal' to others, and therefore free. He agreed that this was part of his experience. I did not insinuate that it was also linked with his ego-mastery over a sexual object, though I had a fair hunch of that, because so far he had held back all data that could have justified such an intrusion into his secret psychic life. I am utterly of Freud's (1937*c*) persuasion, with some modifications, regarding 'a certain man' who had come for re-analysis with him and later complained of its incompleteness. I quote the relevant passage in full because these days more is read about Freud than by Freud:

> A certain man, who had himself practised analysis with great success, came to the conclusion that his relations both to men and women – to the men who were his competitors and to the woman whom he loved – were nevertheless not free from neurotic impediments; and he therefore made himself the subject of an analysis by someone else whom he regarded as superior to himself. This critical illumination of his own self had a completely successful result. He married the woman he loved and turned into a friend and teacher of his supposed rivals. Many years passed in this way, during which his relations with his former analyst also remained unclouded. But then, for no assignable external reason, trouble arose. The man who had been analysed became antagonistic to the analyst and reproached him for having failed to give him a complete analysis. The analyst, he said, ought to have known and to have taken into account the fact that a transference-relation can never be purely positive; he should have given his attention to the possibilities of a negative transference. The analyst defended himself by saying that, at the time of the analysis, there was no

> sign of a negative transference. But even if he had failed to observe some very faint signs of it – which was not altogether ruled out, considering the limited horizon of analysis in those early days – it was still doubtful, he thought, whether he would have had the power to activate a topic (or, as we say, a 'complex') by merely pointing it out, so long as it was not currently active in the patient himself at the time. To activate it would certainly have required some unfriendly piece of behaviour in reality on the analyst's part. Furthermore, he added, not every good relation between an analyst and his subject during and after analysis was to be regarded as a transference; there were also friendly relations which were based on reality and which proved to be viable.

Jones (1953) identifies the 'person' as the famous Hungarian psychoanalyst, Sandor Ferenczi. It is also worthwhile to read James Strachey's succinct and illuminating Editor's Note (1964) to this paper.

Mr X told me that he had not started the 'real' 'girly-cycle' drawings until he went to college in London as a day-student. During the week he lived in his father's flat with his father and Tom the butler, and they all returned to the country home for weekends. He also told me that he took the utmost precaution never to be found drawing such 'girly-cycle' drawings and that I was the first to have seen any of them. I had rather jokingly interpreted that I did not know whether to take it as a gesture of trust or a manoeuvre to make me an accomplice to his 'secret life' with himself. I used this phrase for the first time. I keep repeating, 'for the first time', because slowly over time I build up clinically – for future use – my own private 'card-index' of the potentially significant little details of idiom, gesture or manner of speech from the patient's narrative; at the time, their referents are not clear to me. I had no clue, still, from the patient's spoken material whether he used these 'girly-drawings' only as a means of controlling and mastering his gathering state of elation, or whether he actually ended up masturbating. This was to become clear much later. I said that I had decided on an ego-approach to his fantasy in its final form. I shall summarize the significant changes in his ego and self-experience that we were able to discover from the analysis of this fantasy and its precursors. Here I took the initiative again and pointed to one aspect of object-relating in the fantasy, namely, that he and the girl meet by chance and stay anonymous to each other and, gradually and teasingly, they try out a way of *cooperating* with each other. With my voice I had underlined the verb 'cooperating' (cf. Khan 1964*a*, 1964*b*).

Mr X agreed with me far too readily, which put me on guard; I thought that I had got a quarter of the truth but the essentials were missing. Mr X went on to say that it had never occurred to him to think that way about the fantasy, and he added: 'So far as I am concerned, there was no difference between the wooden cycle and the girl.' This remark struck me as a vital clue to his way of relating to the sexual object in his masturbatory fantasies. We shall shortly see the nature of the girl's role in the complete fantasy, when Mr X had found the trust in the 'impersonality' of the clinical setting to tell me how the fantasy grew further and how, at around nineteen years of age, he would masturbate after each 'girly-drawing' was finished. But first I want to summarize how much we were able to recover from dissociation, repression and amnesia of what he had suffered 'secretly' during his long and painful invalidism, and the various ways this had been worked into the 'girly-cycle' drawings, through his learning to draw. He had brought under ego-mastery his helplessness from the 'handicap' and his dependence on the *other*. Winnicott (1960*b*) has stated: 'In psycho-analysis as we know it there is no trauma that is outside the individual's omnipotence.' But I would add that omnipotence is not mastery; in it there is a tremendous denial of both inner and outer psychic reality, and of recognition of the *other* as a person in his or her own right. We shall see later how omnipotence, when it succeeds, can destroy the person's sense of his own identity and alienate him from himself (cf. Winnicott 1935, Khan 1980).

I have already recounted Mr X's sense of humiliation at not being able to feed himself, his refusing the nurse's help and accepting only his mother to feed him. Mr X emphasized again and again how different were his experiences of hospitalization and his operations in London from those in Switzerland. In London and at home, he soon started to treat his arm in plaster as a 'thing' he carried around. He had experienced the three major operations as inevitable but futile. He expressed no protest at any point. But as he recalled his subjective feelings, he realized that he had felt 'mistreated' (his word) and deprived of having a say. As he talked, I could feel his rage and disillusionment. At one point he said that he had lost complete faith in his parents and the surgeons in London, after overhearing the surgeon's remark to his father about the possibility of amputation and never being told about it himself.

Now I shall finish telling Mr X's 'girly-cycle' reverie. I am deliberately deleting the adverb 'masturbatory' because now I began to suspect that the 'girly-drawing' activity and the reverie ('story', to use Mr X's word) gathering from it were different in psychic quality and experience from the act of masturbation. Mr X had told me the complete reverie, which had led to his first masturbatory act, during a Friday session, with only the next week (that is, three sessions) left for us to analyse it before the four-week Easter break. I had agreed to his wish to have a long four-week Easter break, instead of the customary two in England, because he had said that this would be the last time for more than a year that he would be able to go away with the whole family to their country house, which the children loved, since he was to leave for the foreign country in early August. Though I had agreed, I noted how necessary it was for Mr X to have his way in analysis, to tantalize me and keep me suspended in attention, and also to tease me to make him work harder in analysis. He had become a very demanding perfectionist in the execution of his work and he expected nothing less from others.

Mr X's final fantasy ended with his tantalizing the girl to try sitting on the cycle and his saying: 'Bet you can't touch the pedals.' (The pedals in the drawing were horizontally parallel.) The girl accepted his challenge and teased him, saying: 'By shifting on the saddle, I shall certainly succeed in touching one peddle.' This no girl succeeded in doing. Then he introduced another tantalizing provocation: 'If you fail next try, I will give you one stroke with this stick.' He had the stick handy and never gave more than five strokes. In his fantasy he could see the welts from the five strokes under the shorts.

The fantasy had gone on in just this way for a long while, when eventually – after a year at college where he had worked very hard at improving his capacity to draw and to use tools – he drew a *perfect* 'girly-drawing'. (The qualifying superlative was his.) While looking at this drawing, he had felt the urge to masturbate for the first time. His fantasy, while masturbating, was that the girl protests mildly that it is uncomfortable and slightly painful, as he rubs against her buttocks, because of the soreness from the strokes. (He and the girl are *both clothed*.) And then he would ejaculate.

Mr X had brought the drawing to show me in the sessions in which he completed the recounting of his reverie. I scrutinized it very carefully and was delighted by the excellence of his line; it was firm and supple. And though the drawing was remarkably sensual, it was utterly non-pornographic. It is a great pity that I cannot reproduce the drawing here; it would tell more than I can possibly state. It further convinced me that the 'girly-cycle' drawings and the accompanying reverie were different in psychic character and function from the act of masturbation and the little bits added to the reverie, such as when the girl protests discomfort and a little pain. However, his latent sadistic wish and the girl's masochistic complicity were quite obvious. What had struck me as most significant in the drawing was the very subtle way he drew the toes of the girl nearly touching but not reaching the pedal. He asked me quite explicitly what I had understood about him from his drawing and his 'story'. We had reached the end of the session and this time I decided to suspend interpretation. I said to him: 'We shall discuss it on Monday,' which he accepted with his customary politeness.

I thought a lot about the last session and the patient's explicit demand and readiness for 'deeper' interpretation of his material. I knew what I could interpret in terms of unconscious incest fantasies; vengefulness turned into playful fantasy; the need to reverse his helplessness during long periods of hospitalization; and the very important role of sexualization (or libidinization) of his anger and rage, that is, his aggressive feelings against *the other*. I was pressed for time and had to choose what elements to elaborate and work through in analysis in the three sessions before the Easter break. I was also equally conscious that I knew nothing of the events or circumstances that had led to his ego-collapse in the depressive breakdown.

The patient arrived in a rather expectant mood on Monday and I decided to start the session by offering what I had understood from the 'girly-drawing' and his 'story' (now I used his word). I stated bluntly, without the subterfuge of any type of jargon, that I was most struck by the excellence of his drawing skill and the playful sensuousness (I chose that word rather than 'sexuality') of the whole atmosphere of the drawing and his 'story'. I also told him that I thought the act of drawing and the theme of the 'story' belonged to a different category of psychic experience from the sexual relief of tension and excitement through masturbation (cf. Winnicott 1960*a*).

Mr X was meditatively silent for a long while, and then remarked: 'You are very astute. I have always sensed that there was a difference, but I could not put it the way you have, and you are right. I will tell you why: when I masturbate from boredom or find myself with a spontaneous erection and laboriously use the "story", the ejaculation gives relief but little pleasure. Whereas there is a lusty joy when I masturbate after completing such a "girly-drawing", with the "story" brewing (his word). And though I have had no sexual difficulties in my marital life, intercourse lacks this extra quality of lust and a strange atmosphere of triumph. I have never tried to analyse these feelings.'

The analytic interpretative work and his associative material were very rich and rewarding during the three sessions before the Easter break. I shall skip most of it and meagrely recount the essentials. I avoided linking the 'girl-object' (I used that phrase to him, too) to his sisters (that is, incestuous wishes) and emphasized, especially from what I had seen in the drawing, the link with his accident and the consequent traumata. For example, he meets the girl in his 'story' *accidentally*. Also, I had noticed in the drawing that, though he had chalked the shorts white, there were smudges of very light pencil shading on the shorts. This I rather brazenly linked with his arm in plaster and later in bandages, which could never be kept completely white. This really surprised him. Thus the shorts were a displacement, into a pleasurable area of play, of what had caused him so much pain, discomfort and stasis. I avoided using the concept of projective identification, though it was in my mind. The next interpretation that I gave concerned his active mastery, through and with an *other*, of what he had suffered silently and alone in his periods of hospitalization.

In the last session before Easter, Mr X arrived looking rather grumpy, which somewhat alarmed me. Fortunately, it had little to do with analysis. He was very angry with himself for being unable to finish a chair, which he could have done if he were not handicapped. 'It takes me so much longer than anyone else, and I don't care when they say that my work is so subtle and superior to everyone else's, because I am always behind.' I decided to *reassure* him and support his morale a little at this point, since I wanted him to enjoy his holidays and I knew by now that he had a very taxing ego-ideal. I said to him that he was very ingenious, in terms of his self-care and self-cure, to have found a secret space and unlimited time to make his 'girly-drawings' and sustain himself with his 'story', since he had become rather a loner after his accident and did not readily mix with people other than his family and colleagues in his workshop (cf. Chapter 6, and Winnicott 1971*c*). I shall shortly be telling about the workshop. He remarked: 'You are being very positive today; not that you have ever been negative with me but I feel that you often say much less than what you are thinking about my material.' I told him that he was right but since it was the last session before the Easter break, I felt that I must try to help him regain his positive mood of the week and not get dislocated by the delay in finishing his project. I felt that I owed it to him and his family. I ended the session, however, by giving him one interpretation, which set him a task. For the first time, I deliberately introduced an analytic concept to make my point. Referring to the whole varied range of cycle drawings and 'story', I said that they really belonged to a type of psychic functioning that includes mastering, which had been described by an analyst, Donald Winnicott (1951), as 'transitional objects, and transitional phenomena'. He was very intrigued by this and asked where he could read more about it. I gave him a reprint of the paper as a goodwill gesture.

Thinking about the past three months and the three months ahead, I felt rather nonplussed. I was not sure about introducing Winnicott's concept and giving Mr X the paper, and yet I felt, deep down, like Hamlet when he says: 'the play is the thing wherein I shall catch the conscience of the king.' I was apprehensive that he might use my gesture to evade telling and working through the experiences that led to his breakdown. And I felt very strongly that unless we got some clue to what had made him describe himself as 'evil' at the start, everything we had worked on would be of little use to him. I must add, however, that since January his apathy and depression had totally cleared up and he never mentioned them, speaking only of fatigue from overwork and occasional dismaying boredom. I knew that boredom and dismay had been features of his inner psychic life from very early childhood, screened by his always being eager to please and participate and by his genially 'giving up all too quickly' when losing.

Mr X returned from his break looking relaxed and said that they had all had a very happy time together and the weather had been good. Then he added: 'The present-day youngsters are so different from us. My children are already drawing up lists of pop music records and other things that they want me to bring back when I go abroad. I could never have asked that of my father.' Then he mentioned the paper by Winnicott and said that, though it was written so lucidly, most of its implications had escaped him. I told him that it did not matter. I was now determined to take a *risk* and confront him with the fact that we had little time left to work together, and he had still told me nothing about what his physician had called his 'depressive breakdown', or what led to it. I said that, clinically, I had no evidence of real depression in him. He quickly joined in and said: 'I have told my wife and my physician all along that I was not depressed; hence I have refused medication and any type of psychiatric treatment. I just found it impossible to live with myself.'

Here, I insisted that he had better start telling me why and how it had come about so suddenly. He parried me by paying me a compliment: 'The one thing I have really learnt to my advantage from you is through watching your style of working.' Of course I knew that Mr X was always alert to my way of handling his material. He added: 'I don't want you to feel that I think you haven't helped me with my problems – you have a great deal, indeed. But I am talking of something different: it is your style of working – how much you say and how you say it. This is why I respected my Swiss surgeon so much, compared to the English ones. What I have learnt from your style, I am putting into practice in teaching the apprentices in my workshop. I no longer instruct them to do what I know they cannot yet execute, because of their lack of skill and experience.'

In spite of all my efforts, it was not until the beginning of June that he eventually told me what had led to his 'collapse', as he called it. In the meantime, we had done a lot of analytic work on his difficulties in social and professional relationships and his over-demand from himself, all the time, to do better and more. I must state that when Mr X came to me, he was already famous in his profession, not only in his own country but also throughout the world. He had taken no advantage of this, however, and had continued to work privately and to enjoy his family life.

If Mr X was being tardy and evasive in telling me what had led to his ego-collapse, I must take responsibility for my uncertainty about the wisdom or desirability of intruding into a focalized area of experience that he had dissociated and now seemed to manage very well in living. I feared that I might disturb that balance. I also had reason to fear that his super-ego might be as taxing as his ego-ideal, and an unwarranted intrusion on my part could mobilize severe internal conflict and guilt, leading him to regress into apathy and withdraw again from living. Mr X decided it for me, during one session in early June, by his reaction to a casual remark I had made: namely, that aesthetics and control (mastery) played a large and crucial part in all his life-activities and relationships. He had laughed sardonically, and said:

'You wait until you hear the rest. Sense of beauty and control, what you call mastery of oneself, or the instruments one uses, can all go to pieces from one chance, accidental event.' He added, 'Let me fill in some of the gaps in what I have told you of my life-history,' and then he recounted:

> I married young, while still at college, a very charming and lovable girl. I knew her from childhood but we had lost contact because she went abroad to study. We met again, after some ten years, and found ourselves willing to marry each other. My parents knew her family well and were happy about it. Ours was not a great romance but we have lived happily together and have reared three adorable children. The lustful sensuality, I have kept to my drawings, 'story' and occasional masturbation, to this day.
>
> As a wedding gift, my father bought me a huge warehouse to turn into a workshop in time. Her father bought a house for us in a fashionable area of London and I have *inhabited* [his word] these spaces for over twenty years now.

I noted that he had again used 'accidental' to qualify the event and also that he had not said 'lived' but 'inhabited'. From this, I surmised that he had never lived as a whole person with himself and others. Also, once again, he had told me this during a Friday session, leaving me tantalized, expectant and suspended, as the 'girl' in his 'story' always is. In the following session, without much ado, he recounted the circumstances and events that had led to his 'collapse', as he now referred to it. I summarize:

> In late January or early February last year, my wife went with the children to our country house for the weekend, leaving around noon on Friday. I stayed behind, because I had to attend a conference that weekend. The conference was attended by specialists from various disciplines related to my work and it had newspaper coverage. At the end of the day [Friday], we all had dinner. Seated with me at my table were four colleagues and a young woman, whom I did not know. She was attractive and you might say cute. One of my colleagues knew her and introduced her to us. She was a freelance journalist. She said on introduction that she knew of me and had seen my work. I really didn't take much notice of her, until she got up to get something. I noticed that she was wearing very tight white trousers and a loose sweater. She had a slim, 'boyish' body. While I was thinking how to tell all this to you, I was startled to recall that – seeing her from behind, with her young bottom squeezed into those white trousers – I had begun to feel the same excitement as I do before starting my 'girly-cycle' drawings. I didn't talk much to her. The meal ended and we all parted. As I left I found

it was pouring with rain, so I waited for it to ease up a little. I intended either to catch a taxi or take the underground. Of course, I haven't told you I don't drive. I can get an 'invalid driver's' licence, but I can't bear to advertise my handicap with a plate on the back of the car stating, 'Handicapped Driver'.

I must have been waiting for a quarter of an hour when a small car pulled up in front of me. It was that young woman and she asked me whether I was waiting for my car or could she give me a lift. I accepted her offer because it was very windy and cold. As we drove she talked on, and said she would very much like to visit my workshop. God knows what came over me but I found myself offering to show her the workshop there and then, saying that it was quite near where we were. With hindsight, I now realize that a silent complicity had already started between us. I felt a strange mixture of 'excitedness' [his word] and misgiving. We arrived. I showed her the workshop and told her how it was run. She noticed I had built a sort of studio for myself in one corner of the workshop, which was separated from the rest of the working space and was built on wooden stilts. She wanted to see it. I hesitated for a while and then gave in.

As soon as we entered my studio, which is always kept locked, she saw a fullscale wooden cycle (like the one in the drawings you have seen) in one corner of the room. It is really beautifully made and carved. It was the second *object* I had made in the studio. The first was an object that I gave as a gift to my Swiss surgeon. I must add that this cycle was designed and made by me nearly twenty years ago. The cycle amuses all visitors, and my children, when young, were always climbing on it and playing with it. It was joked about as my toy. Whilst the young woman was examining the cycle, I went over to my desk to make sure I hadn't a sketch of a new 'girly-cycle' drawing lying around.

The next thing I saw was her seated on the cycle and I heard her say: 'But I cannot reach the pedals.' I said blandly: 'You are not supposed to.' 'Then what is the point of putting them there?' she replied. Thenceforth, everything went berserk and I really can't recall the sequence of events exactly, but I found myself petting her as she sat on the cycle. She teased me by saying: 'Men are strange. They all think only they have perverse sexual desires and fantasies. You know, women often lead them on, without them realizing it.' So I challenged her to tell me her fantasy of lusty sex, and she unhesitatingly replied: 'I like being beaten a bit before intercourse.' I asked: 'Would you like it now?' and she said, 'Yes!' I replied: 'So the contest is on!'

By now, I really felt like a man possessed; I was in a tense, maniacal state of sexual excitement. It was quite a new experience for me. I went downstairs to find some suitable object to beat her with but couldn't find one; so I rushed out to the small garden, broke off a branch from a tree and tried to smooth it down hurriedly, before coming up.

When I returned, I was really quite taken aback to find she had completely undressed herself and was seated naked on the cycle. She asked me with a trembling, excited voice: 'What posture shall I take? Please tie my hands to the handlebars.' I felt she was taking over my initiative. I went down, found some string, tied her hands to the handlebar, and asked her to stick out her bottom and try to touch one of the parallel pedals. I told her again: 'This is a "contest". If you fail to touch the pedal, I will give you one stroke per failure with this branch/stick.' She replied laughingly: 'And if I do succeed, what can I do to you?' I said: 'Whatever you please.' Well, she couldn't touch the pedal and I gave her one stroke. She tried again and again and I realized I had beaten her nearly ten times. I had also taken off my clothes by now. It was not so much an orgy, as being possessed, without any awareness of her or myself. What really horrified me was to see her bottom bleeding a little, because I had not quite smoothed out the branch. Also, I had no experience of this before – fantasies are all right but action and practice are different. She insisted I 'fuck' her. She used the word and I did it with a diabolical ferocity of lust and vigour. I wasn't aware of her pain or discomfort at all; she had groaned a little but had neither complained nor tried to stop me.

Afterwards, we said little and she drove me home. I held back my actual address and said: 'Drop me here by the corner of the street.' She said that she was leaving for another congress tomorrow noon, so she wouldn't be seeing me, but she hoped we'd meet again. She gave me her professional card. I thanked her and walked away. I was completely in a daze, as one is when waking from an anaesthetic. On the way to my house, I tore up the card and scattered it in the street. Well, that's it! Now you know the circumstances and the event.

He had talked for nearly two hours, nonstop, and I had let him as he was the last patient and it was possible to allow him more time. The only nuisance was to my staff but it happened so rarely that they did not mind. Mr X left rather shaken by his own narrative. I sensed that he was relieved to have got it off his chest, but I was worried about him, all the same, especially about his need to 'confess' to his wife. So I offered to see him the following day, saying that I had that hour free because another patient was away, which was true. I say this because, with Mr X, I had learnt to be very explicit and use no ruses. I gave him my reasons, namely, that he had told me the 'event' but I really could not see why it had such a traumatic after-effect on him and led to his 'collapse'. I needed to know more about how he had re-experienced the previous night of 'contest' and what he had made of it.

When Mr X came for his next session, he was wearing casual clothes, so I surmised that he had not gone to work. He told me that he had been so overwhelmed by recalling hundreds of small details from that evening and the 'event', that he really thought it was better for him to stay at home. He added: 'I am working on a very difficult piece of furniture, which I have designed, and it entails very precise and sensitive use of electric tools. I could not take the risk of damaging it or myself from lack of concentration.' I responded that he had acted wisely. Wilfulness is not always the sagacious route to mastery. However, I noted his capacity for self-preservation, both from himself and others. Mr X continued:

> I recall nothing more of that night. I had fallen asleep with my clothes on, and only the phone ringing woke me the next day [Saturday], around mid-day. At first, I was confused as to where I was, just as I had always been on waking from each anaesthetic. [He gave some examples, which I skip.] I didn't answer the phone, and when I was fully awake, I decided not to go to the conference. After breakfasting, I went to sleep again and woke early the next morning with the 'statement', 'I am an evil man,' vivid in my mind, as if I had dreamt it.

I asked him, because it was important for me to know, whether in his self-experience he felt that *he was an evil man* or that he had *done an evil thing*. He assured me that it was the former. He went on to say how he recollected the details of beating the girl: the blood, his *savage lustful disregard* of her and his equally *brutal pleasure* (all these are his phrases). He felt that he had lived dishonestly, all his life, cheating everyone including himself; that his idyllic (he said the word with a pungent self-mockery) 'girly-cycle drawings' and his 'story' were fake. He was a ruthless, vengeful and brutal man, and his sexuality was dangerously perverse. He continued again by saying:

> All these and myriad other such thoughts occupied me all day. I didn't eat any lunch. I felt that I had lost all self-respect and wasn't worthy of anyone's affection, and that my work was an alibi to distract myself from becoming a total and criminal pervert: in short, it was evil in reality as I was in myself. I was in this mood of apathy and self-accusative absent-mindedness when my family returned. From that moment, I collapsed into total silence and retired to bed. My wife gently tried to inquire what had upset me but didn't persist. When this condition had lasted for a week, and I was still refusing to eat solid food, she called the family doctor, and that led eventually to my coming to you.

I asked him how he felt now and he replied: 'Upset, but I really feel that you can help me to get some understanding of what happened.' I told him that what had happened – the 'evil contest', as he called it at one point – was not grave, in terms of my clinical experience. I had heard of much more gruesome, premeditated sexual acts of cruelty and savage sensuality from real perverts. What was puzzling me was his extreme reaction, his loss of faith in his own goodness and his extreme need to punish himself. He asked me whether I would agree that it wasn't all his *doing*, that she had set it up as well and urged him on. I said, 'Yes!' and added: 'The passive accomplice is often more in control of such situations and events than the active one.'

From here, we were able to reconstruct, from the period of his year of invalidism, all his dissociated and repressed feelings of rage, humiliation and abject helplessness, as well as his need for vengeance. It is not my intention to recount that data here. Suffice it to say that Mr X gained insight into his reaction to the 'evil contest' (as he called it now) and into what had been waiting in him to actualize in real experience in this way. I stressed his *achievement* in dissociating these feelings in order to overcome his handicap, acquire a skill and raise a family. I made no secret of the fact that in my opinion, if this had happened when he was twenty or so, the results would have been very different. Mr X's last remark to me was: 'Well, I have learnt one more thing: one evil act doesn't make an evil man. Each of us is capable of it.'

Mr X left with his wife for his work abroad in a fairly stable and healthy state of mind and being. He sent me a card at Christmas, which was a reproduction of a native drawing, depicting a coolie pulling a wheelbarrow. The reference to the *wheel* in the drawing was not lost on me.

Finally, I want to say that I have stated four ways in which Mr X was dissociated. I have discussed three of them but I have not talked about the 'hidden self' of Mr X. That is because I know nothing about it and I never tried to work in that direction, realizing how vulnerable he was and what little time we had to work together. I know, however, that the hidden self goes deep into his early nurture and his relation to his mother and sisters. But clinically, one learns not to let one's curiosity take over from one's judgement of limits that are necessary for the well-being of the patient.

I mentioned earlier that Mr X and I moved in the same circles, so I have met him many times in the past ten years. He has made a real success of his life, and is thriving within his family and his profession.

Conceptual Afterthoughts

> De quelle oreille il convient d'écouter?
>
> *Leclaire*

Indeed, most humans can hear with their physiological ear, but since the beginnings of civilizations, humans have needed conceptual apparatuses to enable them to listen to – and make sense of – each other. What these apparatuses are depends on the era and the area of experience; they can range from magico-ritualistic rhythmic noises to the highly abstract symbolic language of present day physics. In between is the vast range of language used in diverse roles. Here I am concerned with 'the language of psycho-analysis' (cf. Laplanche and Pontalis 1973). Even from this repertoire of concepts, I shall select only a few to discuss the case material.

Before proceeding further, I wish to make it quite clear that:

1. it is not my intention to throw light on the aetiology and psychodynamics of perversions. A vast literature exists on these subjects (cf. Freud 1905*d*, 1919*e*, 1924*c*, 1927*e*; Lorand 1956; Aulagnier-Spairani et al 1967; Khan 1980);

2. nor is it my intention to discuss the meaning (conscious or unconscious) and the psychodynamics of masturbation and its accompanying fantasies. Again, a vast amount has been written on

that score (cf. Menninger 1973; Marcus and Francis 1975).

What I hope to do is to explore conceptually how Mr X brought the cumulative trauma, from a year of invalidism, under his ego-mastery.

The concept of ego-mastery is only a variation of Freud's (1905*d*) hypothesis about the role of the instinct for mastery, especially in perversions. Freud never really spelt out, with any thoroughness, his concept of 'the instinct for mastery' (cf. Laplanche and Pontalis 1973). He discusses it in the contexts of cruelty, generally – in children (pp. 192–3) or in sadism and masochism (p. 159) – or in its role in the psychodynamics of obsessional neurosis (1913*i*):

> ... If we wish to bring our hypothesis (about obsessional neurosis) into contact with biological lines of thought, we must not forget that the antithesis between male and female, which is introduced by the reproductive function, cannot be present as yet at the stage of pregenital object-choice. We find in its place the antithesis between trends with an active and with a passive aim, an antithesis which later becomes firmly attached to that between the sexes. Activity is supplied by the common instinct of mastery, which we call sadism when we find it in the service of the sexual function; and even in fully developed normal sexual life it has important subsidiary services to perform ...
>
> In particular we often gain an impression that the instinct for knowledge can actually take the place of sadism in the mechanism of obsessional neurosis. Indeed it is at bottom a sublimated off-shoot of the instinct of mastery exalted into something intellectual ...

It is not an accident that Freud relates closely sadism/masochism, the instinct for knowledge and the instinct for mastery. He had established this equation as early as 1905 in *Three Essays on the Theory of Sexuality* (1905*d*). But Freud was to expand it further in *Totem and Taboo* (1912–13) to the socio-sexual organization of primitive hordes. He quotes the hypothesis Darwin borrowed from Dr Savage: '... when the young male grows up a contest takes place for mastery ...' (p. 125). In *Civilization and its Discontents* (1930*a*), Freud made his position as clear as he could:

> Thus, to begin with, ego-instincts and object-instincts confronted each other. It was to denote the energy of the latter and only the latter instincts that I introduced the term 'libido'. Thus

> the antithesis was between the ego-instincts and the 'libidinal' instincts of love (in its widest sense) which were directed to an object. One of these object-instincts, the sadistic instinct, stood out from the rest, it is true, in that its aim was so very far from being loving. Moreover it was obviously in some respects attached to the ego-instincts: it could not hide its close affinity with instincts of mastery which have no libidinal purpose.

Any reader who wishes to pursue in greater detail Freud's various usages of the instinct of mastery should consult Guttman et al's indispensable *Concordance* (1980).

As I have said earlier, it is not my intention to explicate in detail the clinical material of Mr X. Any sensitive reader can make his own inferences about how this young boy of fourteen gradually brought under the 'omnipotence of his ego' (cf. Winnicott 1960*b*) the traumata that he, at the same time, dissociated. In fact, this dissociation continued, in many subtle ways, to the end of his analysis. For example, while working on a piece of furniture that demanded not only imaginative design but also very sensitive, subtle and careful manual tact and expertise, he had ruefully remarked:

> You know, my two arms, and especially the hands, have developed their own character and competence. My right hand, though handicapped, is subtle and sensitive; it takes time but is idealistic in its efforts. Whereas my left arm and hand are uncouth, vigorous and insensitive to the nature and quality of the material and the limits of the tools used. If not guided and restrained by my right hand, my left hand could savage most of my work.

Later, when he had told me about the 'acting out' of his 'girly-cycle story', I said to him at one point: 'You must have used the branch-stick with your left hand.' He said, 'Yes!' and I added: 'Little wonder that you had no sensitivity regarding the young woman's buttocks and flesh – that you "savaged" it, to use your own phrase.' This parallel had impressed him very much. I think I have made sufficiently clear his near obsessional – or at least explicitly obsessive – determination to master the handicap of his right hand, through sublimations (work) and libidinization of his pyschic life ('story'). Thus, with the help of the instinct for mastery, as well as for self-preservation, he had enlarged and actualized his ego-capacities.

I now want to discuss the theme of his self-damnation: 'I am an evil man.' In the language of psychoanalysis, there is no concept of evil. Even though Guttman et al (1980) have 180 references under the caption 'Evil', one cannot claim that Freud uses the word more than colloquially, and it never gains the epistemological status of a concept. The proof of this is that neither Laplanche and Pontalis (1973) nor Charles Rycroft (1968*b*) has an entry on this topic. Freud (1913*i*), drawing upon the researches of Rudolph Kleinpaul into the ancient belief in spirits, concludes the paragraph: '. . . It was from corpses that the concept of evil spirits first arose.' This is a rather dubious hypothesis.

Fairbairn (1946) in his chapter, 'The Treatment and Rehabilitation of Sexual Offenders', is certainly on the mark when he argues:

> So far as I am personally concerned, it required little experience to discover that the problem of the war neuroses was essentially a problem of morale, i.e. a problem of the relationship of the individual member of a service to that service as a group . . .

Fairbairn continues:

> I regret to say, in my experience, very similar considerations apply to those who commit unnatural sexual offences in civilian life. I know that in recent times there has been a widespread movement among psychiatrists towards the point of view that perverse sexual tendencies are 'symptoms' in the same sense as those which characterise the psychoneuroses; but this is a point of view which I cannot see my way to share. It is a point of view which arises out of a general modern tendency to substitute purely scientific standards for the moral standards of the past; but, in my opinion, it represents an interpretation based upon an erroneous psychopathology.

Of course, the concept of evil is a socio-theological one and only one analyst has challenged the sovereignty of the so-called scientific spirit and its concepts in our field of work, namely, Karl Menninger (1973). In his book *Whatever Became of Sin*, he pungently argues: 'The disappearance of the word "sin" involves a shift in the allocation of responsibility of evil.'

A little later, Menninger candidly challenges: 'But if you think sin is hard to define, try defining evil!'

Menninger ends his book with a long passage from Arnold Toynbee's book *Surviving the Future* (1971). Toynbee's argument is so telling that I shall quote him, like Menninger, but selectively:

> There has always been a 'morality gap', like the 'credibility gap', of which some politicians have been accused. We can first accuse the whole human race, since we became human, of a 'morality gap', and this gap has been growing wider as technology has been making cumulative progress, while morality has been stagnating . . . Science has never superseded religion, and it is my expectation that it never will supersede it . . . It has not been able to do anything to cure man of his sinfulness and his sense of security, or to avert the painfulness of failure and the dread of death . . . I am convinced myself, that man's fundamental problem is his human egocentricity.

Though Toynbee states the case with acuity, he also fails to define evil or what characterizes it. I am not so arrogant or ambitious as to even attempt a definition of evil. All I can say to my reader is that, coming from a different culture and continent (India/Persia) – where *evil* was part of everyone's language and evaluation of himself, others and social events – I have been interested in the *absence* of this concept, or consciousness of it, amongst my colleagues and friends. I have never heard anyone call anyone else evil, though I have heard them berate others with livid execrations. Freud could refer to a patient as 'a scoundrel', but he could never have brought himself to say of anyone: 'He is evil.' Yet from my experience, clinical and social, of persons and institutions in the West, I must agree with Richard Cavendish (1975) when he states categorically:

> The evil entities of the past have descended upon us. A surprising number of people, in what is supposed to be an age of materialism and rationalism, have at heart either a conviction or a strong suspicion of their reality. The revival of interest in magic and the occult owes a good deal to these old fears, and modern occultism has fitted them into its own framework. But on a far broader front, and even among the sceptical, they are part of the furniture of the Western mind. They occupy all sorts of mental lodgments and points of vantage. Even if, or perhaps particularly if, we banish them to the attic and shut the door on them, they make unexpected and alarming reappearances. We are more primitive than we may like to think.

Here I cannot help thinking of a paradox in Freud's sensibility: intellectually, he kept a vigilantly critical stance vis-à-vis parapsychology and occultism, yet in his private life he was prone to superstitious misgivings (cf. Clark 1980).

Before I return to my patient's material, I would like to say that my interest in trying to understand the why and how of his self-designation as evil had resulted, to a great extent, from my diligent, exhaustive study of four nineteenth-century European thinkers, namely, Dostoyevsky, Kierkegaard, Baudelaire and Nietzsche. That personages from such different cultures and disciplines should examine life and living with the theme of evil at the centre of their thinking, I do not consider coincidental. And in all of their writings, the interplay of will (which is the chief vehicle of the instinct for mastery), beauty (human and abstract), evil and violence ending in tragedy, are the primary themes (cf. Charles Dédéyan 1968; Georges Bataille 1973; Paul Evdokimov 1978; Leon Chestov 1926, 1948; Walter Kaufman 1974; and Daniel Halévy 1944).

To return to my clinical coping with Mr X and his material, it is the fashion at present for analysts to 'confess' what they do, a pursuit rendered scientific by the term countertransference (cf. Frank 1977). I will merely try to delineate how, in the total analytic situation and through the analytic process, Mr X and I carried on a benign contest. A certain impersonality was as innate to his style of being and conversing as it was to my way of listening and responding. I do not wish this to be misunderstood as a lack of affectivity in our relationship. Freud (1937*c*) has explicitly stated:

> . . . not every good relation between an analyst and his subject during and after analysis was to be regarded as a transference; there were also friendly relations which were based on reality and which proved to be viable.

I must own up to my style of never giving, if I can help it, a here and now interpersonal (that is, you and me) interpretation. For example, Ella Sharpe (1930) has stated:

> We shall treat resistances, not as specifically directed against analysis but as what they truly are, defences the psyche has evolved in its attempt to reconcile the claims of the id and the super-ego [I would add, also, of the ego-ideal] in the world of reality.

What I am stating as 'a contest' between Mr X and myself is, in fact, a variant in verbal terms of Winnicott's (1971*b*) famous 'squiggle game' consultative therapeutic work with children. Winnicott, in his Introduction, tells us:

> . . . one thing that will be noticeable to the reader is that I never (I hope) make interpretations for my own benefit. I have no need to prove to myself some part of the theory that I use by hearing myself verbalise the material of this case.

After watching Mr X for a half hour during the first consultation, or to use his word, during our first meeting, I was convinced that he was not a case of depression, in the psychiatric sense of that concept. He struck me as a dismayed man, who had not so much 'collapsed' as decided to opt out of active relating and living in any area of life. But I had said nothing about this. Instead, I had made it quite clear to him (as he told me more than a year later) that I considered his self-damnation to be the crucial issue. Again, I did not rush to evaluate it as the result of a harsh super-ego (that is, conscience), even in my own thinking. Since I had regarded our relating and working as a 'contest' from the very beginning, I was not surprised to hear him use that word in his 'story'. Thus one can see that the transferential displacement of the crucial active element in the 'story' had already come into operation in the clinical process and setting. I had initiated playing, and here I am again profoundly influenced by Winnicott (1971*c*). He writes it so clearly that I can do no better than quote him:

> Psychotherapy takes place in the overlap of two areas of playing, that of the patient and that of the therapist. Psychotherapy has to do with two people playing together. The corollary of this is that where playing is not possible then the work done by the therapist is directed towards bringing the patient from a state of not being able to play into a state of being able to play.

I felt sure that enabling Mr X to 'play' verbally *into* conversation, what was so rigidly controlled intrapsychically, was more important than intruding with insightful interpretations.

Listening to his poised and measured elegance of phrasing, I felt certain that *mastery* in all functions played a primary role for him. Once I heard about his learning to draw with the damaged and crumpled hand, I had no doubts that he had set himself the highest standards for effort and achievement. Nowhere, in my opinion, does the instinct for mastery reinforce the ego's efforts so much as in the pursuit of the ego-ideal. It is a very treacherous balance, as Mr X himself stated, after telling me about his *actual* sexual contest with the young woman. And the shift from good to evil can be not only rapid but catastrophic. We see this in human civilizations, too, where all devastating and ruthless wars are mostly in pursuit of ideals rather than vengeance. One sees clearly in European cultures how contest changes into conquest, from the crusades to the Second World War; evil is legitimized as serving one's nation and is gilded with honour and glory (cf. Freud 1933*b*). It is only too well known how wars galvanize individuals and nations into unexpected, unbelievable effort and vigour, while previously they had been carrying out quite ordinarily their day to day living.

It is precisely this sudden discovery and experience of lusty, desperate energy and power that had shifted Mr X's intrapsychic balance and self-evaluation. The self-confrontation after the 'sexual contest' paralysed his ego, and even worse, it let loose all the dissociated rage and vengefulness, but now against himself.

As we worked and tossed around various constructions together, as to what constituted the evil for Mr X, we deciphered roughly the following key features:

1. The nature of the use of the object: Mr X was quite lucid about the difference between what he called the 'aesthetic tenderness' and concern he felt for 'the girl' in his 'story', and his total disregard for the young woman's experience and feelings, as well as his own lack of any subjective feelings.

2. We were able to piece together how subtly Mr X had started to 'dismantle' (his word) her as a person, from the moment he had met her. Her complicity rendered it absolute. She was a 'thing' and no longer a person with an ego. I have reported such a way of *using* the object in a case of foreskin fetishism (1979; also cf. Winnicott 1969).

3. There was another feature of what I have called Mr X's 'self-cure' that interested me very much (Khan 1970*a*). Knowing from his account that he was a 'vague' child, benignly adrift rather than positively living from personal initiative, I was surprised how the accident and recovering from it had *awakened* him. One can attribute it to the instinct for self-preservation, yet there was more to it. Though learning a skill (drawing) and weaving his 'story' were supplementary, they had stayed, as it were, parallel in him (like the pedals on the cycle). This had saved him from becoming a mere skilled artisan or just being swamped in the haze of his 'story', by its becoming more

monotonous and unimaginative over time and thus forming a barrier between him and reality, as well as him and the other. In his chapter, 'Dreaming, Fantasying and Living', Winnicott (1971*c*) argues: 'Dream fits into object-relating in the real world, and living in the real world fits into the dream-world in ways that are quite familiar, especially to psychoanalysts. By contrast, however, fantasying remains an isolated phenomenon, absorbing energy but not contributing-in either to dreaming or to living.' He continues: 'In the fantasying, what happens happens immediately, except that it does not happen at all.' Winnicott goes on to describe the fatedness and psychic stasis in his female patient, from being 'locked in the fixity of fantasying', and shows how dreaming had gradually come to her rescue. But even then, for a long time, 'fantasying possesses her like an evil spirit.' Knowing this, I have preferred, in my clinical narrative, to use the word 'reverie', because in Mr X there was a vibrant interplay between drawing and his 'story'-making. I am sure that it was this capacity in him that gradually enabled the clinical process to become playful, productive and mutual.

4. I have talked about Mr X's use of the object (cf. Winnicott 1969), but I have said little about my interpretations to him of his *demands* from the object (girl). Contrary to his reticence and his control of subjectivity and its expression, with respect to pain and apprehension in the hospitals, he makes quite explicit, though very discreetly stated, demands in his 'story', which needed a lot of empathy on the girl's part to become 'mutually playful' with him. And this is why he never outraged her by physical sexuality. The young woman had not been 'playful' but was enacting her own perverse fantasy with him; hence his sense of 'losing initiative' and becoming totally abstract, impersonal and unrelating. I have met this phenomenon in certain forms of what I call 'malignant perversions', which are different from the 'benign' ones. In my clinical experience, if the accomplice is relative innocent but en rapport preconsciously, the balance of active/passive stays positive. But where each party matches actively, from his own explicit need and desire, the same fantasy in the other, the results can reach criminal proportions, with grievous bodily damage to both parties concerned. Sometime in the 'evil contest', Mr X had unconsciously twigged this; hence his collapse into total dismay about preserving his

own self and protecting the other, and his recourse to total dissociation and alienation from both inner and outer life, psychic and interpersonal.

5. Lastly, I want to say that I really cannot account exactly for the *why* of his change in self-relating, from feeling evil to feeling good again. We did not have time and I wonder even if we had whether he would have dared to open up that area of his hidden self. No patient is totally knowable as a person, to himself or to the analyst. And this final privacy is, perhaps, what we should never transgress clinically. That the patient should be able to take the 'contest' into creative and shared living, and to thrive from it, is the clinical ideal – for me, at least (cf. Chapter 4).

9
Infancy, Aloneness and Madness

> fleurir ne suffit pas aux roses
> au fond de son miroir
> il faut que l'amoureuse
> les regarde la voir
>
> *Jean Lescure*

The human infant is the only living organism that emerges out of the womb into its new environment both traumatically and physically immature. Hence the necessity for extensive and extended infant-care by the maternal coverage and/or her substitutes.

Of course Freud was the first to establish this equation. Yet it was some twenty years before it was taken seriously as a *fact* and not merely a concept. We have three persons to thank for this development – Anna Freud, Melanie Klein and Winnicott.

In this article I shall not be concerned with the myriad vicissitudes of infant-mother relating that lead to later psychopathology, but with the infant-in-care *alone* with himself in the quiet states of well-being. A very large part of infancy and early childhood is spent in that state, and little has been written about it by analysts, except for Winnicott.

What is the nature and function of this aloneness in infancy? Primarily, it provides both the *space* and the *time* for the innate biologic capacities to actualize into a personalized psychic state. Gradually *the* infant becomes *an* infant: a person in his own right and in his own privacy of being.

Secondly, much that the infant is maturationally incapable of rendering into psychic experience at that early stage goes into *oblivion*. I believe Freud meant this by his concept of primary repression. But what goes into *oblivion* is not lost – it will turn up later in private mad states of being. And here I am deliberately using the word *mad*, as distinct from the concept of psychotic, because each adult is mad in a very private way, and also alone.

How we experience and actualize this madness and aloneness in adult life is the next question. We do it in three ways: through art and literature; through sharing unexcited mutuality with the *other*; and through mystic states of being, like the Persian sufis or the Zen priests.

The real predicament for the analytic clinician arises when the analysand brings his *mad* state and need to be alone to his session. The latter is often mistaken for resistance, and the analysand hides his true need, screening it with compliant guilt and acceptance.

But that is not the worst that we do as clinicians. We also try to make sense of the *non*-sense of the analysand's spoken madness in terms of our conceptual vocabulary, through which we are addicted to listening to the analysand's normal or pathological material, and interpreting it. Misguidedly, but from concern, we try to make sense of this *non*-sense by either reconstructing *the facts* of infancy (Winnicott) or its *fantasies* (Klein). Neither helps; the creative potential of the madness lapses back into oblivion and the analysand is no longer either mad or alone, but merely lonely and lost!

10
On Lying Fallow

Writing to Countess M. on 10 March 1921, Rainer Maria Rilke expressed a sentiment which in a humbler way is true of us all: 'Ultimately each one of us experiences only *one* conflict in life which constantly reappears under a different guise.'

What for Rilke was '*one* conflict' has been, in my life experience, a preoccupation with a person's relation to himself. Here I shall focus on a rather private, nonconflictual and personalized area of self-experience, namely, *lying fallow*. The noun *fallow* is defined by the *Oxford English Dictionary* as 'ground that is well-ploughed and harrowed, but left uncropped for a whole year or more'.

Through the metaphor of an active verb, I wish to indicate that the mood I am trying to discuss is not one of inertia, listless vacancy or idle quietism of soul; nor is it a flight from harassed purposiveness and pragmatic action. *Lying fallow* is a transitional state of experience, a mode of being that is alerted quietude and receptive wakeful lambent consciousness.

It is indeed difficult to define positive nonconflictual moods and affective emotional states. Language bears a very long and complex relation to conflictual states, be they vis-à-vis external reality or inner psychic reality. Over a long period of time, it has evolved an expertise and competence in defining these conflictual states of angst and fear, hope and despair, elation and depression.

For centuries, writers, sages and priests have cultivated and perfected the instrumentality of the spoken and written word as a way of regulating and organizing human experience, purposiveness and action. The latest arrivals on this scene are the psychoanalysts, and over some seventy years, guided by the researches of Freud, they have said and established a great deal about the human being in a state of conflict. What I shall discuss here is not a neurotic, conflictual or distress state, but an ego-capacity. By this I mean a healthy function of the ego in the service of the individual.

In recent years, both in psychoanalysis and in other disciplines, the need to view the whole human being as an existential entity has been stressed more frequently. Winnicott and Heinz Hartmann have contributed a great deal towards an understanding of those intractably silent states which we associate with the healthy individual. The most effective and persuasive plea on this score, however, has been made by Pierre Teilhard de Chardin. After accounting for the long and complex evaluation of human consciousness over thousands of years, he came to the conclusion: 'Is it not possible that in our theories and in our acts we have neglected to give due place to the person and the forces of *personalization*.'

My argument is that the capacity for lying fallow is a function of the process of personalization in the individual. This process of personalization achieves its sentient wholeness over a slow period of growth, development and acculturation, and its true matrix is a hierarchy of relationships: the mother looking after the infant; the father supporting the mother; the family nurturing the parents; and society maintaining the family in a living and nutrient ambience for the individuating person.

This is a long process and it is waylaid by many traumata – personal, familial and social. But if all goes well – and it does, more often than not – what crystallizes and differentiates into the separate status of adult selfhood is a personalized individual with his own privacy, inner reality and sense of relatedness to his social environment.

Today we live in excessively pragmatic and ruthlessly evangelical societies, where everything is being done for the *individual* through the instrumentality of the state and politicians, sociologists and psychiatrists, psychoanalysts and entertainers. In this excessive zeal to rescue and comfort the individual, we have perhaps overlooked some of the basic needs of the person to be private, unintegrated and to lie fallow. The welfare state, whether idealistically socialist, traditionally conservative or militantly Marxist, has evolved an intrusive concern for the individual's well-being which, instead of promoting his personal growth, is turning him into a depersonalized parasite, as well as a victim, with ready-to-hand rescue measures of skills and programmed endeavours.

I am not jeering at the true virtues of modern civilizations and that civic concern for the well-being of the individual which is one of the great achievements of the Christian cultures. Through my nurture I am able to evaluate the nihilism built into Eastern cultures by centuries of spiritual inertia, and by their obsession with rarified purity of the soul and their utter disregard for the human being as a civic organism. In my early years, I saw such body-misery, poverty and destitution of existence in the Hindu-Muslim culture of India that I will never believe that a civilization is worth a bean if it does not look after the ordinary welfare of its citizens, no matter how excellent it is with the metaphysics of the soul. It is precisely because Western cultures and civilizations have firmly established the civic dignity, freedom and well-being of the individual that we should try to look at the more subtle aspects of the private and silent psychic experiences and their value for human existence.

Let me say outright that the soul has meaning only in a well-cared-for individual. In abject poverty, no person can lie fallow.

Let us try to make a phenomenological statement about lying fallow. To define it negatively, it is not a state of instinctual or environmental tension. We all experience it frequently in fleeting patches. Quite often we register consciously a mellow disinclination to apply ourselves to something that we should be doing. We nag at ourselves with admonitory rigour but somehow fail to move or harass our executive faculties to the task. We sense a need to be somewhat idle and to feel our way out of this benignly languid passive mood. If we are forced out of it, either by our own conscience or the environment, we feel irritable and grumpy. Quite often we are only too ready to blame some external factor for our incapacity to hold and sustain this fallow mood.

Although this fallow mood is essentially and inherently private and personal, it needs an ambience of companionship in order to be held and sustained. In isolation or deprivation one can neither arrive at this mood nor sustain it. Someone – a friend, a wife, a neighbour – sitting around unobtrusively, guarantees that the psychic process does not get out of hand, that is, become morbid, introspective or sullenly doleful. There are endless variations of the failure of the fallow mood. One extreme is the rigorous self-immolating bleakness of a mystical retreat from life and the imprisonment of self by a rationalized idealistic apologia for such states of being. There are also the exotic experiences that some persons strive after and achieve through narcotics, alchohol and other drugs.

What does the fallow mood achieve for us? The answer is a paradox: a great deal and nothing. It is a nutrient of the ego and a preparatory state. It supplies the energic substratum for most of our creative efforts, and through its unintegrated, psychic suspended animation (which is the obverse of organized mentation) allows for that larval inner experience which distinguishes true psychic creativity from obsessional productiveness.

Thus the fallow state is:

1. A transitional and transient mood
2. A nonconflictual, noninstinctual, and intellectually uncritical state
3. A capacity of the ego
4. An alert wakeful mood – unintegrated, receptive and labile
5. A largely nonverbal and imagistic state, kinaesthetic in expression.

Furthermore, I would say that the fallow mood is largely experienced or expressed in silence, even with oneself. It is, however, more amenable to pictorial expression than verbal articulation – doodling, etcetera, can be quite an adequate vehicle for it.

It is perhaps one of the few genuine achievements of modern art between 1900 and 1940 that it divested the pictorial activity of painting of its too close alliance with thematic representation. The cubists (Picasso, Braque, Leger, Gris, etcetera) staked a claim for expressing transitional states of visual experience – a claim that derived from lying fallow rather than from dream states. The enchanting exponent of painting as a vehicle of the fallow mood is Miro, with his wayward somnambulant doodles and blotches of colour, which are so playful in their stillness.

By relating the fallow mood to creative artistic productions, I wish to establish an important value coefficient of this mood – its discipline and relation to *will*. It is not an idle moronic state of being. It is a cogent capacity in a well-established, disciplined and personalized individual. We may all make-believe that we can doodle like Miro, but the strength and vigour of sensibility needed to sustain that state of free-floating animation and to capture its innate aliveness through imagery is no small achievement of the ego. Compare to it the nostalgic escapist efforts of the Sunday painters, and it is not difficult to establish the difference. Lying fallow is, above all, the proof that a person can be with himself unpurposefully.

How does lying fallow relate to leisure? It is, in some ways, the obverse of leisure, particularly as it has become known today. It is a strange and uncanny result of urban civilization and the impact of technology on human experience that leisure has become a pursuit and an end in itself. It has gradually become an industry, a profession and an imperative social need of the individuals in modern societies. Everyone strives for more and more leisure and knows less and less what to do with it. Hence the emergence of a colossal trade in organizing people's leisure. This need is perhaps one of the real absurdities of our existence today, and it reflects the decay of some crucial value-systems, which the wisdom of religions sponsored for ages, in all types and kinds of human beings. The pursuit of frantic leisure, with little capacity to make a personalized experience of it, is perhaps one of the most dissipating qualities of the technical cultures. The individual on whom leisure has been imposed in massive doses, and who has little capacity to deal with it, then searches for distractions that will fill this vacuum. A vast amount of the energy of modern man is spent searching for these distractions, and when he fails to be assuaged by distractions, he concocts states of ill-health and morbidity which then occupy his leisure. A great deal of the distress and psychic conflict that we see clinically today in our patients is the result of a warped and erroneous expectancy of human nature and existence. It is the omnipresent fallacy of our age that all life should be fun and that all time should be made available to enjoy this fun. The result is apathy, discontent and pseudo-neurosis. It may seem rather odd that a psychoanalyst should write about human conflict with such irony. But unless we are honest and distinguish between true conflict and illness, and illusory faked neuroses which derive from misconceptions of human nature, we only confuse our task as therapists and confuse our patients as well.

A craving for leisure, and the concomitant yearning for distractions to fill the void of given-leisure, is the result of our failure to understand the role and function of the need to lie fallow in the human psyche and personality. Over the past six or seven decades we have industriously misinformed ourselves about the essentials of human nature. We have confused the necessity to relieve human poverty and misery with the demand that all life should be fun and kicks. The entertainment media of modern cultures have further exploited this leisure void for commercial gain and flooded the citizens with ready-made switchable distractions, so that no awareness of the need to develop personal resources to cope with fallow states can actualize as private experience.

A pathetic consequence of this situation is that we have a style of personality development emerging that is overdemanding in its claims on the environment and others, and its need to be related to by others, but has little comprehension of the necessity of the responsibility for an inner relation to its own self. Even a superficial acquaintance with our contemporary theatre and literature will show how dramatically and vociferously the isolation, misery, loneliness, bereftness, etcetera, of the individual is portrayed, with no inkling of insight into the person's primary human responsibility for a commitment to sustain and nourish himself.

It has often been said that the failure to find a true relation to the self is the major symptom of our times, and the blame for it has been overgenerously apportioned to parents, society and the scientific revolution. What has not been stressed enough is that very few individuals today regard it as their own responsibility to relate to themselves. We have replaced effort with labour, and lying fallow with idle leisure.

The capacity to lie fallow is dependent upon:

1. Acceptance of self as a separate person
2. Toleration of noncommunication
3. Putting up with reduced relatedness to and from the environment.

Lastly, I would like to say that one of my debts to Winnicott is that he taught me how to enable a patient as a person to find, when he needed to in the analytic situation, his own capacity to lie fallow, without feeling a silent coercive demand from my presence to fill the session with a debris of facts or to berate himself for not free associating. Language and relating are only creative when the person speaks from himself in order to relate both to himself and the other, and thus actualizes himself for himself and the other. For this to happen, the capacity to lie fallow in a quiescent aloneness with the other is an inevitable prerequisite.

CHRONOLOGICAL BIBLIOGRAPHY

1975 'Freud and the crisis of psychotherapeutic responsibility'. Originally published as 'Freud and the crises of responsibility in modern psychotherapeutics'. *Int. Rev. Psycho-Anal.*, 2.

1975 'Grudge and the hysteric'. *Int. J. Psychoanal. Psychotherapy*, 4.

1976 'Beyond the dreaming experience'. Originally published as 'The changing use of dreams in psychoanalytic practice'. *Int. J. Psycho-Anal.*, 57.

1977 'From secretiveness to shared living'. In *The Human Dimension in Psychoanalytic Practice*, K. A. Frank (New York: Grune and Stratton).

1977 'On lying fallow'. *Int. J. Psychoanal. Psychotherapy*, 6.

1978 'Secret as potential space'. In *Between Reality and Fantasy*, eds. S. Grolnick, L. Barkin and W. Muensterberger (New York: Aronson).

1979 'Infancy, aloneness and madness'. Originally published in French as 'Enfance, solitude et folie' in *Nouvelle Revue de Psychanalyse*, 19, and in English in *Int. J. Psychoanal. Psychotherapy*, 8.

1981 'The evil hand'. Published in French as 'La main mauvaise' in *Nouvelle Revue de Psychanalyse*, 24.

1981 'None can speak his/her folly'. Published in French as 'Personne ne peut dire sa folie' in *Nouvelle Revue de Psychanalyse*, 23, and in English in *Int. J. Psychoanal. Psychotherapy*, 9.

1982 'The empty-headed'. Published in French as 'La tête vide' in *Nouvelle Revue de Psychanalyse*, 25.

BIBLIOGRAPHY

Abrams, M. H. (1953). *The Mirror and the Lamp* (New York: Norton, 1958).

——(1971). *Natural Supernatural* (New York: Norton).

Anzieu, D. (1975). *L'Auto-analyse de Freud et la Découverte de la Psychanalyse* (Paris: Presses Universitaires de France).

——(1980). 'Du code et du corps mystiques et de leurs paradoxes'. *Nouvelle Revue de Psychanalyse*, 22.

Auerbach, E. (1946). *Mimesis* (New Jersey: Princeton Univ. Press).

Aulagnier-Spairani, P. et al. (1967). *Le Désir et la Perversion* (Paris: Editions du Seuil).

Bataille, G. (1973). *Literature and Evil* (London: Calder and Boyars).

Bainton, R. (1967). *The Penguin History of Christianity* (London: Penguin).

Balint, M. (1968). *The Basic Fault* (London: Tavistock).

Baudelaire, C. (1846). 'The Salon of 1846'. In *The Mirror of Art* (London: Phaidon Press, 1955).

——(1857). 'Les fleurs du mal', in *Oeuvres Complètes* (Paris: Bibl. Pléiade, 1961).

——(1863). 'L'artiste, homme du monde, homme des foules et enfant', in *ibid* (1961).

Bion, W. R. (1967). *Second Thoughts: Selected Papers on Psycho-Analysis* (London: Heinemann).

Blake, W. (1789–94). 'Songs of innocence and of experience'. In *Poetry and Prose of William Blake* (London: Nonsuch Press, 1941).

Braque, G. (1917–47). *Cahiers de Georges Braque* (Paris: Maeght Editeur).

Burke, K. (1966). *Language as Symbolic Action* (Los Angeles: Univ. of California Press).

Cassirer, E. (1951). *The Philosophy of Enlightenment* (Boston: Beacon Press, 1960).

Cavafy, C. P. (1911). 'Ithaka'. In *Collected Poems*. Translated by E. Keeley and P. Sherrard (London: Hogarth, 1975).

Cavendish, R. (1975). *The Powers of Evil in Western Religious Magic and Folk Belief* (London: Routledge and Kegan Paul).

Chestov, L. (1926). *La Philosophie de la Tragédie* (Paris: J. Schiffrin, Editions de la Pléiade).

——(1948). *Kierkegaard et la Philosophie Existentielle* (Paris: Librairie Philosophique J. Vrin).

Clark, R. W. (1980). *Freud: The Man and the Cause* (London: Jonathan Cape and Weidenfeld and Nicolson; New York: Random House).

Coleridge, S. T. (1817). 'Biographia literaria'. In *Coleridge: Selected Poetry and Prose* (London: Nonsuch Press, 1933).

Cooper, D. (1978). *The Language of Madness* (London: Allen Lane).

Corbin, H. (1980). *Temple et Contemplation* (Paris: Flammarion).

Damon, S. F. (1973). *A Blake Dictionary* (London: Thames & Hudson).

Dédéyan, C. (1968). *Le Nouveau Mal du Siècle de Baudelaire à Nos Jours* (Paris: Société d'Edition d'Enseignement Superieur).

Deleuze, G. (1973). 'Pensée nomade'. *Nietzsche Aujourd'hui?* 10/18.

Descartes, R. (1637). *Discourse on Method and Other Writings*. Translated by F. E. Sutcliffe (London: Penguin, 1968).

——(1641). 'Meditations on first philosophy'. In *The Philosophical Works of Descartes*. Translated by E. S. Haldane and G. R. T. Ross (Cambridge: Cambridge University Press, 1911).

Ducrot, O., et Todorov, T. (1972). *Dictionnaire Encyclopédique des Sciences* (Paris: Editions du Seuil).

Eliot, T. S. (1918). 'Hamlet'. In *Selected Essays* (London: Faber, 1932).

——(1921). 'The metaphysical poets'. In *ibid* (1932).

——(1950). 'The cocktail party'. In *The Complete Poems and Plays of T. S. Eliot* (London: Faber, 1969).

Ellenberger, H. F. (1970). *The Discovery of the Unconscious* (London: Allen Lane).

Evdokimov, P. (1978). *Dostoyevsky et le Problème du Mal* (Paris: Desclée de Brouver).

Fairbairn, W. R. D. (1946). 'The treatment and rehabilitation of sexual offenders'. In *Psychoanalytic Studies of the Personality* (1952).

——(1952). *Psychoanalytic Studies of the Personality* (London: Tavistock).

Fédida, P. (1981). 'Le cauchemar du moi'. *Nouvelle Revue de Psychanalyse*, 24.

Ferenczi, S. (1933). 'Confusion of tongues between adults and the child'. In *Final Contributions to the Problems and Methods of Psycho-Analysis* (London: Hogarth, 1955).

Foucault, M. (1965). *Madness and Civilization* (New York: Pantheon).

——(1970). *The Order of Things* (London: Tavistock; New York: Int. Univ. Press).

——(1976). *Mental Illness and Psychology* (New York: Harper & Row).

Frame, D. M. (1965). *Montaigne: A Biography* (London: Hamilton).

Frank, K. A., ed. (1977). *The Human Dimension in Psychoanalytic Practice* (New York: Grune and Stratton).

Freeman, L. (1972). *Story of Anna O.* (New York: Walker and Company).

Freud, A. (1952). 'A connection between the states of negativism and of emotional surrender'. In *Indications for Child Analysis and Other Papers* (New York: Int. Univ. Press; London: Hogarth, 1969).

Freud, S. (1893*f*). 'Charcot'. *Standard Ed.*, *3.

——(1895*d*). *Studies on Hysteria. Standard Ed.*, 2.

** The Standard Edition of The Complete Psychological Works of Sigmund Freud*, in 24 volumes (London: Hogarth; New York: Norton).

——(1900*a*). *The Interpretation of Dreams*. *Standard Ed.*, 4 and 5.
——(1904*a*). 'Freud's psycho-analytic procedure'. *Standard Ed.*, 7.
——(1905*d*). *Three Essays on the Theory of Sexuality*. *Standard Ed.*, 7.
——(1905*e*). 'Fragment of an analysis of a case of hysteria'. *Standard Ed.*, 7.
——(1910*a*). *Five Lectures on Psycho-Analysis*. *Standard Ed.*, 11.
——(1912*e*). 'Recommendations to physicians practising psycho-analysis'. *Standard Ed.*, 12.
——(1912–13). *Totem and Taboo*. *Standard Ed.*, 13.
——(1913*i*). 'The disposition to obsessional neurosis'. *Standard Ed.*, 12.
——(1914*d*). 'On the history of the psycho-analytic movement'. *Standard Ed.*, 14.
——(1919*e*). 'A child is being beaten'. *Standard Ed.*, 17.
——(1923*c*). 'Remarks on the theory and practice of dream-interpretation'. *Standard Ed.*, 19.
——(1924*c*). 'The economic problem of masochism'. *Standard Ed.*, 19.
——(1925*d*). *An Autobiographical Study*. *Standard Ed.*, 20.
——(1925*i*). 'Some additional notes on dream-interpretation as a whole'. *Standard Ed.*, 19.
——(1926*e*). 'The question of lay analysis'. *Standard Ed.*, 20.
——(1927*e*). 'Fetishism'. *Standard Ed.*, 21.
——(1930*a*). *Civilization and its Discontents*. *Standard Ed.*, 21.
——(1933*b*). 'Why war'. *Standard Ed.*, 22.
——(1937*c*). 'Analysis terminable and interminable'. *Standard Ed.*, 23.
——(1950*a*). *The Origins of Psycho-Analysis* (London: Hogarth, 1954; New York: Basic Books).
——(1961). *Letters 1873–1939*, ed. E. L. Freud (London: Hogarth; New York: Basic Books).
Gay, P. (1966). *The Enlightenment* (New York: Vintage Books).
Giovacchini, P. L., ed. (1972). *Tactics and Techniques in Psycho-analytic Therapy* (London: Hogarth; New York: Science House).
——(1972*a*). 'The blank self'. In *ibid* (1972).
Girard, A. (1963). *La Journal Intime* (Paris: Presses Universitaires de France).
Granoff, W. (1976). *La Pensée et le Féminin* (Paris: Les Editions de Minuit).
Green, A. (1973). 'Le double et l'absent'. *Critique*, 312.
——(1980). 'Le myth: un objet transitionnel collectif'. *Le Temps de la Réflexion*, 1.
Greenson, R. (1967). *The Technique and Practice of Psychoanalysis* (New York: Int. Univ. Press).
Grinstein, A. (1968). *On Sigmund Freud's Dreams* (Detroit: Wayne State Univ. Press).
Guttman, S. et al. (1980). *The Concordance to the Standard Edition of the Complete Psychological Works of Sigmund Freud*, published in 5 volumes (Boston: G. K. Hall & Co.).
Halévy, D. (1944). *Nietzsche* (Paris: Bernard Grasset, new edition, 1977).
Hartmann, E. (1973). *The Functions of Sleep* (London: Yale Univ. Press).

Hazard, P. (1935). *The European Mind 1650–1715* (London: Penguin).

Heimann, P. (1956). 'Dynamics of transference interpretation'. *Int. J. Psycho-Anal.*, 37.

Holland, R. (1977). *Self and Social Context* (London: Macmillan).

Jones, E. (1953). *The Life and Work of Sigmund Freud*, published in 3 volumes (London: Hogarth; New York: Basic Books).

Joyce, J. (1922). *Ulysses* (Paris: Shakespeare & Co.).

——(1939). *Finnegans Wake* (London: Faber).

Jung, C. J. (1963). *Memories, Dreams, Reflections* (London: Collins and Routledge & Kegan Paul).

Kaufman, W. (1974). *Nietzsche: Philosopher, Psychologist, Antichrist* (London: Vintage Books).

Khan, M. M. R. (1960). 'Regression and integration in the analytic setting'. In *The Privacy of the Self* (1974).

——(1962). 'Dream psychology and the evolution of the psychoanalytic situation'. In *ibid* (1974).

——(1963*a*). 'The concept of cumulative trauma'. In *ibid* (1974).

——(1963*b*). 'Ego-ideal, excitement and the threat of annihilation'. In *ibid* (1974).

——(1964*a*). 'Ego-distortion, cumulative trauma and the role of reconstruction in the analytic situation'. In *ibid* (1974).

——(1964*b*). 'Intimacy, complicity and mutuality in perversions'. In *Alienation* (1980).

——(1970*a*). 'Montaigne, Rousseau and Freud'. In *The Privacy of the Self* (1974).

——(1970*b*). 'Towards an epistemology of the process of cure'. In *ibid* (1974).

——(1970*c*). 'Le cadre thérapeutique de Freud'. *Nouvelle Revue de Psychanalyse*, 1. Published in English as 'The hermeneutic triangle'. *Bulletin of the British Psycho-Analytical Society* (1974).

——(1972*a*). 'Dread of surrender to resourceless dependence in the analytic situation'. In *ibid* (1974).

——(1972*b*). 'Exorcism of the intrusive ego-alien factors in the analytic situation and process'. In *ibid* (1974).

——(1972*c*). 'The finding and becoming of self'. In *ibid* (1974).

——(1972*d*). 'On Freud's provision of the therapeutic frame'. In *ibid* (1974).

——(1972*e*). 'The use and abuse of dream in psychic experience'. In *ibid* (1974).

——(1973). 'The role of will and power in perversions'. In *Alienation* (1980).

——(1974). *The Privacy of the Self* (London: Hogarth; New York: Int. Univ. Press).

——(1979). 'Fetish as negation of the self: clinical notes on foreskin fetishism in a male homosexual'. In *Alienation* (1980).

——(1980). *Alienation in Perversions* (London: Hogarth; New York: Int. Univ. Press).

Krailsheimer, A. G. (1971). *The Continental Renaissance* (London: Pelican).

Lacan, J. (1953). 'Fonction et champ de la parole et du langage en psychanalyse'. In *Ecrits* (Paris: Editions du Seuil, 1966).

Laplanche, J. (1970, Eng. trans. 1976). *Life and Death in Psycho-Analysis* (Baltimore: John Hopkins Univ. Press).

Laplanche, J., and Pontalis, J.-B. (1967, Eng. trans. 1973). *The Language of Psycho-Analysis* (London: Hogarth; New York: Norton).

Lautréamont, I. D., Comte de. (1868). 'Les chants de Maldoror', in *Oeuvres Complètes* (Paris: Bibl. Pléiade, 1970).

Lavie, J.-C. (1980). 'Servir'. *Nouvelle Revue de Psychanalyse*, 22.

Leclaire, S. (1968). *Psychanalyser* (Paris: Editions du Seuil).

Leroi-Gourhan, A. (1964). *Le Geste et la Parole* (Paris: Albin Michel, 1978).

Lévi-Strauss, C. (1962, Eng. trans. 1966). *The Savage Mind* (London: Weidenfeld and Nicolson).

——(1978). *Myth and Meaning* (London: Routledge & Kegan Paul).

Lewin, B. (1946). 'Sleep, the mouth and the dream screen'. In *Selected Writings of Bertram Lewin* (New York: Psychoanal. Q. Inc., 1973).

Lorand, S., and Balint, M., eds. (1956). *Perversions, Psychodynamics and Therapy* (New York: Random House).

Macksey, R., and Donato, E., eds. (1970). *The Languages of Criticism and the Sciences of Man: The Structuralist Controversy* (Baltimore: John Hopkins Univ. Press).

Mandel'shtam, O. (1973). *Selected Poems* (Cambridge: River Press).

Marc, O. (1972). *Psychanalyse de la Maison* (Paris: Editions du Seuil).

Marcus, I. M., and Francis, J. J., eds. (1975). *Masturbation from Infancy to Senescence* (New York: Int. Univ. Press).

McLuhan, M. (1962). *The Gutenburg Galaxy* (Canada: Univ. Toronto Press).

Meltzer, D. (1967). *The Psycho-Analytical Process* (London: Heinemann).

Menninger, K. (1973). *Whatever Became of Sin* (New York: Hawthorn Books).

Merleau-Ponty, M. (1960, Eng. trans. 1964). *Signs* (Chicago: Northwèstern Univ. Press).

Milner, M. (1969). *The Hands of the Living God* (London: Hogarth; New York: Int. Univ. Press).

Montaigne, M. (1965). *The Complete Works of Montaigne*. Translated by D. M. Frame (London: Hamish Hamilton).

Nietzsche, F. (1882). *Joyful Wisdom* (New York: Unger, 1971).

——(1969). *Selected Letters of Friedrich Nietzsche* (Univ. of Chicago Press).

Olney, J. (1972). *Metaphors of Self* (New Jersey: Princeton Univ. Press).

Ortega y Gasset. (1948). *The Dehumanization of Art* (New York: Doubleday Anchor).

Passmore, J. (1972). *The Perfectibility of Man* (London: Duckworth).

Podach, E. F. (1931). *L'Effondrement de Nietzsche* (Paris: Gallimard, 1978).

Pontalis, J.-B. (1955). 'Michel Leiris ou la psychanalyse sans fin'. In *Après Freud* (Paris: Gallimard, 1968).

——(1972). 'Penetrating the dream'. In *Frontiers* (1977).

——(1973). Preface to Rousseau's *Les Confessions* (Paris: Gallimard).

——(1974). 'Dream as an object'. *Int. Rev. Psycho-Anal.*, 1.

——(1977, Eng. trans. 1981). *Frontiers in Psychoanalysis: Between the Dream and Psychic Pain* (London: Hogarth; New York: Int. Univ. Press).

——(1981). 'Non, deux fois non: tentative de définition et de démentelement de la "reaction therapeutique negative" '. *Nouvelle Revue de Psychanalyse*, 24.

Pouillon, J. (1970, Eng. trans. 1972). 'Doctor and patient: same and/or the other?' In *The Psychoanalytic Study of Society*, Vol. 5, eds. W. Muensterberger and A. Esman (New York: Int. Univ. Press).

Rickman, J. (1951). 'Number and human sciences'. In *Selected Contributions to Psycho-Analysis* (London: Hogarth; New York: Basic Books).

Ricoeur, P. (1967). *The Symbolism of Evil* (New York: Harper & Row).

——(1969). *Le Conflit des Interpretations* (Paris: Editions du Seuil).

Rimbaud, A. (1873). 'Une saison en enfer', in *Oeuvres Complètes* (Paris: Bibl. Pléiade, 1972).

——(1973). *Complete Works, Selected Letters.* Translated by W. Fowlie (London: Univ. Chicago Press).

Robert, M. (1964). *The Psycho-analytic Revolution: Sigmund Freud's Life and Achievement* (London: George Allen and Unwin, 1966).

Rosolato, G. (1976). 'Le non-dit'. *Nouvelle Revue de Psychanalyse*, 14.

Rousseau, J.-J. (1762). 'Profession de foi du Vicaire Savoyard'. In *Emile.* Translated by B. Foxley (London: Dent, 1911).

——(1782*a*). *Confessions.* Translated by J. M. Cohen (London: Penguin, 1954).

——(1782*b*). *The Reveries of a Solitary.* Translated by J. G. Fletcher (New York: B. Franklin, 1971).

Rycroft, C. (1962). 'Beyond the reality principle'. In *Imagination and Reality* (1968*a*).

——(1968*a*). *Imagination and Reality* (London: Hogarth; New York: Int. Univ. Press).

——(1968*b*). *A Critical Dictionary of Psychoanalysis* (London: Nelson).

——(1975). 'Freud and the imagination'. *The New York Review of Books*, 3 April 1975.

de Sade, Marquis. (1775). 'Voyage d'Italie', in *Oeuvres Complètes* (Paris: Au cercle du livre précieux, 1961).

Sainte-Beuve. (1849). 'Étude sur Blaise Pascal', in *Oeuvres* (Paris: Bibl. Pléiade, 1960).

Sandler, J., Dare, C., and Holder, A. (1973). *The Patient and the Analyst* (New York: Int. Univ. Press).

Schneiderman, S., ed. (1980). *Returning to Freud: Clinical Psychoanalysis in the School of Lacan* (New Haven: Yale Univ. Press).

Segal, H. (1964). *Introduction to the Work of Melanie Klein* (London: Hogarth, 1973).

Sharpe, E. F. (1930). 'Survey of defence mechanisms in general character-traits and in conduct'. *Int. J. Psycho-Anal.*, 11.

——(1937). *Dream Analysis* (London: Hogarth).

Sheridan, A. (1980). *Michel Foucault: The Will to Truth* (London: Tavistock).

Smirnoff, V. N. (1977). 'Le mot de la fin'. *Revue Freudienne*, 18.

Smith, J. H., ed. (1978). *Psychoanalysis and Language. Psychiatry and the Humanities*, Vol. 3 (New Haven: Yale Univ. Press).

Starobinski, J. (1970). 'Hamlet et Oedipe'. In *L'Oeil Vivant*, II: *Le Relation Critique* (Paris: Gallimard).

——(1971*a*). *Les Mots sous les Mots* (Paris: Gallimard).

——(1971*b*). *Jean-Jacques Rousseau: Le Transparence et l'Obstacle* (Paris: Gallimard).

Strachey, J. (1964). Editor's note to 'Analysis terminable and interminable' (S. Freud, 1937*c*).

Szasz, T. (1971). *The Manufacture of Madness* (London: Routledge and Kegan Paul).

Toynbee, A. (1971). *Surviving the Future* (London: Oxford).

Trilling, L. (1955). *Freud and the Crisis of our Culture* (Boston: Beacon Press).

——(1967). *Beyond Culture* (London: Peregrine Books).

——(1972). *Sincerity and Authenticity* (London: Oxford).

Trombley, S. (1981). *All that Summer she was Mad: Virginia Woolf and Her Doctors* (London: Junction Books).

Tseu, L. (1961). *Le Vrai Classique du Vide Parfait* (Paris: Gallimard).

Veith, I. (1970). *Hysteria: The History of a Disease* (Univ. Chicago Press).

Voltaire. (1746). Letter to Comte de Tressan. In *Correspondence and Related Documents*, Vol. 10, ed. T. Bessermann (Geneva: Institut et Musée Voltaire, 1970).

Wade, I. O. (1971). *The Intellectual Origins of the French Enlightenment* (New Jersey: Princeton Univ. Press).

Winnicott, D. W. (1935). 'The manic defence'. In *Through Paediatrics to Psycho-Analysis* (1975).

——(1941). 'The observation of infants in a set situation'. In *ibid* (1975).

——(1945). 'Primitive emotional development'. In *ibid* (1975).

——(1951). 'Transitional objects and transitional phenomena'. In *ibid* (1975).

——(1955). 'Clinical varieties of transference'. In *ibid* (1975).

——(1956). 'The antisocial tendency'. In *ibid* (1975).

——(1958). 'The capacity to be alone'. In *The Maturational Processes* (1965).

——(1960*a*). 'Ego distortion in terms of true and false self'. In *ibid* (1965).

——(1960*b*). 'The theory of the parent-infant relationship'. In *ibid* (1965).

——(1962). 'Providing for the child in health and crisis'. In *ibid* (1965).

——(1965). *The Maturational Processes and the Facilitating Environment* (London: Hogarth; New York: Int. Univ. Press).

——(1967). 'The location of cultural experience'. In *Playing and Reality* (1971*c*).

——(1969). 'The use of an object and relating through identifications'. In *ibid* (1971*c*).

——(1970). 'The mother-infant experience of mutuality'. In *Parenthood: Its*

Psychology and Psychopathology, eds. E. James Anthony and Therese Benedek (Boston: Little Brown).

——(1971*a*). 'Dreaming, fantasying, and living: a case-history describing a primary dissociation'. In *Playing and Reality* (1971*c*).

——(1971*b*). *Therapeutic Consultations in Child Psychiatry* (London: Hogarth; New York: Basic Books).

——(1971*c*). *Playing and Reality* (London: Tavistock; New York: Basic Books).

——(1972*a*). 'Basis for self in body'. *Int. J. Child Psychotherapy*, 1.

——(1972*b*). 'Mother's madness appearing in the clinical material as an ego-alien factor'. In *Tactics and Techniques in Psychoanalytic Therapy*, ed. P. L. Giovacchini (London: Hogarth; New York: Science House).

——(1975). *Through Paediatrics to Psycho-Analysis* (London: Hogarth; New York: Basic Books).

Zetzel, E. R. (1968). 'The so-called good hysteric'. In *The Capacity for Emotional Growth* (New York: Int. Univ Press; London: Hogarth, 1972).

INDEX

INDEX